THE AUTHORS

Plantagenet Somerset Fry has written over thirty historical books, the first while still an undergraduate at Oxford in the 1950s. His titles include a standard work on British castles, the *David & Charles Book of Castles* (1980), of which a substantial part is devoted to Scottish castles, and *2,000 Years of British Life* (Collins, 1976), of which about a third deals with the social history of the Celtic nations of Scotland, Wales and Ireland. Among his other works are the best-selling *Children's History of the World* (Hamlyn, 1972, 8th edition, 1981), *Great Caesar,* a biography of Julius Caesar (Collins, 1974), and *Chequers: the Country Home of Britain's Prime Ministers,* which is the official history (HMSO, 1977). He has also been a journalist and public relations director in both private and public sectors, was Head of Information at the Government's Council for Small Industries in Rural Areas, and was the first Editor of Books at Her Majesty's Stationery Office, from 1975 to 1980. He now writes full time and is also an editorial consultant. Mr Somerset Fry is a Visiting Senior Member at Wolfson College, Cambridge.

Fiona Somerset Fry is an author and journalist who was introduced to the history of Scotland by her mother and her maternal grandparents, Scots who lived in England but who retained a fervent attachment to 'my ain, my native land'. She has worked on newspapers, in advertising and in publishing, and in public relations in Kenya. As well as newspaper and magazine articles, she has written for radio and television, and is the author of *Horses* (A. & C. Black, 1981).

THE
HISTORY
OF
SCOTLAND

THE
HISTORY
OF
SCOTLAND

By

PLANTAGENET AND FIONA
SOMERSET FRY

ROUTLEDGE & KEGAN PAUL
LONDON, BOSTON, MELBOURNE AND HENLEY

First published in 1982
by Routledge & Kegan Paul Ltd
39 Store Street, London WC1E 7DD,
9 Park Street, Boston, Mass. 02108, USA,
296 Beaconsfield Parade, Middle Park,
Melbourne 3206, Australia and
Broadway House, Newtown Road,
Henley-on-Thames, Oxon RG9 1EN
Set in 11 on 13pt Palatino by
Rowland Phototypesetting Ltd, Bury St Edmunds, Suffolk
and printed in Great Britain by
Thomson Litho Ltd, East Kilbride, Scotland
© Plantagenet and Fiona Somerset Fry 1982

Library of Congress Cataloging in Publication Data

Somerset Fry, Plantagenet
The history of Scotland.
Includes bibliographical references and index.
1. Scotland – History.   I. Somerset Fry,
Fiona, 1927 –   . II. Title.
DA760.S6   941.1   82-3715

ISBN 0-7100-9001-3   AACR2

CONTENTS

CONTENTS

ILLUSTRATIONS

The decorative motifs are reproductions of some of the Stirling Heads (see page 128) and are used by permission of the Royal Commission on the Ancient and Historical Monuments of Scotland.

Maps

Plates

CHAPTER 1

FROM
STONE TO IRON:
THE
FIRST
FORTY CENTURIES

(*c*. 4000 BC – first century AD)

This is the story of a great nation. It is the history of the various peoples who have occupied the land of Scotland over the past 5000 years or more, how they got there, what they have done and what marks they have left upon the story of world civilization. It is an account of the deeds of men and women, great heroes and humble folk alike, who have made a small country assume an importance far greater than its size and population would ordinarily merit. And it is a tale of the political, economic and social progress of a people who have made the word 'Scottish' famous for an unique blend of bravery, cautiousness, diligence and inventiveness.

Scotsmen and Scotswomen have for centuries been pioneers, played leading roles, in a variety of areas of human activity in lands all over the world. This will become clear as the history of Scotland is unfolded, but we may take a few examples at random to show what we mean. Mungo Park and David Livingstone opened up the continent of Africa to European discovery and settlement. Alexander Fleming discovered the antibiotic properties of the mould penicillin. John Logie Baird passed pictures down electrical waves to give the world television. James Simpson enabled women to have their children without the accompaniment of prolonged and terrible pains, and so opened up the world of anaesthetics. John Napier invented logarithms and advanced the usage of mathematics. Alexander Mackenzie traced the great river of his name in Canada through to the Arctic and opened up a whole new area to the world of trade. Robert Adam, with his brothers, introduced a style and philosophy of architecture and interior design that influenced the whole of European building design and furnishing, and spread across the Atlantic to America. Adam Smith revolutionized the study of economics with his *Wealth of Nations*. One could go on.

There have never been many more than 5 million Scots in Scotland. In 1978 the population of Scotland was 5,179,000, and that is about three-quarters of the number of people in present-day London. Large areas of Scotland have been uninhabitable or, at best, capable of sustaining only the simplest way of life. To many visitors, from the days of ancient Rome to the eighteenth century AD, much of Scotland seemed wild, barbarous, on or perhaps beyond the edge of civilization. A sizeable part of Scottish history has been little more than a catalogue of inter-family warfare, squabbling and dark acts of treachery and murder. For centuries, some of the best of Scotland's people have left their native land and sought careers or fortunes in other parts of the world, near and far. Yet those left behind have continued to be vigorous, brave and hard-working, capable of producing the very highest inventive genius. And they are still doing so today, increasingly, as a new spirit of national pride is spreading across the entire land of Scotland.

What is the reason for this seemingly inexhaustible reservoir of national talent? What makes the Scots *tick*? Who are the Scots? These are the three questions that underlie the structure of this book, and for the answers we have first to look at the land of Scotland itself.

A nation's history is shaped by its geography. The character of its people is moulded by the problems they have to face in communicating with each other, in travelling around and in making their country and its resources productive enough for them to live, work and trade in. It is also affected by the people's relations with peoples of neighbouring lands, how easily they can get to and from the next-door country, whether it is warlike or not and how they cope with this if it is. And in turn, over the centuries, the people help to shape their landscape, through ploughing, tree-cutting and planting, even changing the course of rivers. The interaction between a people and its geography is continuous.

Let us look at the map of Scotland. It occupies the northern part of the British Isles, a group of islands that enjoys a very unusual climate, one of the most agreeable in the world. Some readers may smile at this when they think of the rain, the fog and the spoiled holidays, village fêtes and sporting events that are so much part of British life, but it is useful to look at the main features to see what we mean by agreeable. While some parts of Scotland are swept by north-east winds that come almost uninterrupted from Scandinavia and across northern Europe from Russia, bringing severe winters with heavy snowfalls and blizzards, other parts lie in the Gulf Stream, which gives in sharp contrast a warm, sub-tropical air for much of the year and very little snow in winter, with palm trees growing here and there on the western side (such as Wester Ross). This mixed climate is such that people can on the whole spend more time out of doors during the year than almost anywhere else in the world.

The advantages are not hard to grasp. They were as valuable to the first peoples who settled in Scotland thousands of years ago as they are to Scotsmen today. Pioneers who want to make new lives in new lands can put down their roots much better if they are helped by the prevailing climate. But that is not all. What is the land like? The landmass of Scotland is roughly a rectangle, with a southern border with England in the Cheviot Hills, some of it along the river Tweed. It is nearly three-quarters bleak mountain or high hill, difficult if not impossible to cultivate and not often suitable even for pasture for animals. A reference book of 1977 stated that only 8 per cent of Scotland is really fit for pasturing. Here and there the landscape is fissured with great cracks by its rivers that seem to eat into it, almost threatening to cut it in half between Loch Linnhe and the Moray Firth. In fact Scotland is in two halves by virtue of the Caledonian Canal. Three of the four sides are bounded by sea, cold, misty and stormy much of the year. Its westward side is a maze of inlets and islands off the coast, resembling the scattered pieces of a jigsaw puzzle waiting to be fitted together. Of the remaining quarter of landmass, only about half is really fertile, chiefly the Midland Valley which stretches from the Lothians along the eastern coast up to Moray.

This fertile stretch attracted some of the earliest farming settlers 4000 or more years before Christ, and it has been a major source of Scottish wealth ever since. Stone Age, Bronze Age, Iron Age men, Celts, Romano-Celts, Scots from Ireland, even Normans from France and Anglo-Normans from England found good livelihoods there and held on to them with stubborn determination. So did the Vikings. There was also fertile land in the valley of the Tweed, and in the south-western counties like Wigtown, Kirkcudbright and Dumfries. With the Midland Valley, these lands became the focus of Scottish economic and political life. It was there that trading activities began and were to develop right down the centuries to the Middle Ages. Most of the trading towns, called burghs, are in this valley and along the east coast, for Scotland looked eastwards towards Europe, the Baltic and the Low Countries for trade.

Elsewhere in Highland territory, the great mountainous massif from Loch Lomond up towards the northern mainland of Caithness, the land has always been rugged and bare, unable to support much agriculture. In prehistoric times the communities were small, strung out and separated from one another by great uninhabited (and uninhabitable) distances. Their peoples struggled hard to eke out livings. They clung together in closely knit families, becoming over the centuries tough and self-reliant individuals who despised (and perhaps were also a little jealous of) the people of the lower lands who had an easier life. It is interesting and understandable to note that Highlanders have a very similar opinion of Lowlanders today.

These different types of countryside and their respective productiveness have divided Scotland into two distinct parts, as no king or government or foreign conqueror ever could. The Highlands and the Lowlands were regions created by geography and they have been kept separate by economics and politics, even by language and culture. From the earliest times there were two Scotlands, and today it is no less true. And it makes Scottish history and the Scottish character much more interesting and rewarding to study if one bears that in mind. Here, we are concerned with the physical map of Scotland and how it affected the earliest peoples who came from Europe over 8000 years ago.

If you study Map 1 you will see how difficult it must have been

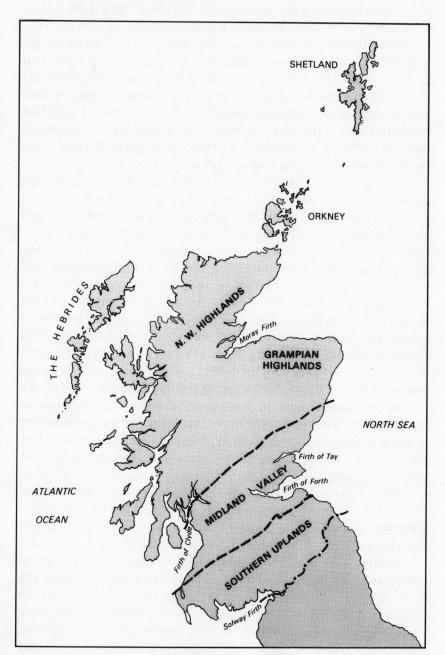

Map 1   Simplified physical map of Scotland

for these early peoples to move about, once they had got to Scotland, to communicate with each other. In the high ground the mountain massif, the forests and the misty lochs and glens between were all formidable natural obstacles. Tracks and paths had to be worked out across the hills. It was not much better on the lower ground which was either swamp or marsh, or dense woodland stretching down to the edges of the rivers. Thus forest had first to be cleared. It was really easier to look for land that was ready for working. This took them to the islands of the Hebrides, along the mainland coast of the north (Caithness and Sutherland) with its fearful storms, to the Orkneys and Shetlands, to Morayshire and of course to the great Midland Valley.

The first settlers travelled by sea in short hops around the British coast, coming from other parts of Britain and the Low Countries. They arrived on the western side of Scotland and occupied the islands where they found refuge in the natural harbours provided by the inlets. Many ventured up the river estuaries and sea lochs on the mainland and made their way inland. Bitter experience of the stormy coasts taught them to search for overland routes from west to east, and quite early on they discovered ways through the Great Glen (Glen Mor) from Loch Linnhe to Moray, from Loch Earn to the Tay and from the Clyde to the Forth. They moved along the rivers and lochs, using boats which were probably canoes dug out of tree trunks, or possibly frames covered with leather hides. On land they went by foot and hauled their families and possessions on sledges. Some used dogs as pack animals. Here and there they felled the trees with stone-bladed axes and cleared the ground which they could plant. But on the whole the Highlands were regarded by the settlers as land for passing through, not staying in. They lived a hunting and wandering existence, killing animals by trapping or harpooning, rather like the early trappers in North America and Canada centuries later.

Sometime about 4500 BC, or perhaps earlier, fresh groups of people reached Scotland. They made homes in places along the Western coast, the Western Islands, in the Forth and Clyde estuaries, and in the Orkney and Shetland Islands. They were farmers who understood how to grow crops such as wheat and barley, which they brought from Europe in the form of seeds and young shoots, and who knew about rearing cattle, sheep, pigs and goats. Some were experienced fishermen and caught bream, had-

6

dock and dogfish in the sea, the rivers and the lochs. They made simple forms of pottery for the table, cooking and storage, and sometimes they decorated it with grooved patterns. This is called Grooved ware, and appears to have emerged in Scotland some time before similar Grooved ware first saw light in England. Most of these people were also skilled makers of weapons, utensils and tools of stone, and they were adept at building houses and storage barns, burial chambers and tombs in stone. These people were the New Stone Age, or Neolithic, people and they have left much evidence of their movements, settlements and way of life in several parts of Scotland. Perhaps their most dramatic remains are the chambered tombs and the cairns (artificial burial mounds of stones). These can be roughly grouped in three types: passage graves, gallery graves and stone cists, and the types will become clear below.

One of the finest of the chambered tombs, though not the earliest, is at Maes Howe, near Stenness, on Orkney mainland. It is a passage grave, of megalith construction, that is, built with large stones, many weighing several tons. Maes Howe was discovered in 1861 and excavated and examined several times. Professor Renfrew, who carried out a new set of excavations in 1972–3, puts the date of this remarkable structure at about the late 4th millennium BC (c. 3400–3200 BC). The grave has a large central chamber approached via a passage, with a small cell leading off each of its other three sides, all reached by means of a square opening through the appropriate wall of the chamber. The plan of the passage grave is cruciform. The whole grave is covered with an earth mound some 116 feet (35 metres) in diameter and over 20 feet (7.6 metres) tall. The vault of the chamber is corbelled, that is, each roof stone is laid horizontally to overhang the one below until the vault is completed with a capstone. The passage leading to the chamber is lined with standing slabs and is for the most part roofed with megaliths. There is a special recess for a solid stone door.

The skill employed in putting this tomb together was amazingly workmanlike, considering that many of the stones, vertical and horizontal, weigh several tons each. The joins are 'so well made that a knife blade can hardly be inserted into the cracks', wrote Euan MacKie.[1] It is even more remarkable an engineering feat when one remembers that the builders had no metal tools or lifting gear. Professor Atkinson has suggested that the large stones of a chambered tomb may have been lifted by hauling them up the ramp of the earth mound surrounding the tomb, which was in part raised before the stonework inside was completed.

One of the key points about Maes Howe is the new dating accorded by Professor Renfrew to its construction,[2] namely, 3400 –3200 BC. For a long time it used to be thought that Neolithic people in western Europe were influenced by the 'superior' civilizations of the Near East, that their culture and technologies were the result of diffusion of Near Eastern skills and knowledge. But radio-carbon dating and tree-ring calibration techniques have recently helped to displace the diffusionist ideas and have led to an extensive re-think about the dating of much European pre-history. The new date for Maes Howe, for example, puts it several hundred years before the great Pyramids of Egypt, and so the technology to build it cannot have been diffused from Egypt, nor indeed from anywhere else in the Near East since the Pyramids were the first stone buildings in that region. Many other megalithic tombs in western Europe, notably in Brittany, Denmark, Portugal and Spain, are now dated in the fourth, or fifth, millennium. Earlier than Maes Howe is another Scottish chambered tomb, at Monamore, Isle of Arran. It is dated approximately 3500 BC, is compartmented and has tall portal slabs. Scotland is rich in Neolithic graves of one kind and another, and hundreds have been found, dating between about 4000 and 2000 BC. They were by no means all like Maes Howe or Monamore. Some were pits dug in the earth and lined with walls of stone, roofed either with slabs or covered with heaps of stones. Some were gallery graves, that is, long tombs consisting of a rectangular gallery-like space whose entrance at one end is the width of the gallery. These were sometimes lined with slabs and similarly roofed, and then covered with earth. Some gallery graves contained a number of rounded chambers clustered end-to-end within them. It was once thought that these were meant for whole communities or large families, but some specialists now think that a long chamber was a special burial place reserved for privileged people such as rulers, in much the same way as the special chapels built to house the graves of successive kings at Iona, at El Escurial in Spain, and at Windsor in England.

But while we have much evidence of Scottish Neolithic burial customs and structures, there is little remaining to tell us what kind of homes they built for themselves during their lives. To obtain an idea, though it can only be an approximate one, it may help to look at the remarkable small dwellings that have been found in the Neolithic site at Skara Brae, on Orkney mainland. These were originally thought to date from the 2000s BC but we can now say that radio-carbon dating and tree-ring calibration adjustment has put the earliest buildings at Skara Brae at about 3000 BC.

The Skara Brae Neolithic Village was discovered in the middle of the last century – by accident, after a terrible storm shifted huge quantities of sand from the shore where the buildings are. Since that time, much work has been done on the site by a variety of archaeologists, the latest major excavation and examination being in 1972–3. There appear to have been many generations of settlers in the eight houses found in the village. The Skara Brae people were stone users, for they did not yet know copper or bronze. They appear to have grown few crops, though some grain was found in the 1972–3 examinations. They raised sheep and cattle and collected sea food, notably shell-fish. Huge heaps of sheep and cattle horns have been unearthed, and refuse from shell-fish was found in midden levels. And yet these people built some fascinating and quite advanced types of housing. It is too early to say whether these were typical of those of contemporaries in Britain, but the Skara Brae structures are worthy of description, for something of the style was to be repeated in later generations.

The walls of the houses at Skara Brae have survived to at least several feet in height. They were built of local stone, large brick shapes for the walls, larger slabs for the floors (like flagstones), seats and so forth. Nearly everything else in and around them was of stone. They actually made furniture of stone slabs and bricks. Some of the houses had beds of stone, recessed into the walls, which would probably have been mattressed with straw and then covered with a bedspread made of animal skins. One house had a kind of kitchen dresser, with stone shelves, and nearby a cupboard, also recessed in the wall. The tools and utensils found were nearly all of stone, including axe heads, several types of flint tool, knives, and so on. There were also utensils of bone, and even some handles for tools that were made of wood, and these handles were found in very good condition. Among the debris in the settlement were found pieces of pottery, some of them Grooved ware.

The houses were squat and low, with half their structure actually below the surface of the earth. They consisted chiefly of a main

9

square-shaped room, perhaps 15 feet across. The entrance was through a low and narrow doorway; the inhabitants of those times must have been very short people. The door was a huge slab of stone, and evidence has been found of grooves in the door jambs to take a stone bar which was used to lock the door. The stone bricks for the walls were laid one on the other with no cement, rather like a dry stone wall such as you can see in many parts of Scotland today. Draughts were kept out by piling up huge heaps of what is called 'midden' round the outside. Midden is a jumble of ash, rubbish, sand and sewage. The houses would have reeked of unpleasant smells unless they were refreshed with the winds that sweep the Orkneys a lot of the time. The houses were linked by a network of passages covered with large slabs weaving through the midden. The whole village was at this low level.

The Skara Brae site has been of continuing interest to archaeologists for a century and work still goes on. The differing building styles pose questions such as, did one generation build upon the remnants of structures left by a previous one, as happened in parts of the Indus Valley civilization in India in the period c. 2500–1500 BC?

The period of the village preceded the first waves of those European settlers in Britain known as the Beaker folk. These were Neolithic people who were farmers and stockbreeders using copper, stone and later bronze, who buried their dead, often in a crouched posture, in small chambers under cairns, singly as a rule, and filled the chambers with an assortment of weapons and possessions, among which were found decorated drinking cups, or beakers. Tombs of the Beaker folk have been discovered in many parts of western Europe. A good example of Beaker burial in Scotland was excavated at Nether Largie, in Argyllshire near the Temple Wood circle of stones. The beakers are thought to have been a status symbol of a male warrior. Many were finely decorated. A good Beaker-folk craftsman need not, one feels, have been ashamed to compare his pottery with that made in ancient Greece fifteen hundred years later.

The Beaker folk reached Britain in the middle of the third millennium, about 2500–2400 BC, and among the earliest settlements were groups in north-east Scotland. Beaker folk put down their settlements beside rivers so that they could travel inland in search of cultivable land, or hunt, trap or fish. They may even have tried to irrigate their fields near the river banks. Over the centuries they mingled here and there in Scotland with less advanced people, building up communities. A good example of a settlement beginning in the third millennium in Scotland is at Cairnpapple Hill, near Torpichen in West Lothian. This site was occupied by a succession of peoples over many centuries, and during that time a variety of burial customs were followed. At first, Cairnpapple was a kind of sanctuary for the dead, who were cremated and their ashes put into pits arranged in an arc. Three large stones were erected in front of the arc. Next, twenty-four stones were raised in an egg-shaped ring, surrounded by a ditch cut into the rock and encircled by an earth bank. Both Beaker graves and early Bronze Age graves were found in this area. Then, a third stage of use followed. The tall stones were taken down and laid on their sides as edging for mounds under which the dead were buried, not cremated. Later still, more stones, this time in the form of rounded boulders, were put up outside the area where the mounds were continuing to be built, though by this time the mounds were substantially bigger. Finally, in the Iron Age, the site appears to have been a burial ground again.

In western Europe, the Beaker culture gradually gave way to the Bronze Age, towards the middle of the third millennium BC. This advance did not immediately affect Britain. Scotland had its own sources of copper ore, and craftsmen were already making some weapons and tools, jewellery and ornaments, from the reddish metal. But it was the Beaker people, some of whom came to Scotland from Ireland, who showed the inhabitants how to anneal copper, thereby hardening and toughening it to make it more useful for tools, and, later on, how to alloy copper with tin (some of it obtained from Cornwall) to make bronze. Thus the Beaker people led Scotland into its Bronze Age, in about 2300–2200 BC.

Scotland's Bronze Age lasted for many centuries, probably as long as thirteen hundred years, from about 2000 to about 700 BC. Scotland did not lag behind the rest of the British Isles, as was once thought. Scottish craftsmen were quick to develop their own bronze-working skills and originality of design. Tombs of the early Scottish Bronze Age have been found to contain objects such as pins and dagger blades, some of which may have been made in western Europe, as well as necklaces of amber that could have come from as far afield as ancient Mycenae.[3] Later in the Scottish

11

Bronze Age, their craftsmen began to make swords, which are in effect lengthened daggers. They had broad blades and thus heralded a style of sword that was to be made and used in Scotland, made of iron, right into the seventeenth and eighteenth centuries AD. These could be wielded with slashing movements and were much more effective in battle than daggers. Bronze weapon-makers also produced socketed axes. These imports of design and material from Europe show that Scotland was trading with European peoples, and this must have been accompanied with exchanges of ideas on many things. Perhaps they communicated in a language which was understood on both sides of the North Sea. It is clear that they also originated many ideas of technology.

In the last centuries of the second millennium, Europeans were beginning to form themselves into small kingdoms or states in those areas which were good for farming and stockbreeding. More definable class structures were emerging, for there was some form of hierarchy even in Neolithic times, and leaders were those who secured bronze weapons and made better use of them than their fellows, or perhaps grew better crops and so were able to acquire greater wealth. The top people emphasized their superiority by building larger and more impressive homes,[4] wearing distinctive ornamental jewellery round their necks or arms, and taking over the ritual connected with the burial of the dead. They reintroduced cremation, but put ashes into urns instead of heaping them loose in tombs or special cemeteries. They also gained control over the supplies of copper and tin, so monopolizing the manufacture of weapons. Stone weapons were no match for metal. And perhaps now the first few men of intelligence appeared, men associated with the rituals over death and burial, who because of their greater knowledge exercised real influence throughout society. In some respects they may be seen as the forerunners of the Druids.[5]

The Bronze Age was followed by the Iron Age. Iron was brought in the eighth century, probably by iron-using immigrants from the Hallstatt peoples of central Europe (see below), who were the first Celts to come to Britain. The term Celts comes from the Greek *Keltoi*. The Greeks used the word to describe in general terms the mass of loosely associated peoples in central and south-western Europe contemporary with them. They regarded the Celts as barbarians. The Celts spoke two branches of the Indo-European family of languages, known as P-Celtic and Q-Celtic, and speakers of one probably understood speakers of the other. The Celts were descendants of the European Bronze Age people mixed with wanderers from the Near East and from as far afield as central Asia. Some of the wanderers from Asia brought horses to Europe for the first time. They knew how to ride and to manoeuvre them with great skill.

The earliest groups of Celts who settled in Europe are called the Hallstatters because of a settlement discovered in the 1860s AD at Hallstatt in Austria. This was peopled by iron users who buried their dead in timber chambers underneath heaps of earth. But it was only one settlement: many others like that at Hallstatt have been found. We are talking in fact about a whole scattering of them in Europe when we use the word Hallstatters, and they are characterized by their use of iron and by their wagons with four wheels, with spokes in each wheel in place of simple circular discs.

Sometime in the sixth century BC the Hallstatt period gave way to another and more advanced age, the La Tène period, named after the Swiss village of La Tène on the bank of the river Thiele that leads into Lake Neuchâtel. Here, in the 1860s and 1870s, another exciting find was made – the remains of a village, or town, which contained many interesting objects. Some were of metal, like Hallstatt objects, but in a noticeably different style. Here, too, were remains of a new vehicle, a two-wheeled chariot drawn by two horses yoked to a central pole. The wheels were spoked and the rims were fitted with an iron band round the perimeter, like a tyre. The chariot body was not much more than a platform with two semi-circular sides of basketwork. There were also a variety of weapons, including an iron version of the slashing sword of bronze.

The two types of Celtic civilization were blending, and as they advanced the people began to spread out further in Europe. Some then crossed the Channel to the British Isles. They did not all come to southern Britain: many headed straight for Scotland, others for Ireland. They were attracted by a variety of things: Cornwall's tin mines for bronze-making; Wales for iron deposits; Scotland for fish and furs; England for its low, flat, fertile plains. Their movements over the last centuries of the first millennium are difficult to trace, and indeed we do not need to do this in any detail. Some excavations have yielded objects so different in style and age that the pattern of settlement in the British Isles can only be guessed at. What is clearer is that one main characteristic of the Celtic way of life, inter-tribal warfare and raiding, affected many parts of Britain, including Scotland. Settlements were always vulnerable to attack by people from other settlements, for one reason or another, and farms, houses and villages had to be protected. So they constructed fortifications, as they had been wont to do in numerous parts of Europe. Scottish fortifications of this period are particularly fascinating, and it is to these that we now turn.

The earliest Celtic fortifications in Britain date from the eighth century. The Celts erected timber palisades on the tops of ramparts, which were created from earth thrown up by digging out ditches and lacing them with stone. These were often put up round whole villages, groups of houses, even (occasionally) individual farmsteads, on low ground and high. Sometimes the walls were interlaced with stone and timber, and on high ground these structures are generally called hill-forts. Among the best-known hill-forts in Scotland of the Iron Age are the White and Brown Caterthuns near Brechin in Angus. Brown Caterthun is a fort that has six concentric lines of ramparts and ditches, and these were supplied with many entrances and causeways. White Caterthun is an oval fort that has a double stone rampart once laced with timber. It dates probably from the sixth century BC. This use of timber with the stone in ramparts and walls led to an interesting feature. Some of the ramparts in Iron Age hill-forts and other fortifications have been uncovered to show the timber-lacing to be fused with the stonework, producing a kind of glazed surface, a slippery mass. This was the result of the wood being set alight and becoming so hot that it melted the surface of the stone, especially if it was a sandstone, to create the mass. Forts with this feature are often called vitrified forts, but there is still discussion as to whether this vitrification was done deliberately as a defensive bonding to the rampart or by accident during a raid by attackers, such as in the fighting with Rome in the first and second centuries AD. A good example, dating to the eighth century BC, is Finavon, in Angus.

Another interesting type of fortification in Iron Age Scotland is the *broch*, or large stone tower. It is unique to Scotland and the remains of many brochs indicate a very considerable degree of skill in architecture and engineering. Elsewhere the brochs have been described as among the most ingenious and impressive military works of prehistoric man in western Europe. And about 500 sites of brochs have been found in Scotland, the great majority of them in the north-eastern tip of the mainland (Caithness) and in Orkney and Shetland. Some have been found much farther south, in the Forth region and even Galloway.

A broch was a tall tower of dry-stone walling construction. The stones were broken and roughly hewn into square, rectangular or oval shapes. The tower was round or oval in plan. Its base was thick and enclosed a courtyard that was lit by the daylight coming down through the opening at the top. Some towers were concave in shape. A splendid example has survived at Mousa in Shetland. It is about 13 metres high and its inner diameter is about 6 metres. The wall enclosing the circular courtyard is 4.5 metres thick and in the wall are several rooms, on different levels, connected by spiral staircases. There is a small entrance from the outside at ground level. Otherwise, there are no outer windows or openings.

Many brochs were situated near the sea, but despite this they had wells for fresh water. Some had hearths for fires and some appear to have had roofs. In the courtyard of some timber buildings leaned against the inner walls, or used the inner walls as the fourth side.

Brochs were built for important people in Scottish society. They served a dual role. They provided residences, though if Mousa is anything to judge from, it would have been very uncomfortable to live inside a broch for more than a day or two at a time. They acted also as forts against predatory neighbours or against raiders who came across the sea.

Brochs were not, however, the only type of home or fortress of the Iron Age Celts in Scotland in the second and first centuries BC. There is evidence for crannogs, island forts that were also a feature of the Celts of south-west Britain (Somerset and Devon). These are sometimes called lake dwellings, and several sites have been discovered in Galloway, the Clyde Valley and in the Highlands. They were low structures with roofs, probably surrounded with a palisade of stakes, put up on tiny islands lying naturally in lakes, or on artificial islands created by submerging logs and stone blocks and brushwood into the water until a platform emerged above the water line. A causeway was constructed from one edge to the mainland, and this would not be in a straight line but more in a maze-like pattern to make it difficult for raiders to approach. A group of crannogs was found in a loch in Wigtownshire about 120 years ago. From the objects found there it is thought that the crannogs began in pre-Roman times and continued to be occupied for some time afterwards.

Another kind of residence of these times was the weem, or *souterrain*. This was a long stone-lined passage built underground leading into a chamber whose floor, walls and roof were of stone slabs. They are sometimes called earth-houses and some of them were getting on for eighty feet long. Here and there are traces of round huts on the surface near the passages, and it is thought that the owners or occupants lived in the huts in warm weather but removed underground in the cold. Remains have been found at Ardestie in Angus, where the underground part is thought to have been a stable for cattle rather than a residence for human beings. There is another at Castle Law in Midlothian.

We have outlined the earliest centuries of Scottish history, and reached the first century AD when Scotland first had a taste of Roman arms. Far from being savage and uncultured, the Celts in Scotland were by then a fair match for the Romans. They were experienced ironworkers, they built some of the most durable structures in Europe outside of Italy and Greece, and they made jewellery and pottery that compared well with anything else available north of the Mediterranean. In some areas they were living in well-built and fortified hill towns, leading interesting and energetic lives, farming with considerable skill and getting good results. They had well-developed language. (They were still speaking P-Celtic and Q-Celtic. Possibly the P-Celtic tongue was the same as that spoken by the Celts in Wales.) They had mastered the art of boatbuilding. They were becoming aware of themselves as a distinct group of people. They were ready to meet the challenge which was to come from the Romans in the second half of the first century AD.

CHAPTER 2

CELTS, CALEDONIANS AND ROMANS

(first century BC – fifth century AD)

When Caratacus, leader of Celtic resistance to the invading Roman forces in southern Britain, was defeated somewhere in Wales in 51 AD, he was captured and sent to Rome. As he was led down the streets of the then greatest city in the world he marvelled at the grand buildings of stone and brick, so many of them faced in marble. Brought before the Emperor Claudius, who had himself visited Britain eight years earlier, Caratacus said to him: 'With so many marvellous buildings here in Rome, what could you have wanted with our poor huts in Britain?' The emperor's reply is not recorded, but he will have had to agree that there was all the difference in the world between the palace of Augustus and a Celtic chief's thatched round hut.

Most Celtic houses in Britain were simply constructed. They were generally round as in the remains of the house at Little Woodbury in Wiltshire, the wheelhouse at Jarlshof in Shetland, or the house on an unenclosed platform at Greenknowe in Berwickshire. The Greenknowe house is one of the earliest timber houses found in Scotland. It was built on a platform of earth dug out of the hillside. Its wall was made of a double line of wattle fencing laced

17

with twigs caked with clay. In between was a level of stone and rubble, on top of which was packed grass and other vegetation. There was another of this type found at Glenshee in Perthshire.

The roof of the Greenknowe house was conical. It had rafters fanning outwards from a high top, like the spokes of an umbrella. You can see why it is called a wheelhouse. The rafters were held at their lower ends on a horizontal ring of timber that rested on vertical posts with Y-shaped tops. The house needed no central pole to keep it up. It was one of several on the hillside. Settlements sometimes had as many as twenty such houses, but there were many places where these stood singly surrounded only by a fence. Further up in Scotland where timber was not so plentiful, wheelhouses were more generally built of stone, with stone slabs for the partitions.

How did the Celts live in these houses in Scotland? What comforts did they enjoy? Living in them was certainly no luxury, nothing that any Roman, even the humblest occupant of the Suburra,[1] could possibly envy. The Scottish climate in the eastern half was bracing, as it is today. In the west the rainfall was greater, and perhaps it was as sultry at times as now. If the Celts had animals they brought them indoors out of the cold or rain and shared their rooms with them. This meant trails of mud and muck, like living in a pigsty, but the Celts cared little for cleanliness in the home, though they were very fussy about their personal cleanliness. They did not worry much about how they slept. A heap of straw or heather on the ground or on a stone slab was enough: not for them the padded, bronze-plated and carved wood-frame couches the Romans loved so much.

It was the Celts who introduced trousers into Europe, probably learned from the Scythians – and how glad the Scottish Celts must have been of them in the cold! We have evidence of brightly coloured check material from which they were woven. The Celts wore flowing capes, too, like modern ponchos, and tunics down to the knee, in bold colours, often red or purple. The tunics may have been like the Highlander's kilt which has become world-famous. The women wore garments of linen and wool, also in the gayest colours and patterns. They loved wide skirts, almost down to the ankle, and they, too, wore long tunics, belted at the waist. They had cloaks, warm, bright and rainproof, made from wool of sheep that roamed the Scottish hillsides.

Celtic clothes were adorned with jewellery. Indeed, the Celts were famous for it. They had brooches for cloaks or ponchos, made of gold and silver with intricate animal designs, or sometimes more abstract ones, as well as rings for their fingers, bracelets of gold or bronze, torcs (necklets) of gold, longer necklaces of jet and other stones, metals, coral and so on. Their weapons were richly ornamented, too, and many a Celtic warrior had a jewelled sword hilt or scabbard, dagger handle, shield boss or helmet decorated with bronze inlay, red glass or enamel. Enamel work was a Celtic speciality, and for centuries the Celtic peoples produced the best in Europe.

A great deal of our information about those times has been carefully pieced together over recent years from studies of the things the Celts left behind, their weapons, jewels, garments, pottery, gold and silver, buildings, chariots and so forth. The picture is sadly incomplete, and they left no literature for us to check against the artefacts. They had no script, or if they did it has not come down to us. We learn something from Latin authors who came into contact with the Celts, like Julius Caesar, or Diodorus Siculus, a Sicilian writing in about 35 BC, and the historian Cornelius Tacitus, whose father-in-law, Julius Agricola, was governor of Britain from 78 to 84 AD. But they wrote as Romans or historians in Roman employment. They did not think of the Celts as civilized.

But if we have no contemporary Celtic account or diary of the life of a chief in, say, Perthshire, in the first century AD, we can reconstruct how he may have spent his time. And there is some corroboration for our reconstruction from the earliest written works of the Celts, in Ireland in the fifth and sixth centuries AD, when scribes began to write down accounts that had been handed down to them from generations past. Much of the early literature is taken up with legends of heroes and heroines, gods and goddesses, performing impossible feats, and of villains and devils capable of unreal cruelties and wickedness. But there is a lot about everyday life, too, and it relates to the life of more down-to-earth Celtic leaders and their people.

The Celt enjoyed fighting, if the quantity and variety of weapons left behind is anything to go by. But he was not always fighting his neighbours, or his enemies. He hunted wild animals like boar and deer, and looked upon the chase as a kind of war. His life was a hard one and he had to keep fit. On occasions, he played games or

19

took part in sports with his friends. The fast ball-game of hurling is thought to have stemmed from these times. He enjoyed music and dancing, singing and dressing up, possibly even acting. By now he had also developed his fondness for reciting poetry which, in those days, was not verse as we know it but rhythmical use of words, sung in musical tones, to express his thoughts, his hopes and fears, or simply to tell the story of some hero or gallant friend.

The Celts loved a feast. It seemed an appropriate end to a good day's hunting to eat and drink hugely, sometimes to the point of insensibility. They had some powerful drinks, not the delicate wines of Rome or Greece, but crude, home-brewed ale that burned your throat, or sickly-sweet, treacly mead. But the Celts were not just fun-loving, boisterous exhibitionists. They were extremely hard workers. Most of the men who went to war or hunted for food were also farmers. They left their farms, probably grudgingly a lot of times, took their swords off the wall and met up with their fellows on the battlefield or in the ditches dug round a settlement, or on a hill-fort rampart, summoned there by a chief's heralds blasting out the clarion call on a bronze animal-headed horn called a carnyx. As soon as they could they returned to the land. They cared that their families had enough to eat. They wanted their children, especially the boys, to grow up healthy and strong. They expected them to be well able to take care of themselves by the time they were in their teens.

Those who did not farm may have been skilled craftsmen – blacksmiths, coppersmiths, carpenters, stonemasons, potters, weavers, thatchers and jewellers. There was a continuous demand for the services of all of them, but blacksmiths were the most eagerly sought. Whatever else you needed or wanted you had to have tools and weapons. Smiths shaped the swords and the daggers, repaired the broken ploughshares, fashioned all manner of tools and weapons, pressed the metal rims upon the wheels of chariots,[2] and they did so travelling about the countryside, stopping here and there to set up temporary workshops and deal with the orders that poured in.

If the Celt was not a farmer or a skilled craftsman, he might be a trader or merchant, journeying up and down Britain, perhaps even crossing the sea to Europe. Many things produced in Scotland were wanted in Europe, leather, coral, salt, fish, furs and iron, and there was plenty of cross-channel business. Traders from Scotland could also make a living selling in Ireland or among communities farther south in what is now England.

In the last century BC and the first part of the first century AD Scotland was a relatively peaceful land, seldom bothered, it seems, by enemies in the rest of Britain. The Celts of Scotland had mingled with the earlier peoples they found there and were living in scattered communities in many parts. They had some sort of class structure, though it is not easy to define other than by saying it had a dominant class of warriors, and that people of greater knowledge were generally accorded high status. Though the peoples were not all of the same stock, clear distinctions cannot easily be made between them. There were those whom the Romans called the Caledonians, who occupied all northern Scotland. In later years these were called the Picts, because they tattooed their foreheads and other parts of the body.[3] Farther south were other tribes, later to be named by the Romans, like the Damnonii in Argyll, the Novantae in Galloway, the Votadini in the Lothians and the Selgovae in the Cheviots. They had their hill-fort towns which the Romans called *oppida*. Probably the Caledonians had some sort of sway over the others, perhaps because they had better weapons and used them with greater skill.

In 55 BC Julius Caesar, then Roman governor and commander-in-chief in Gaul, and later to become the greatest man of the ancient world, embarked with an invasion fleet from north-west Gaul (France) and headed across the Channel to Britain. His expedition was only a limited success: he defeated the Kentish Celts, exacted hostages from them and returned to Gaul. A year later he came again, this time with a larger force, and pushed as far as the Thames, crossed it, probably near Wandsworth, and at a great battle at Ravensburgh in Bedfordshire with the Belgic Celtic chief Cassivelaunus, leader of the Catuvellauni tribe that dominated the area in England now known as the Home Counties north of the Thames, defeated him. Caesar took more hostages, fixed a substantial sum in tribute and went back again across the Channel.

Britain was left alone militarily speaking for about a century, which was long enough for the British to forget how a Roman army could behave in foreign territory. And we do not know to what extent, if any, Caesar's adventures were ever heard of at all in Scotland.

Sometime in the summer of AD 43 the Roman general Aulus

21

Plautius embarked from Gaul to Britain, with an army of some 40,000 legionaries and auxiliaries. The progress of this invasion and conquest is not part of Scottish history, until the late 70s AD, by which time Roman troops had reached Carlisle and Newcastle and were ready to advance across the Cheviot Hills.

In 78 a new governor was sent to Britain. He was Julius Agricola, who had been born a Gaul (and therefore must have had Celtic blood) and who had already served in Britain, as a young officer. He knew the British: he may have come across Celts from southern Scotland or even some Caledonians from the north. By 78 his province consisted of virtually all England and Wales. Agricola was soon to become the first Roman general to advance into Scotland and to fight the Celts in a major battle, though not the first to send Roman troops across the Cheviot Hills. That had been done by his predecessor, Sextus Julius Frontinus.

The Celts in Scotland will not have remained idle while Roman armies were working their way up Britain towards them. There was no central government or dominant chief in Scotland to co-ordinate the national defences. Celts did not work like that; they never did, to their cost time and again in their history. But individual tribes and communities made some preparations. A hill-fort or two may have been additionally fortified. Crannogs in Galloway were strengthened. New duns were built and older ones repaired.[4] Some brochs in the southern areas were put in readiness. One hill-fort thought to have been strengthened at this time is The Chesters, near Drem in East Lothian. It received extra ramparts.

In 80 Agricola launched a full-scale two-pronged invasion of Scotland. One army moved up the Annan river valley, known as Annandale, and the other through Lauderdale. Both paths were extremely difficult for a fully equipped army to march through. There were no proper roads as Agricola had had no time to build them, as his predecessors had done farther south, and the country-side was in turn hilly, marshy, thickly forested or filled with lakes. If the Celtic tribes could have combined their forces they would have been able to descend upon both columns, one after the other, and cut them both to pieces. They knew the terrain while the Romans did not. But the Celts did not get together, and the Romans succeeded in meeting as far north as Inveresk. Agricola then took the two columns together further into the land between the Forth and the Clyde. Detachments were filtered off south-westwards into Galloway, there to deal with Novantae warriors who would not yield to Roman persuasion to join them. The Roman forces in Galloway built forts of their own with which to overawe the Novantae and to police the district.

By 83 Agricola was ready for an attempt to break into the northern part of Scotland. He had sent a fleet from his harbour on the Solway up towards the Western Isles to explore the possibility of attacking the Caledonians from the west by seaborne invasion, and another fleet similarly went up the eastern side towards Aberdeen. But the idea seems to have been abandoned, for in 83 Agricola advanced on land from a line of forts he had established in the Forth–Clyde district, up into Tayside territory, and the edge of the Highlands. It is thought his route went through Strathallan, Strathearn and Strathmore. Some 30,000 troops marched towards Stirling, then on to the foothills of the Grampians in search of the main Caledonian forces.

There was a minor skirmish with the Caledonians, probably near Inchtuthil, near Dunkeld, where a legionary fortress was built, though not finished, in the years 85–7, after Agricola's departure from Britain. Under cover of darkness a Caledonian raiding party attacked the camp of the IXth Legion and killed the guards. Agricola came to the garrison's relief with a force of infantry and cavalry, and drove the attackers off. But he realized that a major battle had still to come. Britons captured by Roman forward patrols revealed that the Caledonians were planning an all-out assault on the Roman forces. This may have been the first time that Agricola actually heard the name of the Caledonian leader, which was Calgacus. That is the Romanized form of the Celtic word *calgaich*, meaning swordsman.

The story of the Agricolan adventure into northern Scotland is well told by his son-in-law Tacitus. We may be sure that Tacitus's military details were substantially correct but the time factor is difficult to grasp. The skirmish took place in 83, but the show-down was not until 84. Does this mean that though Agricola beat off the preliminary attack he did not think his position yet strong enough to take on the full brunt of the Caledonians? Was the skirmish a bigger affair than Tacitus suggests? It would be under-standable for him to play down the reverse. What sort of forts and roads did Agricola establish at the time? The picture is not yet clear.

Some authorities believe there were no Agricolan forts north of the Forth–Clyde isthmus. Both sides withdrew after the skirmish more than ever determined to bring the matter to a head. 'We must drive deeper and deeper into Caledonia and fight battle after battle till we have reached the end of Britain', was the feeling among the Roman troops. Meanwhile, every man among the Caledonians was urged to arm himself, put his wife and children into a place of safety and bury any differences he might have with any neighbour or rival. The Caledonians realized they must unite if they were to have any chance of success. Would they be able to do so?

By the summer of 84, Agricola was ready for the critical battle. To this day, the actual site of the battlefield is not known with absolute certainty. The northernmost military camps of the period have been found as far as Aberdeenshire and Banff-Moray. In 1970 it was persuasively argued by Richard Feacham that Duncrub, in the Earn Valley, between Perth and Auchterarder, was the site, but in 1978, J. K. St Joseph published results of fresh research by himself and David Wilson, both of the Cambridge University Aerial Photography Unit, taking the site much higher up the north east to the hill mass of Bennachie, 5½ kilometres south-west of Durno (site of an Agricolan camp), which is not likely to be contested in the foreseeable future.[5] It has the additional merit of helping to explain the year's delay by Agricola in bringing on the clash. Tacitus calls the site Mons Graupius which has led to it being confused with the Grampian mountains. That summer day saw 30,000 Caledonians, fearless warriors, 'tall, fair or red-haired . . . in primitive tartan, their shields and helmets gay with enamel . . . followed by thousands of half-naked, barefoot infantry, bearing small, square, wooden shields, with a metal boss over the hand-grip, and spears, with a knob at the butt end, which could be clashed with a terrifying noise,'[6] assembled on a hillside ready to meet some 8000 well-drilled auxiliary infantry backed by some 5000 auxiliary cavalry, and with short, cutting, stabbing swords, led by a commander who, in the heat of the battle, was to dismiss his horse and fight on foot at the head of his men.

The only account of the battle is that of Tacitus. Ten thousand Caledonians fell. The rest fled from the field back to the hills. Fewer than 400 Romans were slain. 'On the succeeding day, a vast silence all around, desolate hills, the distant smoke of burning houses, and

24

not a living soul descried by the scouts, displayed more amply the face of victory.' Agricola ordered the commander of the Roman fleet, which had sailed along the eastern coast while the army was moving northwards inland and, presumably, was in harbour somewhere near the battlefield, to proceed north and 'sail round the island'. This is thought to be the Orkneys. Agricola, meanwhile, pulled back his cavalry and infantry, marching slowly to impress more deeply the might and majesty of Roman arms upon the conquered peoples, south to winter quarters, probably in the Forth–Clyde area, to forts established during his earlier campaigns. Soon afterwards, Agricola himself was recalled to Rome and a new governor was sent out in his place, who may have been Sallustius Lucullus.

Tacitus described Mons Graupius as a great Roman victory: who can blame him? But was it? The fact remains that Agricola retired southwards when it was over. Moreover, when he left Britain a few months later, the frontier between the Romans and the Caledonians was nowhere near Moray. It was more than 150 miles south, and over the years that followed, the Roman occupation of Scotland contracted and contracted. It probably never consisted of more than the holding of key forts and fortlets, and as time went by less and less of them. By 117, the year of the succession of Hadrian as emperor, there was fresh trouble in northern Britain. Some kind of revolt had broken out, possibly among the Selgovae and Novantae tribes (who were not Caledonians) in Galloway, and it is thought they may have linked up with discontented elements among the Yorkshire/Lancashire Brigantes.

Hadrian visited Britain in 122, and this is the year generally given as the one in which he ordered the construction of his famous wall. It eventually became 73 miles long and 12 to 15 feet high, with mile-fortlets and towers, from the Tyne to the Solway Firth. It was built to keep separate peoples like the Selgovae and Novantae from the Brigantes who were prone to creating trouble. It was also intended as part of Hadrian's policy of consolidating the frontiers of the Roman empire. When he arrived in Britain there was not much that was Roman north of the Cheviot Hills.

In one respect this puts the 'victory' at Mons Graupius in a different light, certainly from the Caledonian point of view. But if Calgacus, or a succeeding leader, learned not to confront the Romans in open battle, that does not make Mons Graupius a decisive victory for Rome. At best it must have been only a tactical success, and the Caledonians could rightly feel they had discouraged the Romans from pushing any deeper into their territory. If Tacitus's figures are right, 10,000 Caledonians slain left 20,000 still living, from a total force of 30,000. Perhaps half of these were unhurt, fit and ready if need be to fight again. Calgacus himself may have survived. If he did, he would have learned, as Boudica had learned twenty-four years before,[7] that confrontation in the field of battle was not the way to beat the Romans. Harassment of Roman camps, marching columns and so on by small, swift raiding parties of well-armed guerrillas was much more effective, and this is what followed, whether organized by Calgacus or by a replacement chief.

The building of Hadrian's Wall was by the standards of the Roman world an impressive achievement, but it did not keep the Caledonians, or any other enemies, out of Roman Britain. The actual work took about eight years, and this included building a milecastle every 1620 or so yards, as well as several forts for garrisons of infantry and cavalry and the buildings they needed. To begin with, part of the wall was made of stone and part of turf and timber (where stone was in short supply), though all turrets were of stone. There was a ditch on the northern side, 8–12 m. wide and 3–4 m. deep, separated from the wall by a space 20–40 feet across. Below the south wall was another ditch, with ramparts on either side. This was the Vallum. Between the ditch and the wall was a road.

While each milecastle had accommodation for twenty-five to thirty men, and each turret for a handful, and several larger forts like Housesteads and Chesters accommodated several hundred men each, it still proved impossible to stop raids from the north altogether. The Caledonians moved about in small, well-trained teams of 100 to 200 tough warriors, and unless they came up against the full force of 1000 men, both cavalry and infantry, from a fort, they were often too much for the smaller roman garrisons. We do not know how often or where the Caledonians broke through, but in the 140s things had got so bad that Hadrian's successor as emperor, Antoninus Pius, sent fresh forces to Britain. He ordered Scotland to be invaded again. In about 142 the governor of Britain, Lollius Urbicus, marched into southern Scotland and compelled the Novantae, the Selgovae and the Votadini to submit. Then he advanced to the line between the Forth and the Clyde where a few earlier forts and fortlets stood, desolate, unused, damaged, but strategically valuable. He rebuilt some and constructed new ones, making a chain of forts spaced out at regular short intervals along a turf and timber wall, on firm stone foundations. One fort you can see remains of today is Rough Castle, near Bonnybridge in Stirling-shire.

Each of the ends of the fort line was accessible from the firths and could be guarded by ships. It came to be known as the Antonine Wall and it was garrisoned for at least 20 years. It was breeched several times. There were many ways in which the Caledonians could raid Roman-occupied territory. They could make a frontal assault on the wall. They could sail down either east or west coast and land somewhere ashore below the line of the wall. Or they could draw the Roman garrisons out of their forts, fight them in the field and defeat them, and then charge into Roman land simply by running through undefended gateways.

Both Hadrian's and the Antonine Wall were psychological as well as physical barriers. They marked boundaries, as it were. But neither side for a moment imagined them to be impregnable. Perhaps the Romans did not even intend them to be.

Towards the end of the second century the Roman empire sus-tained a series of nasty shocks. The emperor, Marcus Aurelius, by nature a quiet, reserved man, given to studying philosophy, took command of the armies in the Balkans and was defeated. Almost simultaneously, the whole empire was ravaged by a terrible epidemic, about as crippling as the Black Death in the mid-fourteenth century in Europe. Marcus Aurelius died in 180, and was succeeded by his worthless and vicious son, Commodus, who degraded the imperial dignity by participating in gladiatorial and wild beast fights in the arena in Rome. He was assassinated in 192 and the throne was offered to Pertinax, an old soldier who lasted less than a year. On his death there was a struggle for power, in which a splendid north African general, Lucius Septimius Severus, emerged as winner.

The Caledonians were quick to exploit the discomfiture of their enemies. By the end of the second century they had compelled the Romans to abandon almost everything they had in Scotland. In about 208/9 Severus came to Britain, led the legions into north-east Scotland and dealt the Caledonians several sharp blows, but he

27

achieved no major victory. He headed back to York and died there, in 211. Almost at once Roman forces north of Hadrian's Wall were recalled to strengthen the wall. And apart from short intervals it was to remain the frontier up to the middle of the fourth century, although it was breeched several times.

Severus's invasion was the last. Thereafter, the Picts (Caledonians) were left alone, only meeting the Roman army whenever they attacked Roman forts or tried to get into occupied Britain. An uneasy peace reigned between them. In the late 300s Picts moved southwards in some force and swept across the wall. They did so when Saxon pirates from north-west Europe sailed across the North Sea and raided the east coast in a sweep from the Firth of Forth down, probably, as far as the Humber. On the west side, meanwhile, Cumbria and south-west Scotland were attacked by parties of fierce warriors coming by sea from northern Ireland. They were known to the Romans as the Scotti, a word meaning raiders. It is the first time the name appears in history. They came from the area of Antrim and landed in Cumbria where they seized both men and women and took them back to Ireland, enslaving them. These Scots were in time to challenge the power of the Picts in Scotland.

The Romans might have held their own if the assault had come only from one quarter, and their forces had not already been reduced because troops were needed so urgently back in Europe. But the combination of attacks was too great. Moreover, the wall had been neglected and it was not adequately manned. Many of the fortlets were deserted or were held by a fraction of the usual size of garrison. The frontier was edged downwards so that by about 400 there was no effective Roman presence north of York, over 100 miles from the wall. Nearer to the middle of the fifth century the Romans abandoned Britain altogether, leaving the British to fend for themselves against growing danger from Saxon pirates from Europe, Scots from Ireland and, of course, Picts and other tribes from Scotland.

CHAPTER 3

THE
COMING
OF
CHRISTIANITY

(*c*. 450 – *c*. 840 AD)

By the middle of the fifth century the Picts had become the most powerful people in Scotland. Apart from mastering the country-side from the Orkneys and Shetlands down to the Forth and the Clyde, they were also capable of sustaining raids right into south-ern Britain. They did so for short-term material gain. Nothing justified a raid more in their eyes than a series of wagon loads of Romano-British treasure like brooches, belts, helmets, robes, swords and so forth. They were not concerned with conquering territory and settling it on any permanent basis, or else they would have done so. They descended considerable distances into what is now England, and their attacks were strong enough to prompt the Britons of the Home Counties to invite help to ward them off.

The Britons first asked for troops from Rome, but none were available. Italy itself was in dire distress. Attila the Hun, with his huge Asian armies, was marching across Europe towards the great city. So the Britons invited Jutes and Angles from Denmark and Saxons from north-west Germany and Holland to come and help. They offered the foreigners lands in return. The Jutes, Angles and Saxons thought this was not an opportunity to be missed, and they

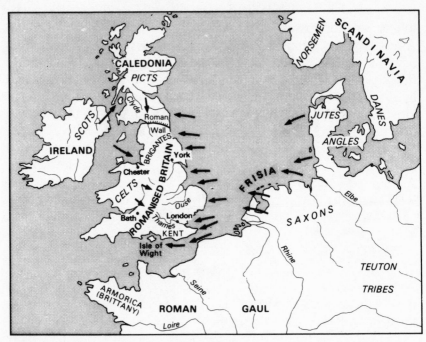

Map 2   The invasions of Britain in the late fourth and fifth centuries AD by Jutes, Angles and Saxons, which coincided with inroads by Picts into Romanized Britain

came over, though not all at once. The Jutes arrived first, in Kent, under their chiefs Hengist and Horsa, and helped the Britons to beat back the Picts. Then they decided to stay. In the entry for 449 the Anglo-Saxon Chronicle says that they fought against the Picts and beat them in every engagement. Then they sent to Germany for more support, telling them that the Britons were a useless and demoralized people, but that their land was very good for farming. Naturally, more Jutes and their families came from Europe; they were under some pressure themselves from neighbouring races who were being threatened by the Huns and the Avars.

The arrival in Britain of these Germanic peoples spelled the end of Roman Britain. Those who did not wish to mingle with the newcomers were gradually edged westwards and north-westwards to join their kinsfolk in Wales and Cumbria, and also into southern Scotland, into the area that came to be known as Strathclyde.

Scotland was by this time divided among four peoples, three of whom were related, for they were Celts. There were the Picts, whose territory was the most spacious. The compilers of the Anglo-Saxon Chronicle said they had originally come from Scythia, which is in Russia, and they may have got this from the first chapter of the *Ecclesiastical History of the English People*, written by the Jarrow monk and historian, Bede. There were the Britons, kinsmen of the Celts in the lands south of Hadrian's Wall, and who occupied territory between Loch Lomond and the Solway Firth, and reaching into Cumbria, known as Strathclyde. Their principal fort and capital town was Dumbarton, otherwise known as Alcluid, or Rock of the Clyde.[1] There were also the Angles, who were not Celts but Germans, and they had settled on the east side between the Forth and the Tyne, emigrating from the Humber and Yorkshire.

The fourth people were the Scotti, those raiders of Roman days. They were Celts from northern Ireland and they settled in the Argyll area and in the western islands. They had not only joined the Picts on raids into southern Britain. They had clashed with them in central Scotland.

The centuries that followed the departure of the Romans were often called the Dark Ages for Scotland. We know better now, though the story of Scotland in this time is not an easy one to reconstruct. The peoples in Scotland left very little in the way of written records of their way of life. We have stones of the Picts and these are revealing. But there is not much else. Yet we need not be surprised at their not writing things down. If a people is in the habit – as the Celts were – of committing things of importance and interest to memory, and then reciting them later on to others with amazing accuracy, and of passing them on and on down the generations in hardly less accurate form, then there is not much need to be able to write or to develop a script. It is through these oral traditions that we get an idea of how the Celtic peoples of Scotland lived in the fifth, sixth, seventh and eighth centuries. And sometime in those years the Celts in Wales and Ireland eventually began to write. It is quite reasonable to suppose that the details about the ordinary things of life, such as what a house was like, what clothes a noble wore, or how a girl was brought up and educated, details that are given in the legends about Celtic heroes written down by Irish and Welsh poets and scribes, were accurate also for Scotland. To build up an idea of those times we can also look at archaeological finds and relate them where possible to the details in the legends.

If we do this a picture emerges of a group of peoples who enjoyed an adventurous and rewarding life and who developed many traditions to hand down to subsequent generations. Perhaps the most striking feature of life among the Celtic peoples of Scotland was the kin, or family group. Though this is found among all peoples of history, it was particularly dominant and most elaborately organized among the Celts. From it grew the clan system of the Highlands, the principal feature of Highland society from that time until today, and this is important because the Highlands were more than half the area of all Scotland. We shall see, moreover, later on, how even in the eighteenth century the English government dreaded the clan system in Scotland and what steps they took to try to stamp it out of Highland society, by, for example, banning the wearing of tartan plaids (see p. 197).

Kin means family, and it is important to understand the role of the kin in Celtic societies in Europe and in Britain. It is a complicated role, with rights and responsibilities which, though different in some particulars in different Celtic societies, were basically the same. It can be simplified thus.

Celtic society was divided into three classes: free men, subjects and slaves. People in the first class claimed to be related to one another, and in the earliest times, when land was shared between everyone who lived on it, they probably were related by blood or marriage. As time went by, this class continued to claim relationship, or kinship, by virtue of descent from the original people in the kin. They had rights not given to other classes. They could carry arms; they could attend the tribal assemblies that were composed of older, more experienced men of their class, though they could not always vote. Some kin grew to be more powerful (by more skilful use of weapons and greater bravery in battle) or more influential (through greater wisdom in giving advice or more subtlety in negotiating political matters). Perhaps a kin acquired power through a long and successful tradition of good, profitable farming. These more powerful kin took the lesser kin under their protection. The latter felt they belonged to the stronger kin. They sent their sons to learn among them and work for them. Their daughters sometimes married into the stronger kin. In this way the lesser families, or septs, became members of the greater kin.

The other two classes had far less rights and did not, or could not, belong to the kin system. The subjects probably carried out much of the work on the land or in small industries like pottery, weaving and ironworking. The slaves were just that – no more. They might be protected by those who owned them, but they had no rights.

The head of the kin was a very powerful man. He was looked upon as father of everyone in the kin, even though he might only be a distant cousin to most. He commanded their loyalty: he had proprietary rights over their land, their cattle; their possessions were in a sense his. His quarrels involved them and they had to take part in them, even to the point of laying down their lives. He called his kinsfolk his *clann*, the Gaelic word for children. So you can see how much the clan system in Scotland meant. And the changing political structure in Scotland down the centuries did not diminish the exclusiveness of the clan, nor temper the spirit of independence that pervaded every clansman who had any land and traditions.

Look a little closer at the power of the chief. He controlled even the division of the clan land among the members of the family, whether blood relations or relatives by marriage. If he sent groups of the clan on cattle-stealing raids (a favourite occupation of the Highland Celt from the earliest times almost to the middle of the eighteenth century) or allowed them to join other clans on similar adventures, he reserved – and took – the right to a proportion of the spoils. In the case of warfare with another clan – and the clans were frequently at war – or with an outside enemy, he led the clan into battle. The clan was expected to protect him as far as they could and fight the enemy at the same time. In and out of battle he had supreme power. His word was law, in fact it was *the* law. Very often his judgments were unfair and his revenges cruel, but, once uttered, they had to stand.

The clan members took the name of their chief, usually sticking the word *Mac* or *Mc* in front of it. Mac means 'son of', and it is found in numerous names, the MacDonalds, the MacLeods, the Macleans, the MacGregors and the MacKenzies, and so on. These names meant much more than just identification. The meanest and lowest member of the MacLeans, for example, was fanatically devoted to his name. He might even die for it, calling it out as his last word. One catchphrase repeated time and again by MacLeans is 'Though poor, I am noble. Thank God I am a MacLean.'

The clan system, which over the centuries grew into a political and social organization that defied the power, the strength and even the laws of the Scottish kings, was already beginning to shape the future of Scotland in those far-off years after the withdrawal of the Romans. It was pointing even then to a Scotland of two parts, of the Highland people and those who went along with the Highland way of life, and the Lowlanders, different in so many respects, who were to be influenced later by the Angles, the Normans and the medieval English. But we should see how before this happened the four parts of Scotland edged towards a kind of unity, what brought them together.

The Scots from Ireland found the Argyll lands and the islands attractive places in which to settle. In the sixth century so many of them came from their kingdom in northern Ireland, called Dalriada, that their new land was also called Dalriada. One of their kings, Fergus Mor, set up his headquarters in Kintyre, while his brothers established smaller kingdoms in the Oban area and on the isles of Jura and Islay. So, we have the odd situation of a king ruling two lands (separated by the sea) with the same name. In both the principles of the kin prevailed, and perhaps some of the old and famous clan names like MacGregor or MacLean originated as far back as those times.

The Scots were warriors, but they were also farmers and fishermen. They were livestock breeders and traders, and cows, sheep and pigs were a staple form of currency. You judged a man by the number of animals he owned, and you bought something with a cow or pig. Slaves were valued in terms of livestock. The Scots were crop-growers and kept their sights on the best farming land they could find when they arrived in Argyll. They also kept bees for honey, which they used both for sweetening and for fermenting to make strong alcoholic drinks. For fishing, the men, like their kinsfolk in Wales, rowed out to sea in coracles, small, wickerwork canoe-like boats covered with skins and made watertight with coatings of tar, or larger craft, called curraghs, which were timber-built and covered with hides that were tar-smeared, and which had oarsmen's benches.

The adventures of the Scots in Argyll and their settlements there did not go unnoticed by the Picts, who had similar Celtic origins, and there were many clashes. The Picts had been in Scotland a long time and regarded all the lands above the Forth–Clyde line as theirs. But it was difficult to move about at any greater speed or in large armies in the Highlands, and the Picts had to deal with intrusions into their territory on the spot, with whatever strength was available. The Scots gradually infiltrated – for that is the word – into the fertile Midland Valley, because they appreciated its great farming potential. Their efforts were not in vain, if some of the place-names still existing are anything to judge from, such as Strathern (Strath of Eire) or Atholl (New Ireland).

But their clashes were not to prevent the ultimate joining of the two peoples. And there were two particular influences that brought them even closer. One was their common reaction to the struggles that went on between Britons in Strathclyde and Angles in Lothian (south-east Scotland) and the threat these posed. The other was the advance of Christianity in the British Isles.

The rivalry between Britons and Angles began soon after the Romans left. British Celtic tribes had occupied the greater part of the territory between the Forth–Clyde line and Hadrian's Wall – today's Lowlands. Some of them, notably the Votadini, had had ties with the Romans, had intermarried and taken Romanized names. The Votadini had their capital on Traprain Law, in East Lothian, a formidable hill-fort and settlement of Bronze Age origin that remained in Celtic hands all through the Roman period. In these districts the Britons lived in villages or groups of buildings, surrounded by wooden palisades. Here and there stone was used for walls, or split to make tiles in place of thatch for their roofs. Generally, one house was markedly larger than the others, and this has been taken to suggest that some kind of manorial system was operating, where a local landlord had sway over the rest of the people.

When the Romans abandoned Hadrian's Wall, the Britons found themselves sandwiched between the fiery Picts in the north and the Angles and Saxons from the south. Gradually they were eased out of Lothian altogether as the Angles crept towards the Forth. They moved to the west, south-west and into Cumbria and Lancashire where they received support from their kinsfolk there and in Wales. But they were cut off from their Welsh compatriots by the crushing victory of the Anglian king Aethelfrith at Chester in 613. The same king had a decade earlier defeated the Scots of Dalriada under King Aidan at Degsastan (probably Dawston in Liddesdale).

Aidan had been marching down to the aid of the Britons in Cumbria when he was intercepted and beaten in the field. These two victories isolated the Britons and in the later part of the century more Angles advanced into south-west Scotland and took the British base at Dumbarton. Yet the Britons survived these blows, and the kingdom of Strathclyde (as it was known) continued to exist, with ever changing boundaries, right into the eleventh century.

The Angles were Germanic in origin and came principally from north-west Germany and Denmark, and a few even from Scandinavia. They had been raiding the east coast of Britain for years, but until the Romans left they had not succeeded in settling. After about 500 they started to make firm settlements. Some came to Lincolnshire, and some to Norfolk and Suffolk (which are still known as East Anglia). Their main base of settlement, so far as this story is concerned, was north of the Humber, in Yorkshire, Durham and Northumberland. They founded two kingdoms, Deira and Bernicia. The first stretched from the Humber up to the Tees and the second from the Tees to the Firth of Forth. To begin with, the Angles moved upwards by sea from the Humber in boats rather than trudging across the Yorkshire Dales and coping with the wild and wind-swept Northumberland hills. They founded towns along the coast. One was Bamburgh, built by their king Ida in about 550. One of his grandsons was Aethelfrith, king of Bernicia from 593 to 617. He was that Aethelfrith who beat the Scots at Degsastan and the Britons at Chester. He also dispossessed his neighbour King Edwin of the throne of Deira and ruled both.

For the next half-century there was rivalry between the two Anglian kingdoms, and this relieved the pressure on the Scots. It is interesting that despite defeating the Scots at Degsastan the Angles made no attempt to invade Dalriada. But they did cross the Forth and intrude upon Pictish territory. In 685, however, the reckoning came when at Nechtansmere (near the present town of Dunnichen in Angus) Aethelfrith's grandson Ecgfrith, king of the Angles, was defeated and slain in a crushing and decisive Pictish victory. As the Anglo Saxon Chronicle admitted, the king was slain 'and a great host with him'. The victorious Pict chief was Brude, and he may have been a descendant of another Pict leader, also called Brude, who had welcomed St Columba in the sixth century (see p. 40).

Nechtansmere is one of the most important battles in all Scottish history. So great was the defeat of the Angles that they had to give up all further attempts to move deeper into Pict territory. As Bede wrote in his *History*, 'their kingdom thereafter had narrower bounds'. When the battle was being fought it is unlikely that either side view it as more than a simple trial of strength. Naturally, the Picts were resolved to stop further encroachment upon their lands. Those Anglian leaders who survived must have thought it best to settle for what they had achieved so far, and that was the territory between the Forth and Hadrian's Wall. But what it did mean was that Scotland was not to become an extension of England. It was a major check on English ambitions north of Lothian. If the victory had gone to the Angles, there might never have been a Scotland at all.

The Picts were the only one of the four peoples of Scotland to keep their territories more or less intact during these turbulent years. It is likely that for some of the time they were divided into two kingdoms, northern Pictland and southern Pictland. There had been a king with a capital at Inverness in the sixth century, in St Columba's time. But the differences would have been of a military kind. Perhaps the southern Picts had leaders who refused to accept the sovereignty of the northern Picts. Certainly, towards the end of the seventh century, the power centre had shifted towards the north-east. And in the middle of the eighth century the southern Picts had another powerful ruler, Angus MacFergus, who apparently was able to bend the Dalriadan kings to his will.

To the chroniclers of the time like Bede the Picts were a shadowy people. The Anglo Saxon Chronicle describes them as having come from Scythia with warships and landed first in northern Ireland. They asked the Scots there if they might settle, but the Scots said there was no room for both peoples. But they tried to be helpful by suggesting that the Picts should try 'another island to the east of us where you can settle if you wish, and if anyone resists you, we will help you to conquer it'. The Picts set off for Scotland and 'took possession of the northern part: the southern part was held by the Britons'. Leaving aside the chronology, this is an amazingly accurate summary of the position of the earliest Celtic peoples in Scotland. And the Chronicle adds that 'after the course of years a part of the Scots went from Ireland into Britain and conquered part of the land: the leader of their army was called Riada, and from this

37

they are called Dalriada.' That is exactly how the first Scots arrived in Argyll sometime in the last years of the Roman period.

Shadowy the Picts may have been to Bede and the chroniclers, but they left behind them a considerable number of fascinating monuments that tell us much about them. These include stones with animal figures, symbols, portraits of men, women, landscapes, and so forth. Some were executed in with considerable artistry, and they are a veritable social history. One of the stones at Aberlemno in Angus tells us also that they used both infantry and cavalry in their battle order. Seven feet six inches tall, the reverse of this stone depicts a clash between the armies, using cavalry and foot soldiers, both with their weapons.

The Picts were well organized. Their government and laws were based on the clan (kin) system which they had developed. They had strict laws of succession, which were different from those of most other peoples. Succession was passed not from father to son but through the female side of the family. That meant a man became chief because his mother was the daughter of an earlier chief and he was succeeded not by his son but by his brother (his mother's son) or by his nephew (his sister's son).

The Picts built in stone, as well as in wood and thatch. When Christianity had spread among the people in the sixth and seventh centuries they constructed churches and monasteries. One site where remains have been found of very early Christian Pictish religious buildings is the brough of Birsay on mainland Orkney. Here, jumbled among the ruins of Viking structures of the ninth, tenth and eleventh centuries are traces of an earlier Pictish church, possibly of the seventh century. Among these is an interesting stone of symbols which shows three Pictish warriors with shields and spears.

The Picts proved their military superiority at Nechtansmere. There may have been other victories, but for another century or so we hear no more of the Picts. We have traces of buildings, objects, carved stones, which say that they continued in northern Scotland, but until they were attacked by the Vikings in the late eight and early ninth centuries, that is about all. The Viking raids on Pictish coasts, and up the estuaries of the Moray, the Tay and the Forth, weakened them and made them vulnerable to attack by the Scots in Dalriada. Their territorial integrity was not to last, and during the reign of Kenneth MacAlpin of Dalriada (c. 825–60) they succumbed to Scottish dominion. In the 840s (the year is generally given as 843) Kenneth, son of a Scots king and descended also from Pictish kings (via the female line), claimed the Pictish throne and was able to win it. He joined the two peoples, Picts and Scots, and formed the state that came to be called Scotia. He is the first king of Scottish history. He moved his capital from Dunadd in Argyll to Scone in Perthshire, and from that time Scone was the royal seat of the Scottish kings.

It was not an easy union to achieve, nor to maintain, and he spent much of the remainder of his rule fighting off Pictish opposition to his government. The Picts were proud, tough, independent, and whatever sense it may have made for them to join up with the Scots to resist the common Viking foe, they loathed the idea of losing their independence. This characteristic has stayed with the Highlanders ever since, who are of course part Pictish in descent.

The Viking threat pushed the Picts and Scots together, and this is traced in the next chapter. The other unifying factor was the advance of Christianity, and to this we now turn.

When the Romans left Britain, many of them were Christians. Their emperors had encouraged the growth of the faith since Constantine the Great declared Christianity the state religion in the early fourth century. This did not mean that Britain was left pagan, with the Celts adhering to their ancient religion, fostered by Druids who had considerable influence over them, worshipping a family of gods and goddesses represented as human beings with supernatural powers. Many Celts had been converted to Christianity and more were probably ready to join them. This was particularly marked in Wales. It was a question more of reviving enthusiasm for the faith, of reorganizing it and injecting fresh meaning.

In Scotland the Britons of Strathclyde and neighbouring lands were Christians, but the Picts were not. In about 400 a British Celtic bishop, St Ninian, who had had years of experience as a teacher in Rome, came to Scotland to build a church and found a school for religious teachers, at Whithorn, near the Solway, in Galloway. There has been much argument about whether what remnants of his community in the Whithorn area are datable to his time, but the Latinus stone in the Whithorn museum is thought to have been erected in his lifetime.[2] He sent missionaries out among the pagan Picts, according to some authorities as far northwards as Caithness and the Orkneys. But the faith did not take much hold, and perhaps only Galloway remained Christian after he died.

About 150 years later, Columba, a bold, gifted, energetic monk who may have been a descendant of one of the Irish high kings, left Dalriada in Ireland with twelve teacher colleagues and sailed to Dalriada in Scotland. They landed on the island of Iona and built a monastery there. Its church was oblong and constructed of wood (but it may have contained some stone, too), and the community's quarters were round timber huts, with clay-coating and thatch roofs, like the houses of any typical Celtic village. The Iona monastery was intended to be the first of a number of religious settlements that Columba planned for northern Scotland. Over thirty-four years his team, joined as time went on by a growing number of converts from Dalriada and Pictland, spread the faith widely and made it take root. They were helped by the powerful Pictish king, Brude, who at first treated Columba with suspicion. Brude had his capital at Inverness and there is a legend that the Columbans were barred from entering through the gates. Then Columba made the sign of the cross and the gates opened of their own accord. This impressed Brude and he took it as a sign that he should accept Columba and his mission. Whether the tough Pictish leader ever accepted Christianity himself we do not know, but he allowed his people to be converted, if they wished.

Columba continued to work largely from Iona, where he trained the men to go out into the wilds of the Highlands. He died at Iona in 597. It was the very year in which St Augustine, an Italian bishop, landed in Kent and began his mission to convert the Saxons to the faith. There had also been other Christian scholars working in Scotland, and one was Kentigern, who was to become better known as St Mungo. Mungo founded a church at the settlement that was Glasgow, sometime in the middle of the sixth century. He was a Strathclyde Briton and after his work at Glasgow he went to north Wales where he is credited with founding a monastery at Llanelwy, which is now St Asaph. His life-story was written in the twelfth century by a bishop of Glasgow who stated that Mungo had actually met Columba. Today, Glasgow's cathedral is called the cathedral of St Mungo.

In the seventh century much of Scotland was converted. There remained that part of the east occupied by the Angles, Bernicia, some of which was not Scotland. The two kingdoms were sometimes ruled by two separate kings, but at other times united under one. The Angles were not excluded from the attempts to make the British Isles a Christian outpost in Europe. In 617 Aethelfrith, the ruler of both Bernicia and Deira, who had beaten the Britons at Chester (613), was slain at another battle by Edwin, whom he had displaced as king of Deira. Edwin thus became ruler of all Northumbria, and he extended his territory as far as Mid-Lothian where he built a town and fortified it. It was to be known as Edwin's burh, and later as Edinburgh. He had driven the sons of Aethelfrith into exile, and two of them, Oswald and Oswy, went to Iona where they were converted to Christianity.

Edwin was killed in battle in 632 by Penda, king of the Mercian Saxons (who occupied the English Midlands), and by Cadwallon, prince of Wales, who planned to take over Northumbria. But a year later the scheme collapsed when Cadwallon was slain at another battle. The victor of that engagement was Oswald and he thus came into the two kingdoms in Northumbria. During a short reign (633–41) he asked the monks of Iona to send a mission into his kingdom, and in 635 they sent out one of their most devout and learned monks, Aidan. He came with followers to the island of Lindisfarne, about two miles off the Northumbrian coast, between Berwick and Bamburgh. Lindisfarne, also known as Holy Island, was connected to the mainland by a causeway. There, Aidan built a monastery and then began to preach the faith on the mainland, sending his followers out into the countryside to do likewise. Among them was Finan, who was to succeed him as head of the church at Lindisfarne.

Oswald, meanwhile, founded a double monastery at Coldingham. This was an establishment for communities of men and of women. He put his sister Ebba in charge. She is commemorated by a promontory near Coldingham called St Abb's Head. Oswald set up another monastery at Melrose (not the same one as that whose wonderful remains can be seen today). From this Melrose another missionary preached Christianity in Scotland, and he was Cuthbert (635–87). Cuthbert was eventually to become bishop at Lindisfarne, and to be made a saint after his death.

The spreading of the faith in the eastern part of the Lowlands of Scotland, therefore, had gone along hand-in-hand, as it were, with that in Northumbria. This helped to bring the interests of the two peoples closer together.

41

One feature of the conversion work was that it began with missions from the Irish Celtic church at Iona but was completed by missions from preachers who accepted the doctrines of the church at Rome. Both churches were devoted to the basic teachings of Christ and his disciples, and the differences were not great. Yet they had to be resolved, partly because the head of the Roman church, the pope, really regarded himself as head of the whole Christian community throughout the world. The differences, which did not amount to much more than disagreement as to how to calculate the date of Easter[3] and variation in what way the head should be shaved to wear the tonsure, could not be permitted to continue as they were seen as threatening to upset the integrity of Christianity. The Irish church did not accept the pope; they probably did not see the need for the kind of elevated dignity that popes had been increasingly assuming at Rome. But in remaining outside the Roman discipline, as it were, the Irish were 'rocking the boat'.

There could not be two styles of Christianity in Britain for long. In 664 a meeting was held at Whitby in Yorkshire, organized by King Oswy of Northumbria (who had succeeded Oswald) but engineered by the church in Rome. It was to determine quite simply which style should be adopted throughout Britain. A strong case was put for taking the Irish model, but Wilfred of Ripon put an even better case for everyone to embrace Rome, and Oswy chose the latter course. It was the beginning of the decline of the influence of the church in Ireland, and within half a century even the Iona monastic community was accepting the supreme authority of the pope at Rome. Thus Christianity became a uniform religion in Britain. And yet the church in Scotland developed in its own way, differing from that in England and in Wales.

The Irish church had lost and it was sad in some respects, particularly when the pioneering work of Columba and his followers is remembered. From the Irish church emerged some magnificent artistic achievements, possibly the finest in all Europe of the time. We are thinking especially of the unique Book of Kells. Irish monks had been the most accomplished creators of handwritten books, but none excelled this remarkable work. It was begun in Iona, sometime in the seventh century. Then it was taken to Ireland after a series of devastating Viking raids on the island in which the monastery and other community buildings were ransacked and stripped of all gold and silver, jewellery and ornaments. The book survived, no doubt because it had no intrinsic value to pagan and illiterate Vikings. Then it was completed in Ireland. Today it is still there, in Trinity College in Dublin. Another most beautifully illuminated manuscript is the Lindisfarne Gospels, a volume containing the four gospels from the New Testament. This dates from about 700 and is decorated with wonderful ornamentation in glowing colours. Remains of church ornaments, stone crosses intricately designed and carved, and other religious objects have been found from Iona and from the western Highlands.

By the middle of the ninth century, Scotland was beginning to become a nation. There was a forceful and effective ruler governing more than half of it, and he was planning to advance southwards to add more territory. The majority of the people were Christian and this provided them with a common interest. And they were facing increasing danger from the Vikings, which they could better resist if they did so together.

CHAPTER 4

SCOTLAND
BECOMES A
NATION

(*c.* 840–1057)

Leaving aside the early saints and missionaries like Ninian, Columba, Aidan and Finan, Kenneth MacAlpin is the first figure of Scottish history we know more about than just his name and an event or two. To begin with, we have some dates for him. Probably born at the start of the ninth century, Kenneth became king of the Scots in about 839 when his father was slain in a war with the Picts, then overlords of the Scots. In 843 Kenneth acquired the throne of the Pictish kingdom. Some say it was after a great victory over the Picts, others that the throne fell to him because he was heir to it by the Pictish rule of succession through the female line. Soon afterwards he moved his capital and administrative centre from Dunadd in Argyll to Scone in Perth, the sacred centre of the Picts. To mark the union between Scots and Picts, and perhaps to stress that he considered the Scots superior, he transferred the Stone of Destiny from Dunadd to Scone. This slab of red sandstone, which is still slung between the legs of the Coronation Chair in Westminster Abbey, was the subject of many legends. It was claimed to be the pillow on which Jacob, son of Isaac and grandson of Abraham, had his dream about the angels and the stairway to heaven.

Another legend was that it had been a royal stone in Irish Dalriada before being brought to Scottish Dalriada, perhaps by an ancestor of Kenneth. Whatever its origin, it was a very important symbol, important enough for Edward I of England to steal it and take it to London some 450 years later (see p. 78).

Sometime in the 840s Kenneth transferred the remains of St Columba from his hallowed grave at Iona to the monastery at Dunkeld, about twenty miles north-west of Scone. The remains were said to have been conveyed in a jewelled and enamelled case, known as the Monymusk Reliquary, now in the National Museum of Antiquities of Scotland. This case is said to have been carried by the Scots into various battles, because it brought them success. There is a strong tradition that one of Robert Bruce's officials carried it on to the battlefield at Bannock Burn in 1314, the greatest victory in Scottish history.

Removing St Columba's remains to the mainland spelled the end of the dominance of Iona as a religious influence and power, and for the next half-century or so Dunkeld was to be the centre of Christianity in Scotland. Then, in the early years of the tenth century, the abbey of St Andrews was founded, and the bishop there became the leading man of the Scottish church. Yet Kenneth – and all his successors for the next two centuries – were buried at Iona.

The remainder of Kenneth's reign seems to have been taken up with trying to beat the Angles of Lothian and bring them into the Scottish kingdom. The Angles, however, would have none of it, and for another 150 or so years they successfully kept the Scots out of their lands. The Britons of Strathclyde, meanwhile, remained independent and Kenneth appears content to have left them so. He is also recorded as having ruled the Picts 'happily' for sixteen years, 'after having brought about their destruction'. This must mean 'destruction' of their independence. He left behind some traces of his building interests. At Forteviot he erected a palace, probably a fine timber-framed hall with thatched or slated roof, and there was another at St Andrews. His wife had a big house at Forfar. Clearly they took to the less mountainous land of the east, so different from Argyll. Kenneth died in 860, and his body was taken to Iona for burial.

Kenneth was the ancestor of all the kings and reigning queens of Scotland. He was succeeded not by his son but by his brother,

Donald (Donald I: 860–2) who was followed by his nephew (Kenneth's son), Constantine I (862–77). The succession was an alternate and an unusual system. It follows no strict order such as one finds with the Anglo-Saxon royal house of Wessex of about the same period. Nor does it observe rigidly the principle of inheriting through the female line, which the Pictish kings followed. It has been suggested that the early kings of Scotland, certainly up to Malcolm II, were chosen from the royal family not in lineal succession but according to merit. The king had to be an adult, to have proved himself in warfare and presumably to be liked by the majority of the circle of royal advisers (many of whom no doubt had ambitions to wear the crown themselves). The system had drawbacks. If one candidate was supported by some people, he would have been opposed by others who preferred another, and the latter generally continued to back the rival until they had got rid of the king. Kings therefore had little chance of living out their reigns to a natural death. Seven kings in succession, from Malcolm I to Kenneth III, were killed, most of them murdered. Then, between 1040 and 1058, three more were killed. It is a terrible record, more so for a kingdom newly formed and struggling to establish good government and to fight off the endless attacks of the Vikings along its coasts.

It is time to consider the Vikings and their impact upon Scotland in the ninth and tenth centuries. 'From the fury of the Northmen, deliver us, O Lord!' was a prayer chanted by priests and monks in every abbey, church and monastery chapel in the British Isles and along the coasts of western Europe. It was a prayer that went unanswered, for these remarkable sea-raiders from Norway, Sweden and Denmark continued to sail across the North Sea and wreak havoc in every town and village, monastery and farm. 'White Gentiles' they were called if they were tall, almost white-haired Norwegians, 'Black Gentiles' if they were golden-haired, a little shorter in stature, and came from Denmark. Their long ships (familiar to everyone since the ruins of two of them buried in mounds of clay and peat, the Gokstad ship and the Oseberg ship, were found in Norway[1]) were clinker-built, that is, the outer planks of the hull overlapped downwards and were fastened by clinched nails. They were driven by oars or by square sail, sometimes by both. The sail was of leather and often gaily painted, with red and white stripes or in a criss-cross pattern. The hulls were works of art.

The high prows were beautifully carved and topped with the head of an animal, often a dragon or a wolf. The warriors hung their shields along the sides, above the holes for the oars.

The Vikings came in waves, as the old history books are fond of saying. The Danes generally came to the English coast and to Ireland, the Norwegians to Scotland, and both to Wales. They started coming in small numbers towards the end of the eighth century. They were bold, dauntless men who made attacks without warning upon anywhere that looked like a source of plunder, on the mainland and on islands alike. The Anglo-Saxon Chronicle records the first raid in 787, an assault by three ships. Lindisfarne was first attacked in 793, in a raid in which the Vikings 'miserably destroyed God's Church'. Between 795 and 806 Iona was raided three times. The monastery and other community buildings were laid waste, the Vikings carrying off all the gold and silver they could find and anything else that seemed to them remotely valuable or useful. Perhaps this is how the great Book of Kells survived (see p. 43).

In the ninth century these daring adventurers, freedom-loving warriors who had the strictest regard for order in their own society and who were governed by a severe but sensible code of laws, began to strike further into the interior. While their compatriots were attacking the coasts of the Low Countries, France, Spain and even northern Italy (where in 860 they burned the town of Pisa), Britain-bound Vikings grounded their ships and terrified the inhabitants of every coastal town. Then they seized horses and rode swiftly inland. By this time they were coming in much larger numbers, several hundred or so together. This is what the Anglo-Saxon Chronicle means when it records that 'the host' stormed Winchester in 860. They were now bent more on settling than on mere plunder. They were hard workers, good builders and intelligent farmers. Their craftsmen were among the finest in Europe, while their shipbuilding skills were second to none in the world. Their nautical prowess had taken them to North Africa and down the rivers of Russia to the very gates of Constantinople, just south of the Black Sea.

The Vikings began to settle particularly along the north-east coast of England, in Northumbria, that kingdom that was refusing to become part of the new Scotland. They also came to northern Scotland, to the Hebrides, the Orkneys and the Shetlands. Their raids and, later, their settlements had some interesting side effects. In many ways, they were to Scotland's advantage. They gave the Scots and the Picts a reason for getting together, their common need to defend their land. They gave Kenneth MacAlpin a motive for uniting the two kingdoms. By occupying the northern islands and parts of Caithness and Sutherland, the Vikings reduced the area that Kenneth and his immediate successors had to govern, which was helpful in the short term. The raids and settlements in Lothian created so many difficulties for the Angles there that the latter were discouraged from trying to enlarge their territory by invading Scottish land.

It was not the Vikings' aim to conquer all Scotland. Even if it had been, it is not likely that they could have succeeded. They did not have the central government and organization to follow up a major invasion with a thorough conquest, as the Romans had had. The Vikings sought new living space. Most of them dwelt on or near the coasts in their Scandinavian lands (elsewhere was uninhabitable because of the cold and the mountains). They were seafarers and much preferred voyages to long treks across difficult countryside. So when they came to Scotland they re-created the environment they had abandoned in Scandinavia, that is, preferred to make settlements on the coast, though some ventured further inland. Once they had formed their communities, they began to follow a more tranquil life. They adapted their ways to those of the Picts and Scots (and the Angles, too), and they brought industry and skills that were extremely valuable to the growing kingdoms. Earlier we said that four peoples combined to make Scotland (see pp. 30–1). The Vikings became the fifth. They intermarried with both Scots and Picts, and from time to time Viking princesses married Scottish kings and princes, notably Ingibjorg who married Malcolm III. They brought new blood to the mixture already there in Scotland and this was good.

We cannot leave these remarkable people without mentioning something of their communities and the people who ran them. Stories of their adventures were written down in later years. These accounts were called sagas, and they combined fact with imagination. One particularly interesting saga is the *Orkneyinga Saga*, about the warlike activities of the 'White Gentiles' in the Orkneys. They had begun with small raiding parties harassing the islands, then part of the Pictish kingdom, in the last years of the eighth century.

In the ninth century some of the raiders stayed. They were farmers as well as warriors, and they were looking for new and better land, because there were too many of them working too little land in Norway. Towards the end of the 800s the Norwegian king, Harold the Fair-haired, decided to add the Orkneys to his empire and he sent a strong force under one of his earls, Rognvald, to occupy them and rule there as regent. Rognvald probably set up his government, such as it was, at Birsay. Here, a seventh-century Pictish monastery had been destroyed by earlier Vikings and a settlement of farms and homes put up on the ruins. The houses were the long kind, two-storeyed, with residential quarters above and byres for cattle below. In the Birsay settlement are the ruins of a great hall, or *skaill* (as the Vikings called it), which has still to be thoroughly explored.

The earls of Orkney ruled like kings. They could do so because their sovereign was 200 miles away in Norway and unable to supervise their activities. The same thing happened in other out-lying Viking dominions in Scotland – such as the Hebrides, where Harold's viceroy was a rough and independent warrior called Ketil Flatnose, who did as he wanted. Some of the Vikings settled as far south as the hills of Galloway, where they lived in harmony with the Britons, married their women and founded a race of energetic and wild people called the Gallgaels, from whom the name Gallo-way is derived. Other Vikings occupied many islands on the western side of Scotland, notably Arran, and even some districts of the mainland like Kintyre. But the main base of Viking power in the Scottish sphere remained in the Orkneys.

The greatest of the Orkney earls was Thorfinn the Mighty, who ruled over practically all the Viking dominions in Scotland from about the 1040s to about 1065. We know something about him. He was a Christian. He was the son of Sigurd the Stout, earl of Orkney, who may have been a brother of Rognvald. Sigurd had married the daughter of Malcolm II of Scotland. Thorfinn built a church at Birsay which in the twelfth century was enlarged into a cathedral. Some of the houses around the remains may well have been built at Thorfinn's directions, too. One became the bishop's palace. It could have been Thorfinn's official residence.

Thorfinn established his power well enough to leave the Orkneys in the 1050s for a tour of Europe. He visited his overlord in Norway, Harold Hardraada (who was seven feet tall and who was

49

to fall at the battle of Stamford Bridge in 1066, trying to defeat Harold II of England). Then Thorfinn went to Denmark to see Sweyn, the Danish king, who was a son of the magnificent Canute the Great (king of England, Denmark, Norway and Sweden in the years between 1016 and 1035). From there he went to the court of Henry II, emperor of the Holy Roman Empire, and lastly he visited the pope in Rome where, it is said, he asked for pardon for his sins. When he returned to the Orkneys he settled down to a peaceful reign, governing his domains which, by then, included the Isle of Man and some parts of Ireland. He had good relations with Macbeth, king of Scotland (1040–57). He died in 1065, and his widow, Ingibjorg,[2] became the wife of Malcolm III, Macbeth's successor.

For a time the kingdom of Scotland which, until the eleventh century, still comprised only Pictland and Dalriada, learned to coexist with the Vikings, and some of the earls became good subjects, or allies, of the Scottish kings. But this could not continue forever. There was a need for all Scotland to be one kingdom, islands and all, and the Scottish kings of the eleventh, twelfth and thirteenth centuries never gave up full unification as their principal policy.

The activities of the Vikings were not the only problem facing the new and developing kingdom of Scotland. Once the English peoples had begun to find their unity under Aelfred the Great of the kingdom of Wessex and his immediate successors, his son, Edward the Elder, and grandson, Athelstan, by overpowering the Vikings and by prevailing over their rivals in Mercia and Northumbria, they began to claim a sovereignty over the Scots and Picts, and over the Strathclyde Britons and the Anglians in Lothian. The Scottish kings naturally refused to recognize this.

In 900 Constantine II came to the Scottish throne and reigned thereafter for forty-three years. Sometime in the period 910–15 he launched attacks on Lothian and Northumbria, but this provoked the English. Edward the Elder held a meeting at Bakewell in Derbyshire and there, the Anglo-Saxon Chronicle says, received the homage of 'the king of Scots and the whole Scottish nation . . . together with the king of the Strathclyde Welsh and all his subjects'. This is exaggeration, but clearly Edward was in some sort of position to get Constantine to leave English interests alone. Twenty years later, in 934, Athelstan invaded Scotland 'with a land and naval force' and ravaged the countryside. Which countryside, one wonders? Some say he reached into the Mearns. In 937 Athelstan went to war again, taking on the kings of Scotland, Strathclyde, Viking Northumbria, other Viking rulers from Man and Ireland and, at a great battle, defeated them all. The battle is known as Brunanburh and yet it has not been accurately placed, though it is believed to have been near the Solway border. It was a crushing victory for Athelstan. Constantine fled from the field, leaving his son mangled from wounds.

The Scottish king is said to have grovelled before Athelstan, recognized him as overlord and agreed to give up his wars with England. Then in 943 he abdicated and his throne passed to his brother Malcolm, who became Malcolm I. Two years later, Malcolm came to an arrangement with Athelstan's brother and successor, Edmund I, whereby he agreed to be the English king's 'fellow worker both by sea and land'. The phrase was meant by the chronicler to indicate that Malcolm would provide troops and ships in any wars for which the English king might demand them. In return, Malcolm was given the kingdom of Cumbria, which must mean that part of Strathclyde that was below the Solway. This was the beginning of that centuries-old belief of the English that they are sovereign over Scotland. No doubt it was dragged out by Edward I in support of his outrageous claims to Scotland at the end of the thirteenth century.

Thirty years after Malcolm's acquiescence, Edgar of England took a fleet through Scottish waters and frightened the then Scottish king Kenneth II (great-great-grandson of Kenneth Mac-Alpin) into acknowledging subservience to England. With six other equally submissive kings in Britain (Irish, Welsh and Viking) Kenneth rowed Edgar in a boat across the river Dee near Chester. It was a gesture, but it was taken seriously by all concerned.

Finally, around 1018, Malcolm II, son of Kenneth II, fought the Lothian Angles at Carham on the river Tweed, not far from Roxburgh, and won a decisive victory. He annexed Lothian and thus brought into Scotland the land from the Forth to the Tweed. He was helped by Owen, king of Strathclyde, who died soon after the battle. His kingdom passed to Malcolm, either as a gift or as the result of another battle. The kingdom of Scotland was now larger than it had ever been before, despite the Viking presence in Caithness and Sutherland and the northern islands. There was to be an almost endless dispute over how much of Cumbrian Strath-clyde should become part of Scotland and how much should remain English, and the border between Scotland and England was to be contested, shifted, agreed, contested again, for many years to come. But the kingdom of Scotland embraced much the same area as it did nearly seven hundred years later, when it was joined with that of England and Wales by the Act of Union in 1707.

Malcolm II died in 1034: he had ruled since 1005. He was succeeded by his grandson Duncan I, who was not the ageing and venerable monarch portrayed by Shakespeare in *Macbeth*. He was actually an impetuous and spoilt young man whose six years of kingship brought glory neither to Scotland nor to his family. Against the advice of his counsellors he invaded Northumbria and attacked Durham. The campaign was a disaster for Scottish arms and Duncan was compelled to withdraw. When he got back to Scottish soil news of his defeat had preceded him, and in no time he was faced with revolt among the lords, particularly those led by his cousin Macbeth, *mormaer* (or lord) of Moray. In a skirmish at Bothgouanan Duncan was slain. He had come to the throne by means of the weird system of succession. Macbeth had an even better claim, as far as strict descent was concerned: so had his wife, Gruach, who was his cousin. Both were descended from Kenneth MacAlpin, and the Moray party were keen to have Macbeth as their ruler.

We have mentioned the term *mormaer*. It was the word for a high official or viceroy in the kingdom of the Scots and Picts. The origin is obscure. There were for a time seven provinces in the kingdom, each governed by a mormaer on behalf of the king. The seven were Angus, Atholl, Caithness, Fife, Mar, Moray, Strathearn. These were not the same districts as those of the same names later in Scottish history. For example, in Macbeth's time Moray was much larger than it was in the fifteenth century or today. The mormaers had great power and influence. Some were, like Macbeth, of royal blood. They could put their candidates on the throne and they could – and did – as easily pull them off again. A strong man who combined firm government with a sense of justice could count on support from his mormaers. Macbeth's relatively peaceful rule of seventeen years, generally praised by early historians, is a good example.

Macbeth's career is interesting. Coming to power among

peoples who were trying to adjust to unity but who, at the same time, did not want to give up their own ways of life, which were not always compatible with those of their neighbours, he organized troops of men to patrol the wilder countryside and enforce some kind of law and order. We can judge how effective this was by the fact that in about 1050 he considered his kingdom well enough ordered and his standing among his supporters sufficiently high for him to make a pilgrimage to Rome. Many kings of these times did this. Such journeys entailed several months away from home, and this involved great risk of things going wrong in their absence. Macbeth set off and in Rome distributed sums of money to the poor, generally expected of visiting monarchs. He then returned to find his kingdom quiet and to enjoy a further seven years of rule.

In 1057, however, one of Duncan's sons, Malcolm, known as Ceanmor (Great Head), who had been in exile for some time, raised an army with the help of the English earl of Northumbria, Siward. They invaded Scotland and reached deep into Aberdeenshire. At Lumphanan they defeated Macbeth, who was slain in the battle. His step-son Lulach was able to gather some support among his father's people in Moray and got himself chosen to succeed as king. But within a few months Malcolm, calling himself Malcolm III, defeated Lulach at a skirmish in Strathbogie and put him to death.

Malcolm III was a descendant of Kenneth MacAlpin. He was also the founder of a new dynasty of Scottish kings, sometimes to be known as the house of Canmore. Some historians say that the name means 'great head' of the dynasty. This is a possibility. But Malcolm lived in an age when rulers were nicknamed as a result of physical or behaviour characteristics, like Thorfinn the Mighty, Sweyn Forkbeard, Sigurd the Stout, Edward the Elder, Aethelred the Unready (or Redeless). Was Malcolm known as Big Head because he had a noticeably pronounced head? His reign was a long one and many changes took place in it, but it is a matter of dispute whether it was a distinguished reign, more so whether it was good for Scotland.

CHAPTER 5

CONFLICT
WITH
ENGLAND

(1057–1249)

Macbeth and Lulach were the last of the kings of ancient Scotland.
They were Gaelic-speaking. They represented the old Pictish and
Scottish kingdom of Kenneth MacAlpin, their ancestor. In a sense
they were, in turn, chief of chiefs in the clan system. Until the end
of his reign, Macbeth's kingdom was not involved with English
arms. Unlike many of his successors, he was not troubled by lords
who, secretly or openly, favoured alliance with England, sometimes even subservience to the English king. Macbeth governed his
country effectively from that part of it which was most familiar and
pleasant to him, the north-east. If he had not lost the battle at
Lumphanan he would have steered Scotland in a direction very
different from that which it took under Malcolm III. But Malcolm
triumphed, with English help, and among his supporters were
Scottish lords who had ties with England. Some perhaps had
obligations. Thus were sown the seeds of an 'English party' in
Scotland, and these were to flourish, with terrible results. It was
the beginning of the process whereby Scottish lords were induced
with money and other gifts to promote English causes in Scotland.
This same process was operating when the English steamrollered
the Scots into the Act of Union in 1706–7.

The system of succession in Scotland was still not a clear-cut one. Under it, Malcolm III would probably not have followed his father Duncan I in 1040 even if he had been an adult. Being but a young boy made it even less likely that he would have been chosen by the Scottish lords in preference to Macbeth. Instead, Malcolm left Scotland and went to live in England. He may have spent some time at the English court of Edward the Confessor (1042–66) who had himself spent much of his youth in Normandy and made many Norman friends. Whether Malcolm did that or not, he fell under English influence. Living away from the land of his native tongue, Gaelic, he learned to speak English and he grew up used to English ways. He may also have spent time in Normandy, where he would have seen at close quarters something of the feudal system of landholding, with service given to the duke in return for land.

Thus, by the time he came of age, in the 1050s, Malcolm had had a thorough grounding in two alien ways of life. Many of the English lords looked favourably upon him as a contender for the Scottish throne, not for his own sake or, indeed, for Scotland's, but because it was established English policy to get the Scots to recognize the English as their overlords by influencing the kings and their counsellors, or if that failed, by force. Malcolm became a pawn of the English. They offered him military support to win the throne of Scotland from Macbeth, but only because they thought this would serve their end. But once Macbeth was slain, Lulach deposed, and the Scottish crown safely on Malcolm's head, he chose to forget his obligations to England. He looked instead to the Vikings in northern Scotland for help and he made an alliance with them. In 1059 he married Ingibjorg, widow (or some say, daughter) of Thorfinn the Mighty. This made him a formidable opponent of England. In 1061 he invaded Northumbria and ravaged the western parts of Cumbria. His sights were set on the strategically important town of Carlisle, but the English succeeded in holding him off. Eventually he withdrew. Then in 1066 the whole political situation in England was abruptly altered. William, duke of Normandy, crossed the English Channel, landed near Hastings and totally defeated the English main army. The king of England, Harold II, was slain on the field, with most of his lords and knights.

Ten sixty-six was also an important year for Scotland. As William of Normandy reduced the Anglo-Saxon people very rapidly to a state of virtual slavery, Malcolm of Scotland had to think again about his policy towards his neighbour England. Some members of the Anglo-Saxon royal family had fled to Scotland for asylum. One was Edgar, grandson of King Edmund Ironside. Another was his sister Margaret, handsome, devout and learned, a woman of gentle manner, whose only aim in life was to become a nun and devote her time to God and to good works. Enemies had now become allies. Malcolm saw this as an opportunity to do something about the Border between Scotland and England, which we have seen was continuously in dispute. The northern counties of England, Northumberland, Cumberland and Westmorland, were wild, bleak and thinly populated. But Malcolm wanted them for Scotland, as did many of his successors. In his reign of thirty-six years he made several attempts to seize them. His motives are not known for certain, but probably he saw them as a kind of 'no-man's land' between Scotland and England proper, in which he would have preferred Scottish influence to prevail, so that if the two countries went to war, his southern frontier had an additional line of protection of some depth.

Malcolm's wife, Ingibjorg, died in the mid-1060s, and in about 1069 Malcolm married Margaret of the Anglo-Saxon royal house. Legend says he had to work very hard to persuade her to give up her wish to become a nun. He was greatly handicapped by the differences between them. She was a cultured and gentle princess, he a wild, unkempt, pleasure-seeking, quarrelsome warrior who fought and drank even harder than his soldiers. Yet she yielded, and this seemingly unsuited pair enjoyed a long and affectionate relationship. Three of their children were to become kings of Scotland. The marriage, however, alarmed many people. The Gaelic-speaking Scots of the Highlands, the Moray men and others of Pictish and Scottish descent saw it as the end of the predominance of the Gaelic language and way of life. Margaret could easily weaken Malcolm's resolve to preserve Gaelic as the national tongue. And that is what happened. Lothian-English[1] gradually replaced Gaelic as the language of the court, and later government, church and legal circles. The Highland clansmen and their dependent families had to learn to speak it if they wanted to communicate with the king or his officers. The decline of Gaelic was accompanied by changes in the legal system and local government. These were hastened in the twelfth century by the introduction of the feudal system.

The Vikings rightly saw the marriage as a threat to their position in northern Scotland. Over the next two centuries they were very gradually edged out of their possessions. Some chose to integrate with the Scots. Others kept up a kind of armed neutrality, though many were to be found joining rebellions against the royal authority. The Gallgaels of Galloway also regarded the marriage with suspicion. Malcolm might, they thought, bring in foreign troops to curb their independence. And the marriage angered William the Conqueror, and not surprisingly, for Malcolm had married the sister of the Anglo-Saxon pretender to the English throne which William had seized by conquest.

In 1071 Malcolm again led his armies south and invaded Cumberland, possibly to establish the border as a line roughly from Carlisle to Newcastle. He discovered that William's new order was much watered down in the northernmost counties, and the lands were almost undefended. He harried the farms and villages, and carried off so many of the population into servitude that, according to one chronicler, there was no village or even large house in southern Scotland that did not afterwards have a servant or two of English origin. William, however, was enraged. The next year, as soon as the campaigning season began, he brought an army, consisting of knights clad in chain mail and wearing special protection pieces for nose and ears, mounted on fast horses, across the Tweed into Lothian. He despatched a fleet of ships up the Scottish eastern coast, to terrorize the inhabitants of seashore communities and to provide supplies for the troops advancing on land. He crossed the Forth and at an engagement near Abernethy in Perthshire he defeated Malcolm's forces. The Scottish army was no match for the most formidable troops of the time in western Europe.

And yet William's victory was not decisive. The Anglo-Saxon Chronicle goes as far to say that 'he got no advantage from it'. It is true Malcolm had to acknowledge William as overlord of somewhere, but was it Scotland or merely the disputed border district? Subsequent English kings made claims to the allegiance of Scottish kings and regarded them as little more than feudal lords who held Scotland at their favour. But whether Malcolm did promise to accept the English king as overlord or not, his successors did not all consider themselves bound by it.

Malcolm invaded northern England at least three times more,

but on his last attempt, in 1093, he was slain outside the walls of the castle at Alnwick, then no more than a fair-sized earthen mound with a wooden tower and walls of timber planks. The news was brought by his son, Edgar, to his adoring wife, Margaret, herself lying very ill in Edinburgh. Within three weeks she died. The church at Rome made her a saint, in 1251.

What had Malcolm and Margaret accomplished in a long reign? Malcolm had been sufficiently patriotic, but in agreeing to the introduction of English ways at his court, through Margaret's influence, he had alienated large sectors of Scotland. Many Scots despised the luxurious taste for fine clothes, exotic foods and wines, gold and silver tableware and so forth, enjoyed by the king's family and friends. They objected to the new idea that only highborn people could attend the king or hold royal offices, instead of these privileges being open to all classes. They resented the encouragement of English and other craftsmen and merchants to settle in the more prosperous parts of Scotland. And they were offended by the king's new bodyguard of armed troops mounted on horses, which went with him everywhere. And of course they were put out by the official language ceasing to be Gaelic.

For the queen they had more respect, although except among churchmen she was never popular. She found many things about the church and its organization that grieved her. The new monastic ideas and spirit of service to God prevailing in Europe had not made any impact in Scotland. Scottish monks and priests were allowed to marry, and many of them did. They did not live in their community buildings but in their own houses. Offices in the church were hereditary; bishops passed their jobs on to their sons. Men and women in the land worked on Sundays as well as the other six days. Churchmen were on the whole much more easy-going about religious observance than their European contemporaries. But the queen did not attempt to put an end to these differences by royal decrees. Instead she tried to get the church to reform and set an example with her own piety. For instance, for several periods of each year she and the king had beggars brought to them every morning. When they arrived she got on her knees and washed their feet. Orphaned children were brought to them and given food. Some may even have found odd jobs around the royal buildings. Malcolm and Margaret founded religious houses and endowed them with money. One was at Dumfermline.

Margaret's devoutness won her the hearts of many Scottish clergy and monks, and when she summoned them to a conference, at which the peculiarities of the Scottish church were to be aired, they came readily, heard her out and discussed how far they could go along with her ideas. Some were willing to make changes in their establishments. This had two effects. First, it brought the monarchy and the church closer together, which enabled the kings in the future to count much more on church support.[2] Secondly, it paved the way for the new monastic ideas in Europe to spread in Scotland.

There was a reaction when Malcolm and Margaret died. Malcolm's brother, Donald Bane, representing the nationalist Celtic elements in Scotland, took over the throne by right of succession according to the Scottish system. His first act was to drive out all officials and supporters of Malcolm who were English or pro-English. In less than a year he was deposed by Malcolm's son (by Ingibjorg) Duncan II, but soon afterwards Duncan was killed, probably by Donald Bane's supporters who restored him to the throne. Three years later, Donald Bane was deposed again, this time by Edgar, Malcolm's eldest son (by Margaret), who was encouraged and supported by the Normans. For the next few decades there was no serious warfare between England and Scotland, but if the pro-English, propping up Edgar, who reigned from 1097 to 1107, and Alexander I (1107–24), welcomed the peace that followed the acceptance of William II (1087–1100) and Henry I (1100–35) as overlords, they were to find out before long what that overlordship really meant. What it did mean was the introduction into Scotland of the Norman feudal system, which had the most far-reaching effects upon the Scottish state.

The feudal system is often said to have been introduced into Scotland by David I (1124–53), who was the younger brother of Edgar and Alexander. As a prince, David had been given some English land by Henry I and, through marriage, had become an English earl (of Huntingdon). However, the feudal system was already beginning to take root in the reigns of his brothers. Feudalism was the European organization of society brought to Britain by the Normans. Its basic characteristic was the holding of land by one man from another of superior rank in return for military service and payment of certain taxes. It involved everyone from the king downwards. The king was in theory (and in the case of William the Conqueror in England, in fact) owner of all land in the kingdom. He granted estates by means of agreements or charters, which set out the terms of the 'contract' and listed the details. Receivers of large estates likewise parcelled out parts of them to lesser men, and so on down to holders of a few acres with probably no more than one house and a barn or two. The king could also confirm by special charter ownership of lands already held, which was like taking away the land from the owner and saying 'You can have it back again, but on fresh terms, that is, you hold it from me.'

In England the system was imposed by force on a conquered people, swiftly and in most cases brutally. The 'feudalizing' of England took no more than twenty years.[3] In Scotland, however, it was 'fed' into the state organization more gently. The sons of Malcolm had Norman friends and, wanting to give them something, often granted them tracts of land, chiefly in the Lowlands. Some of the recipients were the kind of people who would, if they had remained in England, have had to wait for a long time to inherit from their fathers or uncles, and even then not get much, as Normans tended to pass property to the eldest son. So they were granted lands on much the same terms as those which the Conqueror would have adopted, and the Scottish kings, notably David I, confirmed the grants in charters. Among the Norman families given grants in the early years of the twelfth century were some whose names were later to become famous, or notorious, including the de Brus (who received lands in Annandale), whose descendant was Robert Bruce, Walter Fitz-Alan (from Brittany), whom David I made hereditary steward of Scotland (and thus he became the ancestor of the Stewarts) and the de Baillieuls from Picardy, one of whose descendants was to become king, John Balliol.

This feudal society had the advantage of being well ordered. It enabled the king to be in command of a central organization of government, that is, to be strong and powerful and govern effectively without constant fear of revolt among his most wealthy and powerful lords. After all, what they held they could have taken away from them, if they rebelled unsuccessfully. It provided kings with an army which they could call up at short notice to resist invasion or to put down internal disturbance. It enabled the kings to offer protection to property owners. In theory it meant the maintenance of law and order, and in practice it achieved this in

England under William the Conqueror and his two sons, William II and Henry I, because they were all strong kings. But in Scotland it was going to be very different.

If David I did not actually introduce feudalism into Scotland he certainly opened the way for it to spread in the Lowlands. By the end of his reign there was a long roll of families owning land in Scotland, who had originated in France or England, including the Frasers, Grants, Crichtons, Maxwells, Sinclairs, Hays, Lindsays and many more. And they were established in their domains with followings of tradesmen, merchants and craftsmen who, like their masters, gradually took on Scottish ways, adopted the Lothian-English tongue, mixed it with Norman-French and perhaps some Gaelic words as well. Historians are agreed that the new system led to greater prosperity in the Lowlands, particularly for the lords and their dependants. But it was doomed to produce results in Scotland that the king neither bargained for nor wanted. First, it widened the gulf between the king (and his Lowland associates) and the Highlanders, whose chiefs were certainly not going to allow the king to take over their long established rights over their clansmen. Nor were they going to approve the system whereby lords and knights had to give fixed periods of military service to the king each year. Among the first districts to register their feelings was Moray where, in about 1130, a rebellion broke out. The king was compelled to get help from English nobles from the northern counties, who were friends of his. He granted them permission to move through north-east Scotland and in return for their help to set up domains for themselves. They were among the first people to build castles in Scotland.

Castles were one of the weapons used by kings and feudal lords to impose their rule upon the countryside. They were not at that time the huge stone structures (great rectangular towerhouses surrounded by high stone walls with turrets and gates) that in the fourteenth and fifteenth centuries were to become such a feature of the Scottish countryside. They were mounds of earth, naturally formed, or heaped up by gangs of diggers, on the top of which were erected tall, wooden towers, generally two- or three-storeyed, standing anything from about 25 feet to about 60 feet high. The mound was called a motte, it stood inside a park known as a bailey, and both were surrounded by a tall wooden fence or a ditch (with or without water), or both fence and ditch.[4]

Meanwhile, in Galloway, the descendants of the Gallgaels were not prepared to accept feudalism or the laws that came with it. They became restless, fearing interference with their independence, and the king had to let them keep their own customs. Indeed, as late as the 1380s the Scottish King's Council was still accepting that Galloway had its own special laws. And there were the western islands and the northern parts of Scotland still under the Vikings, whose people reacted to the new system by invading Scottish territory. One of the principal opponents of the king was the great half-Scot-half-Viking hero Somerled, who became king of the Hebrides and Argyll in the 1140s, lands which were outside the control of the Scottish kings. Somerled was descended from the earliest Irish-Scottish kings of Dalriada, and he established sway in the west, also in the Isle of Man. The overlord king of Norway recognized his rule largely because Norway was so far from these parts and Somerled was not a hindrance to him.

Somerled managed to get David I to recognize his independence, and in return swore a vague kind of allegiance as vassal, which he threw off immediately David died in 1153. For the eleven years that followed, Somerled ruled his lands well, harried the Scottish mainland and chased the king's ships at sea around the islands. In 1164 he mounted a raid on Glasgow, already a major town, but he was slain by a spear-thrust in a skirmish near Renfrew. His followers melted away, returned to their ships and fled to the islands and to their mainland havens. Somerled's family were the founders of two important Highland clans, the MacDonalds (through his grandson Donald) and the MacDougalls (through his son Dugald).

The opposition to the feudal idea was perhaps never to be fully overcome by the Scottish kings. Worse, the lords began to use it to their own ends and against the king's. The lords created by Edgar, Alexander and David acquired so much land and formed private armies on such a scale that their immediate successors began to threaten the central authority. The lords became more and more warlike, indulging in violence and bloodshed not as the last resort in a private quarrel but as the usual method of settling disputes. And the reigns of David's successors were taken up very largely with efforts, generally unsuccessful, to curb the power and belligerence of these magnates. Even when Scotland itself was threatened from enemies outside, particularly England, the lords did not always bury their differences in the national interest. Indeed, most of them either ignored or were even unaware of any national interest.

David I spent much of his reign introducing Anglo-Norman ideas into Scotland, and yet he remained a staunchly patriotic Scot. He warred with England over the northern counties. He invaded England and was defeated at the battle of the Standard, at Northallerton, in 1138. He took sides with Matilda, daughter of Henry I, in her struggle with her cousin Stephen during the years 1135 to 1154 for the throne of England. He resisted attempts of the English church to persuade the bishops of Glasgow and St Andrews (among others) to recognize the archbishop of York as archbishop of Scotland. Yet he used English help to quell rebellion among his Scottish subjects, steered the church into line with the organization and practices followed in England, and encouraged the construction of castles by his Norman friends, setting a good example by erecting many of his own at strategic points in the Lowlands and the Midland Valley. And he founded some of the earliest royal burghs, that is, new townships generally near castles, peopled mainly with English families of traders, craftsmen and handymen of all kinds.

This is a strange paradox that has never been explained. It is also a feature of some later Scottish kings – indeed of many ordinary Scotsmen, too – that they should remain proud Scots but not hesitate to use their neighbour England and everything it had to offer whenever they wanted to, or were in trouble in their own land. Scottish nobles often turned to the English kings for support when they were in dispute with their own monarchs.

David died in 1153. Before we look briefly at the reigns of his immediate successors, we should mention something of the work he carried out for the church. He was less squeamish than his mother about the changes wanted in the church. In his time he brought it into line with European disciplines and practices. He made the last real break with the old Celtic church and in so doing got it on to his side in his 'feudalizing' work. He encouraged the foundation of many new monasteries, ensuring that they were houses of continental orders such as the Cistercians and the Augustinians. Among those established in his time were Kelso (Tironensian), Melrose (Cistercian), Dundrennan (Cistercian), Holyrood, Cambuskenneth and Jedburgh (Augustinian). There were many others. He also established new bishoprics and restored old ones so that Scotland was divided into ten sees.[5] As may be expected, the new bishops were nearly all Anglo-Norman associates, and this was deliberate, since they would more readily support his feudal schemes.

The king's reforms went beyond the higher levels of church organization. He introduced parishes within the sees and actively encouraged the building of small churches, especially in Lothian and the north-east plains. Probably it was David who introduced the system of tithe-paying, that is, rendering for the upkeep of the church and its priest one tenth of the value of agricultural and other produce from the parish territory. Certainly he organized the system, but he made the mistake of granting to religious houses special exemptions from various state taxes. He also initiated the practice whereby parishes became part of the estates of these religious houses, so the tithes and other funds raised for the parishes went instead to them. The religious houses grew rich, while the parishes got poorer, a circumstance that served to divide the church.

David died at Carlisle, at that time a Scottish possession. He had occupied much of Cumbria without effective opposition from England. He had obtained control of Northumberland (except Newcastle and Bamburgh) by a treaty in 1139 with Stephen, despite having lost – not won – the battle of the Standard. At Carlisle David began to build the great stone castle that overlooks the Eden river, a symbol of his determination to keep the northern counties Scottish. But it was not to be.

David was succeeded by a grandson, Malcolm IV, aged only twelve. Malcolm's father had been Prince Henry, David's son and heir until his premature death in 1152. The new king was surrounded by Norman advisers and friends of his father and grandfather. This was one of the causes of the revolt in Moray that broke out early in his reign. The people of Moray refused to acknowledge Malcolm as king because they considered the family of Lulach had better claims. At almost the same time rebellion broke out in Galloway in protest against the influence of the Normans at court. After several attempts, Malcolm's forces quelled both revolts, with Norman help, but did not remove the cause nor the ill-feeling. Some of the help received had come from Henry II (Plantagenet) of England, who saw Malcolm's difficulties as a good opportunity to bargain over the disputed ownership of the northern counties. In 1157 the English king succeeded in getting Malcolm to give up the Scottish claim to Northumbria.

Malcolm does not appear to have married, and certainly had no children. When he died in 1165 he was succeeded by his brother William, known as William the Lion because he went into battle with a standard consisting of a red lion rampant on a yellow field. Of this king little can be told that is creditable to himself, of advantage to Scotland or, indeed, of interest to the reader. He reigned for almost half a century but achieved practically nothing. He sought early on to reverse the position about the northern counties and even tried to bargain with Henry of England by offering assistance in the latter's wars, but Henry sent him off with a flea in his ear. William returned to Scotland to wait for a chance to win the counties back. In 1173 Henry was distracted by the rebellion of his eldest son, who marshalled behind him a powerful faction of English and Norman lords. William seized his chance and invaded northern England. He was given promises of help by Henry II's rebel son, Prince Henry, but his attack was nevertheless ill-planned and he was driven back by lords loyal to the English king. The following year, 1174, William marched again into Northumberland and spread his forces round the countryside with orders to ravage and plunder. With a small detachment he himself advanced against Alnwick Castle, which he attempted to besiege. It was a foolhardy exercise. He was outnumbered by the garrison and, worse, a relief force of English soldiers under Ralf de Glanvil was approaching from the south. Skirmishing in a mist, William was unhorsed. Before he could get up from the ground, his horse rolled over on to him and pinned him down, so that he was captured by his opponents.

William was sent in chains and under guard to Henry II who was then at Northampton. He was too busy to deal with his captive, so the Scottish king was taken through England to the Kent coast and then across the English Channel to Henry's castle at Falaise in Normandy. In due course, Henry followed, and at Falaise extracted from William an oath of allegiance as feudal superior. This time the English king spelled out to the Scot exactly what the act of homage meant: William held Scotland only by permission of Henry. Scottish soldiers were to be evacuated from the castles at Edinburgh, Stirling, Roxburgh, Jedburgh and Berwick, which were then to be handed over to English garrisons. And the expenses of the English garrisons were to be borne by the Scots.

It was a bad day for Scotland. The people had to endure their humiliating subservience to England and all that meant for the next fifteen years, until Richard I came to the English throne. Richard, completely absorbed with his scheme to lead and to finance the armies of the Plantagenets on the Third Crusade to the Holy Land, agreed to cancel the obligation to pay homage to England for the kingdom of Scotland in return for a huge cash sum of 10,000 silver marks from the Scottish treasury. That was about £700, or about a tenth of the total income the king of Scotland received from his various dues and taxes. Scotland became independent again and the surrendered castles were returned to their owners. But the cash sum was extremely hard to find and it caused much discontent. In the reign of John (1199–1216) of England, William tried to get his claim to the northern counties recognized but the English king refused. William died in 1214 and was succeeded by his son Alexander II (1214–49) who, with the same aims as his father, almost immediately invaded England.

Alexander was a very different person from his father. Even at sixteen, the age at which he succeeded, he had earned a reputation for wisdom and for strong-mindedness. He chose the time well for his inroad into England. John's hands were full with the rebellion of his barons who were soon to force him to put his seal to Magna Carta.[6] But Alexander met unexpected resistance in England and he was checked. Nonetheless the English king was hardly in a position to exact anything from Alexander, and the result of the encounter could be said to have been a draw. Later in the reign of John's son, Henry III (1216–72), Alexander formally agreed to give up the Scottish claim to the northern counties, and accepted in return an income from certain estates there.

Alexander faced other problems during his rule. A rebellion in Galloway required several expeditions to stamp it out. Descendants of Thorfinn the Mighty and Ingibjorg (mother of Duncan II) rose against him in Moray because they did not accept his qualification to be king (his descent from David I). The danger was not removed until in about 1230 the last of the Duncan descendants, a baby girl, was murdered. And the presence of the Vikings in the north and west was a constant irritation, sometimes quiescent, sometimes active, but needing final solution sooner or later. There were incidents which served only to aggravate matters. In about 1230 Vikings attacked the castle at Rothesay in Bute, then a circular stonewall enclosure with turrets on the perimeter, protected by a ditch. It fell to a siege in which a wooden tunnel was built, whose front opening faced the castle wall and through which the besiegers 'hewed into the wall with axes, because the stone was soft; and the wall fell down after that'. Alexander retaliated by constructing, reinforcing, and encouraging others to build, several castles in the Argyll and islands regions, including Dunstaffnage, which was a MacDougall castle, Sween (said to be the first stone castle ever built in Scotland) and Mingarry. He also went to war with the Vikings in Kintyre.

The Viking problem might also be solved by other methods, thought Alexander, and he tried money. Two bishops were sent over to Norway to visit the Norwegian king, Haakon, overlord of all the Viking lands, and to offer him cash for the remaining Viking territories in Scotland, western islands, Orkneys, Shetlands and the mainland regions. Haakon is said to have replied that he did not need money. So Alexander decided to mount an invasion of the western islands. In 1249 he assembled a large fleet of ships, many of which were a particularly fast type of galley belonging to the MacDougalls, then powerful in Argyll and owners of the best warships in Europe. He set out, but only a few miles off Oban he was taken ill and had to stop at the island of Kerrera. There he died, aged fifty. The expedition was called off. The Vikings earned a breathing-space, but the time for the decisive battle could not be put off much longer, and it came in the next reign.

Alexander was succeeded by his son, also called Alexander, who was only eight years old. He had been promised in marriage to Margaret Plantagenet, a daughter of Henry III, who was but a year older. To some it may have seemed an innocent enough match, but it was an important stage in the gradual tightening of the English monarchy's grip on Scotland. The boy Alexander III was one day to pay homage to an English king (Edward I) for the land of Scotland, and to do so without pressure. The fortunes of Scotland were becoming increasingly entwined with those of England. In the next chapter we see how some of the Scots attempted to break out of the tangle.

CHAPTER 6

SCOTS
WILL BE
FREE

(1249–1371)

Alexander III was the last of the kings from the line of Malcolm III. In a sense he was the last truly Scottish king, for all those who followed were largely of foreign descent, mainly Norman or French, with some (though not much) Scottish blood. In many respects Alexander was the best of his dynasty. For once, the provinces that habitually rebelled, like Galloway and Moray, were quiet. His military activity was largely confined to his great and successful campaigns against the Norsemen. He was generally remembered in Scottish history as 'the peaceable king'. In his time the prosperity of all classes advanced. A now forgotten Scottish writer described his rule as one of peace and love in the land, and plenty of 'ale and bread, of wine and wax (cake), of game and glee [happy singing]'. It is a good place at which to look closer at everyday life in Scotland in the thirteenth century.

One result of the 'infiltration' of the Normans and their ideas into Scotland was a gradual change in the economy. Up to the twelfth century it had been an agricultural economy. Even in the least arable parts or those where livestock generally had to roam huge distances to get enough nourishment, some kind of living was possible for all. If you could not grow good crops to sell, you could rear cattle and sheep, and either would bring in enough money or goods you wanted in exchange. Bartering goods was the more usual way of obtaining your needs, as coinage did not become widespread until the thirteenth century. Most people worked on their own patches, even if in the Highlands the patches were part of a clan chief's territory and in the Lowlands leased in some way from big landlords. There were also some towns, small by comparison with what had already grown up in England and elsewhere in Europe. Dumfermline had been a favourite with Malcolm III and Margaret, and there were beginnings at Stirling, Edinburgh and Glasgow. There were also many villages, tiny communities that had probably not changed for centuries. But Scotland was still a land of huge, wild open spaces, farmed haphazardly where the grass or earth was good.

Then, gradually, foreigners were encouraged to move into the Lowlands and the north-eastern plains by Malcolm III, David I and his successors, including Englishmen, Danes and Flemings (from the Low Countries). Many of these people were not farmers, but merchants, traders and craftsmen. They came as followers or dependants of Norman or Flemish lords invited by the kings, or in some instances they were immigrants who were not attached but were anxious to make a new life in a pleasant land. The kings encouraged them with grants of land. Many of these were in the newly created burghs which in the twelfth century were growing up in well-sited positions near rivers, harbours and important tracks in Lowland Scotland.

To begin with, the burgh was a small town, surrounded by a rampart and wooden fence. The idea was based on the earlier Anglo-Saxon *burhs* which were fortified townships specially constructed for communities in England to shelter in and where people could continue everyday life under some kind of protection from the raids of the Vikings. The new Scottish burghs were often sited next to a castle that belonged to the king, or to a lord who had permission to build it. In many burghs, like Berwick, Edinburgh and St Andrews, the main street, or high gait, led directly to the entrance to the castle. This meant they were to some extent protected by the castle garrison. The burghs were called royal burghs because they had been created on king's land and the foundation confirmed in a charter. The people who lived in them had special privileges and duties. They were specially protected from violence; they were exempt from taxes due to feudal lords; and they were allowed to hold their own markets.

Burghs were also created on existing settlements and as a rule these had the same rights. The inhabitants paid tolls such as merchants' fees to sell goods in the market, stallholders' fees and percentages on goods sold. They could, however, raise fees from peasants coming in from outside to sell them goods. They had to provide their own internal police force to maintain order and arrest thieves and vagabonds (the castle garrison was there only to protect them from outside violence). They took turns in patrolling the streets after dark. The high gait had side streets and alleys known as wynds and vennels, and it was by no means safe to wander home in the dark carrying the day's takings in coins in a purse or bag.

Burgh residents, or burgesses, elected their own magistrates, called bailies. Legal and other local business was often dealt with at open meetings. To a large extent the burghs were self-governing. They had their own laws, different from the laws of the land. They even had their own 'mini-parliaments'.

The development of the burghs gradually changed the economy of the country into a commercial one.[1] Burghs and their surrounding countryside produced goods such as fine cloth, wool, hides, woodwork and furs, and they traded them with other burghs, or with England, or Europe. They imported wine, spices, jewellery and also raw materials. And yet the burgh was a small unit, certainly up to the seventeenth century. Berwick, said to have been the biggest in the 1280s and 1290s, had only 1500 people in it. Stirling did not have that number until the sixteenth century. Burghs were at some time administrative centres for the local sheriffs (see p. 71). Not all the burghs were royal; there were episcopal burghs, like Glasgow, burghs belonging to abbeys (Arbroath) and burghs owned by lords, like Dunbar.

The changes in the economic life of Scotland were accompanied by changes in the law. People make laws to meet circumstances and they alter them when the circumstances change. Generally, they leave legislation to elected representatives, or in some cases the laws are made by kings or dictators and the cliques of advisers around them. Sometimes new laws arise from revolution or civil war. At this period in Scottish history there were so many needs for development of the law that the kings and their advisers could not ignore them, but they were not brought about all at once.

The law of the Highlands was the law of the clan chiefs. To a great extent it remained so up to the seventeenth century. In Galloway, the Gallgaels refused to accept the royal writ (jurisdiction) at least till the thirteenth century, and after that they would only admit changes very slowly. The rest of Scotland observed the royal writ, though many of the more powerful feudal lords sidestepped it wherever they could. David I introduced the office of sheriff, but only in the Lowlands and the north-east. The sheriff was a high official whose job was to administer a whole district, about the same as a Scottish shire. In his district there would be at least one royal castle, and generally several more, and one would be his headquarters. From it he exercised a wide range of powers, collecting taxes and rents for the king, hearing lawsuits, trying criminal cases, summoning the levies of men when armies were wanted, and so on. But the sheriff was not able to exercise much control over the feudal baronies which became almost like small kingdoms on their own. It was not easy therefore to bring the whole kingdom under one uniform legal system, and the differences were among the main reasons for the long struggle between king and lords, which is described on pp. 89–105. There is an irony in the fact that the kings who introduced sheriffdoms as extensions of their government were challenged by the same feudal lords who became powerful enough to do so because of the land grants they had had from those kings. Some lords managed to get the sheriffdoms under their control, so that they could make the appointments. Some even arranged for the sheriffdoms to be hereditary offices, inside their families or dependent upon them. It is very doubtful if David I envisaged or wanted that dangerous state of affairs.

Notwithstanding the activities of over-mighty feudal lords, a central administrative authority gradually emerged around the king in Scotland. He could not expect to govern the entire kingdom, or even those parts that accepted his writ, merely on his own or through his sheriffs. He had to delegate specific authorities to other key officials, and over the years the kings built up a kind of Cabinet of government, of men who were loyal, able and in the main fearless. The principal officials were a Chancellor, a Constable, a Chamberlain and Justiciars. The chancellor was perhaps the

71

most important. He was keeper of the great seal, which in practice meant that every document, charter or treaty that required the king's seal of approval had to pass through him or his staff. Generally, he was a cleric, because only people associated with the church were educated enough in those days to handle state business and to talk on equal terms with court officials in other lands. His office remained among the very top offices of state for centuries, though later kings were to have private secretaries who handled matters more closely connected with them, and these secretaries were keepers of the privy seal.

The constable was a military appointment, and his job was to protect the king at home and while travelling. Generally, he was one of the main army commanders in time of battle. The office became hereditary quite early in its history, and the family of Hay, a Norman family, has held it to the present.[2] The chamberlain was the king's chief accountant, or banker. He collected the taxes and paid out the money for the king's expenses, often through the sheriffs. His title comes from the Latin *camera* meaning treasury. Because a substantial part of the monies he collected came from burghs on king's land, he had overall responsibility for the burghs.

There was more than one justiciar (to begin with, there were several), and each had the responsibility of supervising the work of a particular sheriff who was himself a local law officer and magistrate rolled into one. Justiciars travelled about their regions hearing appeals against sheriff's decisions. By the 1300s, however, the number of justiciars had come down to two, one for the north above the river Forth, known as the Justiciar for Scotland, and the other for the south, called the Justiciar for Lothian. As an office, it has survived in the present appointment of Lord Justice General, though the duties have changed.

In addition to these high officials, kings had a council of advisers. It was called the *curia regis*, a term widely used in Europe, in state and in church, to mean King's Court; its content and size varied over the years. Its role was judicial and administrative, that is, it could try cases and it would also carry out official jobs, through its members individually or collectively. Membership included the royal family, high clerics in the church, some feudal lords and the officials we have mentioned. Occasionally its meetings would be extended to include the larger landowners, or tenants-in-chief, and then it would be known as the Great Council. The *curia*, or Council, advised on all kinds of state matters. It sat as a court of justice in much the same way as the House of Lords in London did – and sometimes does today. It could hold special enquiries. It could discuss taxes, customs duties and raising of loans. It even heard lawsuits from ordinary people. Sometimes its meetings were known as parliaments, which is interesting because the first mention of the use of this word occurs in documents of the twelfth century, half a century or more before the first parliament of Simon de Montfort in England (1265). But the Scottish 'parliament' was not then as representative as Simon's; burgesses were not summoned to attend.

All this took many years to evolve. Legal systems generally take a long time to develop; yet there are safeguards in the slowness, for every step is constructed, tested, amended where needed, and that in the long run is advantageous for everyone. In Galloway, for example, the idea of a jury of twelve men to try cases, accepted in most other parts of Scotland, was regarded as quite unsatisfactory. Gallgaels much preferred the older system whereby a man accused could get acquitted if he could find twenty-four people willing to swear that he was not guilty. They were not averse, either, to resorting to trial by combat, where the accuser and the accused fought it out. If the accused won, he was acquitted. After about 1400, the Gallgaels reluctantly accepted the jury system.

Under Alexander III Scotland enjoyed a high degree of justice. Alexander took personal interest in how his justiciars meted it out in their regions, and even travelled about checking up that they were not abusing the law. He sat as judge himself in many local courts and earned a reputation for quick and fair decisions.

For the first years of Alexander's reign, Scotland was managed by regents, first one put up by one group of lords, and then another supported by different lords. This played right into the hands of the king of England, Henry III, who was the father of Alexander's child-wife Margaret. He claimed to be the principal counsellor of the king of Scotland and goaded the pro-English lords into deposing those regents who were not pro-English. He also claimed to be overlord of Scotland. Then in 1262, at a time when Henry was having some difficulty in holding on to his own throne, Alexander came of age and asserted himself. He emerged very quickly as a forceful young man, a patriot, determined to make Scotland a nation that would count in Europe. For this he knew he had to bring about the final reckoning with Haakon of Norway over possession of the Hebrides, the other western islands and if possible the Orkneys and Shetlands. He was supported by some lords who no doubt saw his policy as an opportunity for them to enlarge their own territories: few Scottish lords of those days ever looked at things in a broad national sense.

To begin with, Alexander tried to buy Haakon's interests with cash, as his father had, but again the great Norwegian was not interested. In 1262 one of Alexander's feudal lords, the earl of Ross, invaded Skye, then a Viking possession. Whether he did so with the king's agreement or not, he did it much violence and many Viking settlers were killed or wounded. The islanders sent for help from Haakon and he responded. For years he had let things drift in these outlying Scottish territories. Now he decided that they must be consolidated, and at the same time the Scottish king taught a lesson. So he put in hand the assembly of the biggest armada of ships, filled with troops, ever to be gathered together by the Vikings throughout their history. He sent orders to viceroys in the Orkneys, the Hebrides and the Isle of Man to join him with their fleets and forces. Meanwhile, he set out with about 100 warships and headed for the western side of Scotland.

Somewhere near Oban the various fleets met, though it is likely that some viceroys held back, preferring to see which side would prevail in the forthcoming confrontation. Haakon sent about forty ships up Loch Long and ordered the captains to drag them across the land the other side and then enter the water again, in Loch Lomond. This was to try to carry his invasion right into the heart of Scotland.

But the Vikings did not find Alexander unprepared. He had for some time been fortifying his royal castles near the sea, along the loch edges and also inland in the west, and among these were Sween, Dunstaffnage and Dumbarton. In some cases this actually meant converting wooden palisade walls into thick stout walls of stone, even building – or at least starting to build – towers of stone. Autumn 1263 approached as each side manoeuvred into as favourable a position as it could. Alexander had no great fleet of his own, and the MacDougall fast galleys (see p. 67) were not all ready for use. So he moved about on land hoping to draw the Norwegians and their island allies into battle. Haakon sailed up the Clyde to avoid this trap, but a terrible storm blew up at the end of September and scattered and sank a great part of his fleet.[3] Many ships were driven aground and the men could not get them afloat again. The survivors of those that sank struggled ashore. And by the shore, near Largs, on 2 October, Alexander and his army were waiting for them, rows of archers in front of squadrons of mailed knights on horseback. It was not a large force but the result of the battle was decisive. The Scots drove the Vikings back to the Clyde, cutting many of them down on the way.

Haakon survived, though many of his captains and warriors did not. He abandoned his campaign and set sail for home, stopping at Kirkwall in the Orkneys. There he died, and with him passed his great empire. His fleet was shattered. His successor Magnus had not the capacity with which to enforce any dominion over the western islands, and at the Treaty of Perth, Magnus agreed to hand over to Alexander the western islands in return for a sum of 4000 marks. The Orkneys and Shetlands were to remain Norwegian.[4] The treaty was a good one. It allowed the Vikings to stay where they wanted and even gave them a measure of independence. This was illustrated by the continuance of Viking traditions in Caithness and Sutherland, surrounded as they were by the Highlanders. As for the Hebrides, the most apt comment on the victory of the Scots has been made by the great historian J. D. Mackie, who said 'It made little difference to the Islesmen: hitherto, they had disobeyed the king of Norway; now they disobeyed the king of Scots.'

For the rest of his reign, Alexander ruled wisely and earned great affection and regard. But in the Highlands he was no more success-ful than his forebears. There were few burghs to speak of, the king's law was not widely known and where it was it was ignored. The hold of the clan chiefs on their families remained absolute. Elsewhere, however, Scotland enjoyed sound government and economic prosperity, such as it had not done before, though saying this requires to be qualified by the understanding that the prosper-ity took some time to be felt in the humbler ranks of society, and even then may not have meant more than a stability in the value of goods.

But while the poet sang Alexander's praises, he did not mention that Alexander had been summoned by the English king, Edward I, to the latter's coronation in 1274, and summoned in his capacity as a vassal king. Worse, Alexander had accepted the summons and gone to London for the ceremony. We do not know why he went.

Perhaps he felt he could afford to go and pay lip service to the English king's demand to be acknowledged overlord of Scotland (which he was not), because by so doing it would prevent Edward from mounting an invasion of Scotland.

In 1286 an appalling disaster happened near Burntisland in Fife. The king was riding towards Kinghorn to join his young wife, Yolande de Dreux. It was dark and a fearful storm was sweeping the Firth of Forth. But the king was determined to ride on. Suddenly, he lost his way in the swirling rain and in a moment had ridden over a cliff, down, down to the shore below where he crashed to his death. Scotland was accustomed to violent ends for her kings; few indeed had died in their beds. But Alexander left no male heir. Worse, his heir was his granddaughter, a little girl of four, who had never seen her country. She was Margaret, daughter of Eric of Norway and his wife Margaret, Alexander's daughter. Guardians were appointed to rule her kingdom, and for four years all was quiet. Then in 1290, on her way home, her ship put in at harbour in the Orkneys. There she died, and to this day the cause of her death remains unknown.

When Alexander's death was known, the news was received with the greatest sadness throughout Scotland. In England, however, Edward I heard it with some satisfaction. He had recently conquered Wales and sought to build a united Britain under one king – himself. While Alexander lived, Edward was reluctant to provoke war, for he could not be sure that he would win. But the position was dramatically changed by Alexander's death. Moreover, wittingly or unwittingly, the new queen's father played right into Edward's hands. Eric asked Edward to ensure that the Scottish guardians did their job properly. Edward naturally obliged: he had already decided to persuade them and Eric to agree that the infant Margaret should be betrothed to his young son, Edward of Caernarvon. This should ensure that one day young Edward would become king of both kingdoms – by right. In the meantime Edward himself would act as king of both. The unification of Britain would be achieved. But whether the Scots wanted this or not never entered Edward's head: the Plantagenets were unaccustomed to bothering about other people's wishes when their own desires were involved.

Margaret died in 1290, and Edward's plans went awry. But it opened up an alternative and perhaps more immediate possibility.

There were at least three good heirs to the infant queen's crown: they were all descendants of David I; they all owed something to the English; and none of them would be acceptable to the other two. Civil war would follow as they wrangled over the succession, unless of course they could put the matter to outside arbitration. An arbiter was waiting, eager and ready to back his 'offer' to mediate with force – Edward. The heirs accepted. Then, with an arrogance astonishing even in a Plantagenet ruler, Edward dictated that before he gave his decision, whomsoever he chose had first to acknowledge him (Edward) as overlord of all Scotland.

In the end Edward weighed up the claims of two heirs, Robert de Brus (Bruce), great-great-grandson of David I through his great-granddaughter Isabella, and John de Bailleul (Balliol), great-great-great-grandson of David I through his elder great-grand-daughter Margaret. Both contenders were of Norman descent, were feudal lords in Scotland, with lands also in England. Bruce had the stronger following; he had been named heir twice during the reigns of Alexander II and Alexander III at periods when those kings had had no sons. Yet Edward chose Balliol, probably because he knew that Balliol was a weak and ineffectual man who would not command much loyalty. Edward had got himself a lackey, and he treated him with contempt. He egged on English lords to bring frivolous complaints against Balliol in the Scottish courts and parliament, to irritate and humiliate him. He sent for Balliol to come to England on trivial pretexts, merely to assert his overlordship. On one occasion he ordered Balliol to answer at Westminster some petty claim by a Gascony wine merchant against his predecessor Alexander III for some wines that had not been paid for.

In 1294 Edward went to war with France. He summoned his lords and knights in the traditional feudal manner, and Balliol was included. No distinction was made that he was king of Scotland. This time, however, Balliol had had enough: he ignored the call. Instead, he approached the French court (with which Scotland had had ties for nearly a century) and made a treaty. It was the first of a long line of such arrangements between the two kingdoms, to be known as the 'Auld Alliance'. Balliol formally discarded his allegiance to Edward.

The English king was extremely angry. He took an army across the Tweed to Berwick, then a Scottish town, and besieged it.

Berwick fell quickly. It had hardly any stone walling, only a ditch and rampart, with wooden palisading. To emphasize his fury Edward let his army loose in the town. The garrison was massacred, prisoners were put to death, buildings burned to the ground, shops looted, churches smashed. He sent his principal general, his friend de Warenne, to take the castle at Dunbar, and there the same destruction followed. And as news of the atrocities spread, many other Scottish castles surrendered at once or after token resistance, including Roxburgh, Edinburgh and Stirling, all of them key fortresses. Edward marched on to Scone and ordered the sacred Stone of Destiny to be removed and carried to London. Cartloads of valuable and important Scottish documentary records were also stolen, most of which have never been returned. Balliol was compelled to abdicate and Edward decided to rule Scotland himself, through de Warenne as viceroy. Scotland was to be treated as just another English county. An Anglo-Norman lord was made treasurer, another was appointed sole justiciar, both replacing the Scottish holders, English officials were appointed to collect taxes, English judges heard cases, English soldiers garrisoned castles and made the Scots pay their expenses. Effectively, the arrangements applied only to Lothian, for not even Edward was able to make headway in the Highlands. There was little sign of Edwardian government beyond Stirling, Perth, Dundee and Glasgow.

The English were blind as well as arrogant if they imagined that a great and proud people like the Scots would tolerate foreign domination so tamely and without opposition. They began to resist at once, but it was not the lords and rich landowners who had much to lose if they were caught, but more humble gentry like William Wallace, whose family had a smallholding in Renfrewshire.[5] Wallace's wife had been killed and his household assaulted by English soldiers on the rampage from the garrison at Lanark. Wallace killed the garrison commander in return. This was the signal for revolt. Soon he had gathered about him a small but tough and determined band of warriors dedicated to the task of driving all the English, military and civilian, out of Scotland. They lived and trained in hiding, and would suddenly spring upon an English-held castle or fortified town and take it by surprise. One after another the castles fell. Meanwhile, to the north-west, similar resistance was organized by another minor knight, Andrew de

Moravia, who mobilized the men of Moray. Wallace and Moravia called themselves the Commanders of the Army of the Kingdom of Scotland and even wrote to German trading towns to ask them to continue recognizing Scotland as an independent nation.

In 1297 the two forces took on an English army near Stirling. As the English, led by de Warenne, began to cross the Forth, the Scots attacked them when they were 'bottle-necked' on the narrow wooden bridge, and scattered them. It was a great victory, but it was one thing to ambush an army as it is squeezed between bridge walls, quite another to engage one in the open field. And near Falkirk the English re-formed, brought up more archers and more mailed knights, and defeated the Scottish patriots. Wallace fled from the field; Moravia may have been killed, for he disappears from history.

Wallace was beaten in battle but he was undaunted. With a price on his head he remained in hiding for the next few years, coming out now and again with a small band of patriots to attack an English castle or camp, or raid a town occupied by English people. In 1305 he was betrayed, it is said by the servant of a pro-English lord, and taken to London for trial. He was found guilty of treason – an astonishing verdict when one considers that he had never accepted the overlordship of Edward and was but a patriot fighting in and for his own country. Wallace was hanged, drawn and quartered, the English punishment for treason. His head was spiked on London Bridge and the four quarters of his corpse displayed at key points in Scotland. If Edward thought by this shameful exhibition to cower other patriots in Scotland, he failed. Opposition to the English stiffened, and it was triumphantly vindicated by Bruce at Bannock Burn in 1314 (see p. 81). And Wallace became the greatest hero in all Scottish history.

Feelings about Wallace's end can be well imagined. Men looked for another leader, and they turned to Robert, grandson of the Bruce who had not been picked by Edward in 1292. This remarkable Anglo-Norman lord, then about thirty years old, tough, sagacious, but hot-tempered, had for some time regretted his earlier subservience to the English king. He had come to admire the Scottish traditions and had absorbed many of their characteristics. His claim to the throne was the best among all claimants, and what it would bring was clearly more attractive to him than continuing to be regarded as a feudal lord of a foreign ruler. In a way Bruce was becoming more Scottish than the Scots, just right for one who would lead the Scots out of English dominion.

Sometime in 1306 Bruce decided to assert his claim. To do so he had first to neutralize opposition from other claimants. One was Sir John Comyn (Red Comyn) who was a relative. Comyn and Bruce had been at loggerheads for years: in the late 1290s they had quarrelled when Comyn betrayed a campaign of resistance organized by Bruce to Edward. Now they met at Dumfries, in a church, and quarrelled again. This time Bruce drew a dagger and stabbed Comyn to death. It was a serious crime, made worse because it was in church. But Bruce was unrepentant; indeed, he may have engineered the meeting in order to despatch a dangerous rival. Even Bruce's excommunication by the church for the crime did not deflect him from his course, and with the assistance of a few close friends, notably the countess of Buchan, sister of the earl of Fife, he rode across country to Scone, there to have himself solemnly crowned king of Scotland. To strengthen the meaning of his 'coronation', he was crowned by the countess and the ceremony was attended by three bishops, Glasgow, St Andrews and Moray, as well as the abbot of Scone.

So far, so good, but Bruce had a long way to go. His first skirmish with the English, in 1306 at Methven, was a defeat for him and he had to flee to the Highlands. His brother Nigel was taken and put to death. His family fortress of Kildrummy was besieged and taken. The countess of Buchan was captured and put in a cage at Berwick. In the west Highlands, Bruce ran into trouble with the MacDougalls who were kinsmen of Comyn. They defeated him and almost captured him as he left the field. But in 1307 Edward I of England died at Burgh-on-Sands on the Border, just as he was about to bring yet another invasion force into Scotland. For the moment Bruce could relax. He knew something about the new king, Edward II – gentle, indolent, unwarlike, with no stomach for hard fighting. Edward had been enjoined by his father to continue to 'hammer' the Scots, but hardly had the invasion force got into Nithsdale when young Edward ordered it to return to England. Bruce used the opportunity to mount a campaign of daring raids upon English-held castles and captured them, Edinburgh (taken by stealth at dead of night by his nephew Thomas Randolph), Caerlaverock, Perth, Brechin, Linlithgow and Roxburgh, while his brother Edward Bruce is said to have taken thirteen castles in

Galloway alone. Finally, in 1314, Stirling Castle was besieged by Edward Bruce who rashly challenged the garrison commander, Mowbray, to hand it over if an English relief force had not come to Stirling by Midsummer Day (24 June). Mowbray accepted.

Meanwhile, Robert Bruce had also to deal with a considerable variety of personal enemies in Scotland. There were the Mac-Dougall lords of Lorne and Argyll, still implacably opposed to him; there were Scottish lords who remembered his earlier subservience to Edward I. Bruce defeated the MacDougalls, broke their power and drove them from Argyll. He had good allies as well, and one of these, James Douglas, (known to the Scots as 'Good Sir James') became his most trusted friend and counsellor.

Bruce went from strength to strength. Support came in from many sides, the Scottish church (despite the excommunication), the French king (recognizing him as king of Scotland), many of the Celtic clans, and the Macdonald descendants of Somerled. In 1309 Bruce held a parliament at St Andrews, and the delegates addressed a letter to the king of France declaring Bruce to be their leader and prince. And when in June 1314 the reluctant English king was finally prevailed upon to lead an army of some 25,000 into Scotland to relieve Mowbray at Stirling and try to retake all that had been lost since 1307, Bruce was confident he could challenge him, although his effective military strength was about half that number of men.

June 1314 came, and by the third week Bruce knew it would not be many days before the English reached the open plains near Stirling. On 21 or 22 June he drew up his men on the ridge straddling the Stirling–Falkirk road. To the south just at the bottom was the winding stream known as the Bannock Burn. It joined the Forth River a mile or two north-east across some marshes. There, about 12,000 men waited, ready for battle under their commanders, Thomas Randolph, earl of Moray, Edward Bruce, James Douglas and Robert Keith. The English, meanwhile, were coming up alongside the old Roman road from Falkirk towards Bannock Burn. Edward II detached a 3000-strong force of horsemen and infantry under the earl of Gloucester, and sent it on ahead to attack the Scots on their hill. Simultaneously, he sent a smaller force of cavalry round the back of the ridge to wait to deal with the fleeing Scots as they were dislodged from the hill by Gloucester, or so he thought. But Gloucester's attack was repulsed. Edward had to think again. He led the main army, some 20,000 strong, further towards Stirling, and in the low-lying ground between the ridge held by Bruce and the bend in the Forth where the Bannock Burn entered, he camped for the night. He planned to assault the ridge the next day.

Dawn rose on Midsummer Day and the English king had the call to arms sounded. Soon, the main English force began to move, led by Gloucester. It was a frontal attack; not much had been kept back in reserve. Tactically, it was bad generalship. The Scots, with the advantage of downhill going, advanced in good order. When Gloucester accelerated the pace and charged into the Scottish front line, the Scots infantry men suddenly formed themselves into their famous *schiltrons*, rings of men with spears 'levelled at every point of assault', like a bristling hedgehog at bay, and forced the English back. At that moment the three commanders, Douglas, Edward Bruce and Moray, led their men forward and with a tremendous succession of 'shoves' broke the English front lines, pushing them into the rear lines where Edward and his entourage had their backs to the swampy marshes by the stream. Chaos in the English main ranks followed. The king detached a squadron of archers to the left of the Scots where they did some damage to Douglas's men. But Robert Bruce countered by sending forward Keith's cavalry squadrons in among the English bowmen and scattered them. He then ordered up a strong reserve of horsemen and footsoldiers and led them into the thick of the mêlée. Edward of England recognized the signs of defeat and promptly fled from the field, heading for Stirling. His standard was seen fluttering in the wind by the English soldiery on the battlefield, who disintegrated as a force. Some surrendered where they stood; others tried to fight on but were chased into the stream and the quagmires, there to perish. Edward II reached the great castle on Stirling rock but the garrison commander urged him to flee; there was no security in the castle. He might find refuge at Dunbar, some distance away along the north-east coast of Lothian.

The battle of Bannock Burn was a decisive victory – the most crucial military success in all Scottish history. It did not end the war between Scotland and England, but it put Robert Bruce firmly in the ascendant. He had already demonstrated considerable skill as a general and leader; he had been fighting for a just cause; his reputation was beginning to make an impact in the courts and palaces of Europe. And now this victory enhanced it. At home the people had a king to admire, to respect and in the end to love.

Bruce was to rule for another fifteen years. There were more battles, more castle sieges, more invasions of Scotland by the English, more raids by the Scots over the Border. Edward II accepted military defeat but refused to recognize Bruce as king of Scotland, until in 1323 when he and Robert made a kind of truce. Robert on his part refused to accept letters not addressed to him as king of Scots. Meanwhile, in 1320, the lords and the bishops of Scotland had written their famous Declaration of Arbroath, a letter to the pope, John XXII, insisting on recognition of Scotland's independence and on the sovereignty of their king, Lord Robert. 'For as long as one hundred of us shall remain alive we shall never in any wise consent to submit to the rule of the English, for it is not for glory we fight, for riches or for honours, but for freedom alone, which no good man loses but with his life.' The letter was not answered for a long time, but in 1324 the pope finally recognized Robert's title. Four years later, Edward II's son and successor, Edward III, formally recognized Bruce at the Treaty of Northampton, and sealed it with the betrothal of his sister to Bruce's son, David, both of whom were very young children.

What of those last years of Bruce's reign? Although they were filled with war and aggravation, Bruce also held at least sixteen parliaments, put the collection of revenue on a sound footing, restored order in the administration of justice and opened up the counsels of the realm, that is, the parliaments, to burgesses from the burghs. He made a formal treaty with France, got his lords to accept his son David, at the time an infant of but three years, as his heir, and in default of him, his grandson Robert, son of his daughter Marjorie Bruce, and squared his disputes with the pope and the church that had excommunicated him.

One policy of Bruce's is of interest. As a fugitive in the early years of the wars against England and during the years before Bannock Burn, Bruce had seen the erection of numerous castles in southern Scotland. They were generally built by the English or pro-English lords. Some were the wooden towers put up on hastily scooped-up earth mounds (known as motte-and-bailey castles), which served their purposes well enough in those times. Others were the stronger stone tower type, huge, tall, square-plan fortified houses with great thick walls, tiny windows, battlements on top, great gates with iron portcullises or lattice gates called yetts, sited on hillocks, rock promontories, islands in lochs, by rivers, on the coast or at the edge of important roads. They had been symbols of feudalism, a feudalism Bruce himself had supported because he was a feudal lord. Now they became instruments of terror and aggression, 'police stations' of foreign troops grinding a native population down. So Robert ordered castles to be destroyed, or if not destroyed, dismantled enough for their military parts to be useless. He did not want them to be used again by the English. If they were taken in a raid they were to be slighted, that is, rendered ineffective by removal of towers, battlements, bridges and so forth. Numerous castles were slighted by Bruce's direction.

To the great sadness of the Scottish people Bruce died in 1329, aged about fifty-seven, worn out by his exertions and prematurely aged by the desperate kind of life he had led for so long 'on the run'. His brother Edward had been killed on a vainglorious expedition to Ireland in 1318 where he had tried to make himself king. And his two grand and faithful warriors, Moray and Douglas, his principal counsellors of state, were soon to follow. Douglas joined a crusade to the Holy Land. With him he took in a casket the heart of his king, torn from the lifeless body, but was himself killed in Spain in 1330. Moray died two years later, 'a man to be remembered while integrity, prudence and valour are held in esteem'. A heroic age had come to an end, and it did so with a vengeance, for all that these splendid Scottish champions had lived and fought for was to be swept away in the reign of Bruce's son and successor, David II. They were to be 'dark and drublie days', as the poet Dunbar wrote in a verse about the times.

David II was but five when his great father died and was buried at Dunfermline Abbey. He came to the throne fully recognized as king of Scots by the pope, and probably by other European powers, too. That was what his father had fought for, and yet in David's time Scotsmen lived to see their king accept Edward III of England as lord paramount of Scotland. David's first years were a regency under Moray, a continuation of the sound government of Bruce. But when Moray died, the next regent, the earl of Mar, another nephew of Bruce, was a man of very different stamp. No sooner had he become regent than Edward III encouraged Edward Balliol, John Balliol's son, to make a bid for the Scottish crown. Balliol, accompanied by a gathering of lords and knights who had been banished from Scotland in Bruce's time, landed in Fife and easily defeated an army sent against them under Mar (who was slain) at Dupplin Moor. A few months later, however, Balliol and his followers were defeated in Annandale by great Moray's son and James Douglas's brother, Archibald, and Balliol barely escaped with his life. He fled to England.

Edward III thereupon decided to break the Treaty of Northampton (see p. 83) and he invaded Scotland, with Balliol trailing along behind. He defeated Archibald Douglas at Halidon Hill, near Berwick, in 1333 when the bold Douglas heir was bringing reinforcements for the Berwick garrison, and Douglas fell, along with many of his finest warriors. Balliol was declared king by Edward III. In return the treacherous prince handed Edward the southern counties – just like that, yielded up Berwick and its castle, importantly sited on the north bank of the Tweed, and allowed all Lothian to be policed by English sheriffs and their officers. The habitable castles in the region were garrisoned (again) by the English. It was at least as much as Edward I had won in hard fighting.

Meanwhile, young David and his betrothed had fled to France where they remained for nearly nine years. Regents continued to rule in the northern part of Scotland in his name. Then in 1339 Edward III began his protracted struggle with France to establish his claim to the French throne (the Hundred Years War). This took much of the pressure off the Scots. It also left Balliol unprotected. Men of the character of Wallace and Bruce, notably Andrew Moray and William Douglas (the 'Knight of Liddesdale') continued to attack English towns and take their castles. By 1341 it was even safe enough for the young David to come home to his kingdom, for Balliol had fled, never to return. Edward III had neither time nor resources to intervene.

Scotsmen looked to the youthful son of their hero for good government and peaceful times. They were sick of warfare with England, but were nevertheless determined not to become a mere province of Edward's more populous kingdom. They were to be disappointed. Except perhaps in the matter of personal bravery, David had none of his father's qualities. French life had prevented him from acquiring the natural hardness of fibre and strength of character that are so much a part of the Scottish people. When the king of France asked David for a diversionary attack upon England to take some of the pressure off him in France, where Edward had just won Crécy and was besieging Calais, David rashly agreed and led an ill-planned raid into Northumberland. It was disastrous. At Neville's Cross, near Durham, he was defeated. Worse, he was captured by the Northumbrian English lords. His right-hand supporter, his nephew Robert the Steward (son of his sister Marjorie Bruce) managed to get away, but many Scottish knights were slain.

David, who fought valiantly to free himself from his captors, was sent to the Tower of London to await a decision on his future from Edward. It was to be eleven years before he saw Scotland again. And for most of that time he haggled with Edward about the terms for his release. When at last they were settled, probably in 1357, they were extremely hard on Scotland. The most burdensome clause was that a ransom was to be paid to England for his return, and it was fixed at 100,000 marks, payable in instalments of 10,000 a year. Such a sum would have made a sizeable dent in the English treasury; it well nigh crippled the Scottish national finances. It has been estimated that it equalled three-quarters of the entire revenue raised from the nation in a year through agreed taxation. Every man in the land suffered in some way to help meet it, lords, priests, bishops, merchants, knights, farmers, craftsmen, shopkeepers, peasants, and they had to contribute for years, even after the death of David II in 1371, since by that date it had not been paid off. What made the imposition even harder to endure was that once David was back in Scotland, having sworn allegiance to Edward as overlord, he settled down to a life of luxury and idleness, neglecting government. Worse, he often visited England for this or that reason, and on one of these journeys he offered to bequeath his kingdom to Edward III, if he himself had no son to inherit it, in return for the cancellation of the rest of the ransom. When he returned to Scotland from that visit he put the proposal to a parliament summoned at Scone. In no uncertain terms parliament rejected it. Somehow or other they would find the money for the ransom: *Nullo modo voluerunt concedere nec eis aliqualiter assentire.* (In no way would they agree to such an arrangement.)

David died in 1371. There can have been few mourners, and none who did not hope for better times under his successor, his nephew Robert the Steward, hereditary high steward of Scotland, whose family were to take the name Stewart and become the ruling dynasty right to the Union of the Crowns in 1603 and beyond.

The misery and hardship resulting from the commitment to pay this vast ransom was not the only affliction to press upon the people of Scotland. In about 1348/9 the worst plague in the history of the world struck the Near East and Europe. It was the Black Death. Reaching every country in this part of the world, chiefly through people travelling in ships carrying the infection and passing it to others after they came ashore, it was a killer disease that spared no class, no age, no condition of healthiness. Everyone was vulnerable. Scotland received it later than England, but felt its effects to the full. There was a second visitation in about 1361. When it had blown itself out, so to speak, about a third of Scotland's people had died of it. This affected every aspect of farming, trade and manufacturing, and of course the national wealth suffered acutely. How much the more difficult, therefore, it was to have to contribute towards the swingeing ransom tax every year for so many years.

Yet all was not gloom and despondency for Scotland. There were bright patches. Scottish parliaments increasingly influenced the general direction of government. This was not surprising with the king's long absences. Much of the initiative in making parliament more effective as a check on the king or his associates came from the burghs which survived the ravages of the Black Death better than the countryside. There were several occasions when the royal wishes were curtly refused; we have cited one above. Parliament also ensured that the royal family should not get rid of its lands or revenues but must keep them to help pay for their expenses.

In the burghs there was growing strength and self-reliance. To an extent the inhabitants were insulated against many of the burdens and they steadily expanded their trading and commercial activities, which made a significant contribution to the ransom debt but which also strengthened their rights of self-government. Even by the end of the previous century the burghs had their own law courts and their own laws which differed from those in the rest of the country. Then came the privilege of sending burgesses to the parliaments, to the extent that by the end of the fourteenth century the burgesses had come to be accepted as the third estate in parliament (lords and bishops were the other two). Edinburgh had grown into a major port, Aberdeen already had one of the biggest fishing fleets in western Europe, and Inverness was noted for its shipbuilding.

It says much for the toughness and durability of the Scottish character that the nation survived these burdensome years. But Scotland's troubles were by no means yet over.

1 Aerial view of the houses and streets at Skara Brae. There are ten houses in various states of preservation, some of them older than the others. Skara Brae was occupied roughly between 3100 and 2500 BC

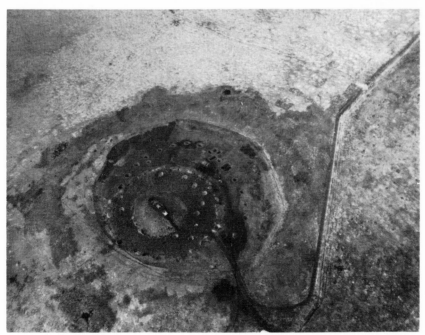

2 The Neolithic and Bronze Age site on Cairnpapple Hill, near Torpichen, Lothian. There were at least five phases of occupation. The earliest, indicated by the arc of seven sockets immediately to the right of the innermost mound, has been dated to about 2700 BC. The site was still in occupation at the beginning of the Iron Age, *c.* 700 BC

3 The Iron Age hill-forts of Brown Caterthun (lower right) and White Caterthun (top left), about five miles north-west of Brechin in Angus-shire. White Caterthun has a massive stone rampart

4 The best-preserved Iron Age broch in Scotland. Mousa Broch is on the western edge of Mousa Island in the Shetlands. Note the small entrance at bottom left. The tower is still over 40 feet high today. At the top it is possible to see an entrance into the galleries in the wall thickness

5 Aerial view of the Carlungie souterrain, about seven miles east of Dundee. The stone-paved sunken passageways are clear. They led to huts on the surface. Carlungie was occupied during the first four centuries AD

6 Looking inside one of the wheelhouses at Jarlshof, Sumburgh Head, 22 miles south of Lerwick, mainland Shetland

7 One of the Pictish stones in Aberlemno kirkyard, near Forfar. The scene on the stone is of a battle, and it illustrates fighting between trained troops, with a clear picture of the skilful use of horses. It has been suggested that the stone commemorates some important battle in Pictish history

8 An illustration from the eighth-century Book of Kells, the Irish illuminated manuscript of the Gospels. The picture is of a Scottish warrior

9 The remains of the Norse cathedral on Birsay Island, at the north end of Orkney mainland. It is basically of mid-eleventh-century construction. The wall in the foreground is the northern wall of the cathedral cemetery

10 A decorated Viking sword hilt, probably of the ninth century, now in the National Museum of Antiquities of Scotland

11 The oldest surviving structure at Edinburgh Castle, the chapel of St Margaret, wife of King Malcolm III (1057–94), in Norman style

12 A mural showing the great Battle of Largs, 1263, when Alexander III crushed the Vikings under Haakon. It was painted by William Hole

13 A fine equestrian statue of Robert I (Bruce), erected in 1964, on the field of his tremendous victory over the English at Bannock Burn

14 Elgin Cathedral, Morayshire; the east front. Founded in the 1220s and built under French Gothic influences, it was burned by Alexander Stewart, 'the Wolf of Badenoch', in 1390. Some rebuilding was done afterwards

15 Aeneas Sylvius, later Pope Pius II, once visited the court of James I (1406–37). The scene was painted by Pinturicchio

16 The magnificent Borthwick Castle, one of the greatest tower-houses in Scotland, built in the 1430s. The damage to its 14-foot-thick walls was done by Cromwell's guns in 1650

CHAPTER 7

STEWART
AND
DOUGLAS

(1371–1460)

The succession of Robert II as the first of the Stewart kings of
Scotland meant that the Scots had a Celtic king once more, for the
Stewarts were descended from Breton Celts in Brittany (north-west
France). Admittedly, the blood had been thinned by their marriages outside Celtic families, but the point was not lost on the
Scots that a Celtic dynasty was ruling again. They could be forgiven
for looking to Robert II to bring about a break with the allegiance to
the kings of England. When he succeeded his uncle David II (who
was actually several years his junior), Robert had already demonstrated his Scottish nationalism for over a quarter of a century. He
believed fervently in the independence of Scotland. He had played
an important part in persuading the parliament of 1363 to reject
David II's preposterous plan to bequeath his kingdom to an
English prince. Certainly, too, he had been right to withdraw his
divisions in good order from the battlefield at Neville's Cross in
1346 (see p. 86), once he saw that the battle was lost and the king
actually captured. If he, too, had been taken, Scotland would have
had no direct heir to the throne. There would have been a golden
opportunity for Edward III of England to supply one – of English
blood.

Robert inherited a kingdom still suffering grave difficulties as a result of the swingeing ransom instalments being collected for payment to England on behalf of David II. He came with years of administrative experience behind him. He was popular. We have descriptions of him: tall and well-built; gentle-mannered; full of good fun and humour; a ruler with the tenderest of hearts; said by the Scottish historian Boece to have paid for the damage done to crops in the fields around Scone when the crowds gathered to celebrate his coronation there in March 1372; affectionately known as 'Old Blearie' because his eyes were more or less permanently bloodshot.

And yet, this lovable old man had lost the fire and vigour of his youth. He was no longer the fighter he had been, and he proved quite unable to give Scotland the firm government she needed so desperately. Power passed to his son John, earl of Carrick, and to feudal lords like the Douglases (who were all-powerful in the Lowlands). In the military sense it was as well that power was in other hands because in the 1380s there were fresh troubles with England. One of Robert's earliest acts had been to reaffirm the 'Auld Alliance' with France, which provoked the English to renew border skirmishing. Neither side made significant gains. The French king, always ready to aggravate his English adversaries, decided to send an army over to Scotland to help step up the war. Led by Jean de Vienne, admiral of France, about 1000 knights and men-at-arms with plenty of armour and weapons set out for Scotland, intending to invade England with the help of their allies. But when they reached Scotland they were to be disillusioned.

The Scots had found that large-scale battles with the English were not worthwhile (though, of course, Bannock Burn was the glorious exception). They preferred guerrilla warfare and refused to be tempted into open battle. Even when the English crossed the border and burned down abbeys like Melrose and Dryburgh and destroyed shops, homes and farms, the French were astonished to see that their allies did nothing to stop them. The Scots explained that while it was a pity about the abbeys, the smaller buildings, mostly of wood, could easily be rebuilt in a few days. They were content to let their homes smoulder and allow the English to rampage around without opposition, for they expected the English to retire across the border, exhausted by chasing and trying to bring to battle a seemingly non-existent enemy. Then the Scots would descend into England, sack the towns and carry off what plunder they could find, meeting little opposition from the tired troops.

The French did not understand this kind of warfare at all. They had come to Scotland to fight battles with the English, but they could not risk major engagements without Scottish help. So they decided to go back to France, disgusted with the Scots whom they considered a rude and worthless people. Before they could leave, however, the Scots compelled them to pay for the damage they had done to Scottish fields and crops during their stay. The French were outraged. They were accustomed in their own land to trampling down crops on farms while on their way to battle and they were not expected to compensate the farmers. Why should they pay compensation in the land of their allies? The Scottish people were equally disenchanted. They had not wanted the French in Scotland in the first place. Why didn't they go home?

In 1390 Robert II died. His son Carrick succeeded. His Christian name was John but so many King Johns had come to grief in one form or another – John of England, forced to seal Magna Carta, John of France, defeated and captured at Poitiers (1356), and John Balliol, disgraced and expelled – that he decided to be known as Robert III. He was actually no more fit to rule than his father. He had been guardian of the realm in his father's last years, but in 1388 had been kicked by his horse and severely injured. He delegated his authority to his brother Robert, earl of Fife, who continued to govern on his behalf for the first few years of the reign. In about 1394 Robert III declared he would govern on his own and he dismissed Fife.

These were very unruly times for Scotland. Even allowing for the natural inclination of chroniclers to exaggerate hard times, especially if the writers were victims of raids on the same religious houses in which they were working, the descriptions do give a gloomy picture of anarchy and lawlessness, of 'horrible destructions, burnings and slaughters'. One of the king's brothers, Alexander, lord of Badenoch, earned a place among the villains of history on account of his particularly wild and violent behaviour. Known as the 'Wolf of Badenoch', in 1390 he had the cathedral at Elgin burned down because he resented some critical remarks about his activities uttered by the bishop of Moray. And the king was too weak to do anything about it, other than reprimand him. It was unfortunate that Alexander did not have his brother Fife's sense of good order and government, for between them they would have brought much stability to the kingdom. Instead, Alexander instigated or encouraged trouble of one kind and another: cattle raids (*creaghs*) in the Highlands, street fighting in Lowland towns, armed robbery on the highways, all in the pursuit of lawlessness for its own sake. 'In those days there was no law . . . the kingdom was a den of thieves. . . . Justice was in exile, beyond the borders of the realm.'

In 1398 Robert decided to appoint his young son David as lieutenant of the kingdom, thus excluding Fife from further service. David was made duke of Rothesay, the first dukedom created in Scottish history. For consolation Fife was given the second dukedom, of Albany. But the appointment of David soon proved to have been an unwise one, for he was a worthless and vicious young man, with no interest in the dignity or responsibilities of a ruler. His life was given over to the pursuit of doubtful pleasures, he abandoned one wife, practically forced another girl to become his second, and almost at once began to ill-treat her. The enfeebled king realized his mistake, and in 1401 David was arrested and confined for safe keeping in one of Albany's castles. The next year it was announced that David had died, and soon it was rumoured that he had been starved to death. Albany was summoned by the General Council to explain the circumstances, and the Council seemed satisfied, for it pronounced that David had died 'by providence and not otherwise'. Curiously, England's Richard II, deposed by his cousin Henry of Lancaster (who became Henry IV) and imprisoned at Pontefract Castle, was similarly rumoured to have died from enforced starvation while in custody, only the year before.

Albany's hour had come, whatever the manner of David's end, and the king, who had for some time been reproaching himself about his inadequacies, at last raised Albany to the lieutenancy.[1] It was a popular move. Albany had already made his mark as a bold and fearless administrator. He was ambitious and ruthless, but withal a patriotic Scot who loved good order and his country in equal measure. He has been condemned by some for his power-seeking, but by the 1400s he was over sixty, an ageing man. He already had power, and the dukedom of Albany had given him added wealth. He still had more to give Scotland than Scotland could give to him. We may look briefly at his period of office, for it covers the last years of Robert III, to 1406, and the first fourteen years of the reign of Robert's son, James I (who was to spend from 1406 to 1422 in captivity in England).

Albany was well-fitted to give Scotland firm government, but as it turned out he was not very successful. He had the authority of a king, but he was not king. Mighty lords who would think twice about defying crowned kings were more reckless with regents, and so it was with him. Many lords in any case resented the succession to the throne of the Stewarts, who were not of direct royal blood in the male line but were there by accident of marriage. Albany, whatever his abilities, was in their view no better than they. He was aware of this, for he attempted to buy peace and co-operation from them by giving in to their demands, turning a blind eye when they seized revenues meant for the crown, or making pacts with them. One was with the great Douglas family, with whose chief, Archibald the Tyneman,[2] the fourth earl, he came to an arrangement in 1409 for mutual support and defence.

In 1406 Robert III decided to send his son James, aged about ten, to France. We do not know why. Some say it was because he was dying and did not want young James to succeed as a minor, merely to become the focal point for fighting among the lords who wanted to oust Albany. Others think he feared for James's life once he was gone and Albany's regency became a monarchy in fact if not in name. This is the view of hindsight, held because of the assumption of royal trappings by Albany. Whatever the reason, James never reached France: his ship was captured by English pirates off Flamborough Head and he was taken to Henry IV and lodged in the Tower of London. He was to remain in confinement until 1424, in the reign of Henry's grandson Henry VI. The news shattered Robert III and in April 1406 he died.

Albany's transition from lieutenant to regent was swift. A General Council was summoned and it appointed him *gubernator generalis*, though a parliament called at the same time declared James to be lawful successor to his father Robert. Albany assumed royal powers. He had a new seal struck for himself, with the phrasing *Sigillum Roberti duci Albanie gubernatoris Scocie*.[3] At first this seemed unexceptional, but suspicions began to grow that Albany was aiming at the monarchy itself when he started to refer in documents to 'our subjects' and not 'the king's subjects'. His great seal began to appear on charters normally granted and sealed by kings. Historians have also pointed to the curious wording of the pact he made with the Douglases, which ran 'and if it happens the said Lord the Duke to grow in time to come to the estate of king, this band (pact) . . . shall expire from thenceforth but all kindness and friendship shall be kept between them'.

But was he aiming at the crown? The contemporary historian Andrew de Wyntoun described him as appearing as a mighty king, and explained that young James could not be regarded as king because he had not been crowned. Men wondered when James would come home, though no ransom money had been demanded from Scotland. Albany has been accused of dragging his feet deliberately over negotiations for the king's return, but he will have remembered the terrible cost of the ransom for David II, which in fact was to have a direct and long-lasting effect on Scotland's economy (see p. 87). He rightly questioned whether the Scots could afford to pay again, this time for a young boy whom no one really knew, who was not yet a king. He had little alternative but to wait. There were other pressures. His own son, Murdoch, had been captured in 1402 by the English and had been held ever since. At least he was a grown man and could straightaway perform some useful services if ransomed and brought home. Should Albany get his son before his nephew? It was 1416 before Murdoch was returned.

If Albany was not over-ambitious, other Stewarts certainly were, and some were troublemakers as well. Robert II had been married twice and had fathered many children. His sons had been given high titles and with them considerable lands. His daughters were married to rich and powerful landowners. By the end of the fourteenth century the Stewart family was 'lording' it over a sizeable part of Scotland, wielding influence in government. Some members of the family, like the 'Wolf of Badenoch', were abusing their position in order to gratify ambitions, settle personal disputes by warfare, or to claim additional titles and the more material things that went with them. In 1411, a son and two nephews of Albany fought it out, along with companions and followers, in a fearful battle at Harlaw, near Aberdeen. Donald, lord of the Isles (son of Albany's sister, Margaret), claimed the earldom of Ross by right of his wife. His cousins, John, earl of Buchan (Albany's son) and Alexander Stewart, earl of Mar (the Wolf's son) resisted this and led an army against him. Donald had already been charging through the Highlands with fire and sword, burning towns like Inverness and Dingwall and he was heading for Aberdeen with arson in mind. But Buchan and Mar defeated him with the help of local levies raised among the burgesses of Aberdeen. The whole fracas had been illegal, but Albany was powerless to do anything. Too many of the protagonists were members of the family.

The expansion of Stewart power alarmed other great families, notably the Douglases who considered themselves – and indeed were – the greatest. The ramifications of Douglas influence were like those of the Nevilles in England in the mid-fifteenth century in England. They helped kings to get their thrones, they used kings, even abused them, but they never aspired to be kings. This was the fundamental difference between the Douglases and other great families, notably the Stewarts (and later the Hamiltons). The fifteenth century in Scotland is as much as anything the record of rivalry between the great families. The rivalry developed in Albany's time and he was unable to stop it. Yet he never attempted to take the throne, which would have been easy and which would certainly have strengthened his hand. He continued as regent until 1420 when, aged over eighty, and in full possession of his faculties, he died.

Albany's rule had in many respects been good for Scotland. The burghs had grown in size and wealth, and there were more of them, many granted charters by Albany. He had summoned meetings of the General Council nearly every year and he had also held parliaments. He had attempted to rule without raising taxation. It was a creditable aim but it actually increased his difficulties. Scotland's first university was founded at St Andrews in 1412 by its bishop, Henry Wardlaw, with Albany's encouragement. And no one ever challenged his position as regent. When he died, the General Council almost at once appointed his son Murdoch as successor – and they did not ask the absent James I for his permission or his views.

Murdoch was not of the same stamp as his father, but he was able enough. He lacked Albany's gift for handling people and had not his head for administration. Yet he should be credited for having negotiated the release of James at the Treaty of London in 1423, an act which put an end to his own high position. When the king came home in 1424 Murdoch retired from the scene gracefully, making no difficulties.

James Stewart, by right king of Scots since 1406 but still uncrowned, was now nearly thirty. We may wonder what his feelings were when he at last reached his homeland. He had had a long period of exile. Captured when he was twelve, an age at which, in those days, he was almost a young man, he had on the whole been well treated in England. Much of the time he lived in comfort, indeed in some state, with a household of loyal Scottish men and women who would have helped to keep alive in him his yearning to return. Though surrounded by English influences, he does not appear to have yielded to them, except that later in his reign in Scotland he did try (unsuccessfully) to recast Scottish parliaments in the English mould. In England he continued to practise speaking and writing in Latin and French, and more especially in his native Lowland-Scottish. He worked hard to keep informed of everything that was going on in his kingdom, from time to time intervening where he could, such as sponsoring the foundation of St Andrews University.[4] But James was also vindictive by nature and for years he planned his revenge upon those in Scotland responsible – as he thought – for his long absence. What he heard from Scotland about the rivalry between some of the great families, including his own Stewart cousins, and what he had learned at close hand about similar rivalry among the English feudal families (Plantagenets, Percies, Nevilles, Beauchamps, *et alia*) served to make him determined once he had recovered his position not to allow any subject lords to become overmighty. And yet there is not much evidence of Scottish lords being overmighty.

James was crowned at Scone in May 1424, soon after arriving in Scotland. Murdoch Stewart, who was earl of Fife as well as duke of Albany, was granted the customary Fife privilege of placing the crown on the king's head. Then James summoned the first parliament of his active reign, hardly a week after the festivities at Scone, and let it be known that he had come to govern his kingdom. 'There shall be no place in my realm where the key shall not keep the castle and the bracken-bush the cow', by which he meant that everybody would be safe under the law. The first acts of this parliament showed that he meant what he said:

That firm and sure peace be kept and held throughout the realm among all subjects of the king; and if any man presume to make war against another, he shall suffer the full penalties of the law.

That if any man presume to rebel against the king, he shall suffer the pain of forfeiture of life, land and goods.

That any man who refuses to help the king against his rebels shall himself be accounted a rebel.

That no men shall ride throughout the country with excessive followings: and all who move through the land shall make full and ready payment for all they need.

That officers of the law shall be appointed who can and may hold the law to the people; that they shall be persons of substance who can be punished in their own goods if they fail to do their duty; and that any now holding office who are incapable shall be replaced by others.

That the sheriffs shall arrest any men who move about the country in bands squatting upon other men's lands and demanding sustenance.

That all the great and small customs and all the rents of the burghs are the king's for his support.

That enquiry be made as to the lands and rents which pertained to the crown in the reign of David II; that the king be informed of those lands, possessions and rents which have fallen into other hands; and that, if he so desire, the king may summon all his tenants to give proof of their right to their holdings.

This last clause is clearly to tighten up the gathering of customs and taxes which had fallen into disarray in Albany's time. In 1422, for example, less than one-fortieth of the revenues due from Edinburgh to the crown actually reached the royal treasury. The shortfall was not simply the result of sloppy collection: greedy hands had helped themselves to some of the dues on the way, as happened throughout the land.

These first acts look good on paper and no doubt sounded good at the time. Certainly they were necessary if James was to make anything of his intention to govern, but it would be fanciful to imagine that they were all carried out at once and effectively.

Soon after the first laws were passed, James embarked upon his programme of revenge. First to suffer were the Albany family. Albany's soldier son Buchan, who had commanded a Scottish army fighting for France against the English, had fallen at the battle of Verneuil in 1424, otherwise he would have gone the way of his brother Murdoch and family who were arrested in 1425 and beheaded at Stirling. They had been tried before a panel of lords presided over by the earl of Atholl, the king's uncle and Albany's half-brother. Sir Robert Graham was imprisoned, his nephew Malise Graham, earl of Strathern, was banished to England, and in 1430 Archibald, fifth earl of Douglas, was imprisoned. Other lords also suffered, and in every case of the king's vengence, lands and possessions were requisitioned. It has been said that there were fifteen earldoms and one dukedom, all with extensive lands, in 1424, but that by the end of James's reign the dukedom had gone, along with seven of the earldoms. The lands and revenues had all passed to the king.

What interests historians of these times is, was the king in any danger from overmighty lords, and if so, how far was he justified in making a pre-emptive strike? Among the families to suffer were the Stewarts. Did James see himself threatened by his cousins or was he more probably interested in their wealth? Certainly the revenues from the lands of those whom he punished reverted to the crown. There was another factor. He had been in England during the reign of Henry IV, a king who had usurped the throne in the first place and had never been secure on it thereafter. Did James see that his own security had to come from the elimination of dangerous relations?

James now turned on the Highlands. He sent for the clan chiefs to come to a conference at Inverness. Some fifty men arrived, chief among them Alexander, lord of the Isles, son of the Donald who had been defeated at Harlaw in 1411. When they arrived they were clapped in irons, and several of them were put to death without warning. It was an appalling act of treachery on James's part. Alexander was kept in custody for a while and then released. He was a very angry man. He burned Inverness to the ground, but was defeated when the king marched against him near Lochaber and was again imprisoned, this time at Tantallon Castle, a huge, gaunt, lonely fortress built on a rock jutting into the sea on the north coast of East Lothian. Finally, Alexander was released in 1431 and restored to his possessions. The king did not feel strong enough to put to death the lord of the Isles.

James did not waver in his determination to rule, and for many this was what the Scottish people had long been wanting. He looked very much a king; broad-shouldered, of medium height and with narrow waist; handsome, dark-haired, with a strong head – clearly a man of intelligence and resolution. He may not have been popular among the nobles, but his parliaments did much to ensure that 'full law and justice' were done to the 'poor as to rich, without fraud or favour'. Many of his laws were geared to bettering the lives of ordinary folk. Acts were published throughout the countryside so that all people would know of his intention to maintain law and order. He started the construction of a royal fleet of ships; he introduced the poor man's advocate, a kind of legal aid scheme of the time; he tried to reduce unemployment by directing people without land or work into learning a craft in order to make a living from it. Some of the good that he did, however, was affected by his greed. He imposed various kinds of tax and some made him unpopular. One tax was raised specifically to finance the marriage of his daughter Margaret to the dauphin of France. Another was to pay for his stay in England (demanded by the English at the Treaty of London negotiations in 1423, but not enforced); the great proportion of this was retained by the king for his own use.

James was a strange mixture of good and bad. His personal accomplishments set him apart from most men. He was one of the best poets of his time; he could play several musical instruments well, and is credited with having introduced the organ into Scottish churches. He was physically very strong, and excelled at most sports of the day, such as running, wrestling, fencing and throwing the hammer. His political and social ideas were sound, and he believed in making them known and explaining them, thus endearing himself to many people. But those men he had wronged, or whose families had suffered earlier in his reign, could not forget, and they plotted to kill him. The leaders of the plot were Sir Robert Graham and Sir Robert Stewart (a cousin of James), and they tried to make the conspiracy more respectable by planning to put Stewart's grandfather, the aged earl of Athol (James's uncle), on the throne. They claimed they were ridding Scotland of a tyrant, but when the king had been killed in a desperate fight with his assailants in the cellar of a monastery in Perth, few people regarded his murder as either heroic or necessary. Before long, everyone was repeating a verse: 'Sir Robert Graham that slew our king, God give him shame'. The murderers were hunted down until they were all taken and tortured to death, which is said to have taken three days of agonizing torment. James's son, James, aged only six, was hurriedly crowned, not at Scone as his ancestors had been, but in the greater safety of Holyrood, outside Edinburgh.

It was one of Scotland's difficulties that time and again her kings succeeded when they were still children, leaving the government in the hands of regents, or king's widows, or powerful lords locked in feuds with other lords. These periods of Scottish history have generally been described as periods of anarchy. It is true that one faction or another would attempt to gain control of the king's person, giving a veneer of respectability and authority to their actions, but such a state of affairs is not necessarily anarchy. Indeed, there were so many instances where government continued without breakdown that the generalization becomes untenable. In the case of James II's minority, perhaps the worst that can be said is that for a few years the excellent developments inaugurated by his father were held up. They were carried on by James when he became master of his own kingdom.

The General Council retained Bishop Cameron of Glasgow as lord chancellor and appointed as governor, or regent, Archibald, fifth earl of Douglas. He was the son of the fourth earl who had been killed alongside the earl of Buchan at Verneuil in 1424 (see p. 97). Archibald was a grandson of Robert III. His appointment was not a success. He had none of the courage or energy of his family and was not suited to administrative work. He would not even exert himself when the country was threatened by the activities of two lesser lords who were competing for custody of the king.

William Crichton was governor of Edinburgh Castle, one of the major royal fortresses in Scotland. He had been a friend of James I and no one thought it odd that he should become protector of the boy king who was taken to the castle by the widowed queen, Joan. After a while, however, the queen became restless. She may have feared for her son. Crichton was a stern man, and he was ambitious to advance his own position and to share the benefits with his family. Joan decided to take the king to Stirling Castle, another major royal fortress, where the governor, Alexander Livingstone, gave them refuge. Livingstone was another ambitious landowner, and he was quick to appreciate the power the queen had, unwittingly, given him by putting herself and James in his care. He appealed to Douglas to confirm that he should be guardian of the king, officially, because he feared Crichton would try to recover the king. But Douglas would do nothing. Crichton, meanwhile, also asked Douglas for assistance, but Douglas would not help him, either. Crichton thereupon suggested to Livingstone that they join forces and form a party strong enough to dominate the government, and Livingstone agreed. Very conveniently, Douglas died from the plague while these negotiations were proceeding, but Cameron had to be dismissed. Crichton took his place as lord chancellor, embarked on a rebuilding programme at his great square-towered castle at Crichton, and generally set himself up as a grandee. Livingstone became official guardian of the king, and likewise enriched himself and his family.

Douglas was succeeded by his eighteen-year-old son, William. He struck up a friendship with the young king, but this was seen as a threat by both Crichton and Livingstone, for the Douglas possessions were vast, and with them went enormous potential military strength. At the time, Douglas was lord of Galloway, Annandale, Ettrick, Lauderdale, Eskdale and Teviotdale, and owner of more lands in the north. He was lord of the greatest area of land in Scotland, except for the crown. It was said that at any time the Douglases could raise a full army from the numbers of people who paid them rent or who were employed by them. So the two men had Douglas murdered. They were helped by Douglas's great uncle, James the Gross, who was his heir. James had a long record of violence from his earlier days, but by the time of this conspiracy, 1440, he had become so overweight that it is thought unlikely he could have been of any use in an active capacity. Possibly the Crichton–Livingstone party deliberately engineered the plot because they knew they would have no trouble with the old man.

James the Gross died in 1443. His successor was another eighteen-year-old, his son William, a cunning, able and forceful young man who was determined to consolidate the family power and break the Crichton–Livingstone alliance. Douglas's efforts to set the Crichtons and the Livingstones at each other's throats produced a great deal of disorder in Scotland. The earl of Crawford, owner of huge estates in north-east Scotland, was involved on the Livingstone side, while the bishop of St Andrews, James Kennedy (a grandson of Robert III), was for the Crichton party. Each side ravaged the houses, lands and villages of the other in a kind of free-for-all in which only the Douglases profited. The Douglases held three of the eight remaining earldoms in Scotland at the time:

101

William's brother Archibald was earl of Moray and his brother Hugh was earl of Ormond.

In 1449 the king became eighteen and decided to assert his authority and govern. He was much like his father in character, a man of action, tough and determined, but with his father's streak of vindictiveness. He was born with a disfigurement; half of his face was a blotchy purple, earning him the nickname 'Fiery Face'. One of his first acts was to make a good marriage, handling most of the negotiations himself. His bride was Marie, niece of the duke of Burgundy, and the match reinforced the ties with France as well as bringing commercial advantages through agreements with states in the Low Countries. James was obsessed, like his father, with the desire to break the power of the great families, including his Stewart cousins. His first victims were the Livingstones who by 1449 were holding several high offices, such as controller of finances, chamberlain, warden of the mint, and governor of Stirling and Dumbarton castles. Alexander Livingstone was arrested and imprisoned in Blackness Castle. Other Livingstones followed into prison, and two were put to death. The Crichtons, with fewer in high office, were warned to curb their ambitions and the king looked to his cousin Bishop Kennedy to control them.

Curbing the power of the Douglases was a different matter. The king knew it would take several years to undermine the influence they had in so many spheres, but he was prepared to be patient. In 1450 he sent the young earl to Rome as his representative at some important celebrations being held by the pope. James encouraged him to take with him his brothers, the earls of Moray and Ormond. The journey lasted more than a year, and in that time both James and Douglas took steps to strengthen their respective positions, for both knew that sooner or later there would be a confrontation which would determine which of them was to dominate Scotland. The king's first parliament rushed through a series of measures as forceful as those of James I. Some were financial, some were calculated to strengthen the royal authority, particularly in a judicial capacity, and some were designed to help the poor against the greed of the mighty. James also appropriated some Douglas lands in Wigtown and seized several Douglas castles on the pretext that local disturbances on Douglas lands required royal action. When the earl of Douglas returned from Rome, he found to his dismay that the balance of power had shifted away from his family.

He had not, however, been idle himself. On his journey he had had what must have been treasonable discussions with the duke of Burgundy, and also with the Yorkist lords in England (who were about to begin the civil war known as the Wars of the Roses).

When Douglas got home he found that the king had learned of his 'discussions' and he was called upon to explain them before parliament where, ironically, his cause was pleaded by the queen, who was the duke of Burgundy's niece. The king appeared satisfied, but of course he was not and Douglas's days were numbered. James was particularly angry when he discovered that Douglas had come to some kind of pact with John MacDonald of the Isles, son of the Donald of Harlaw fame (see p. 94), and with the earl of Crawford, and he insisted that Douglas attend him at Stirling. It was February 1452. Douglas would not come without a safe conduct. The king granted it. When Douglas arrived, the two men confronted each other across a dinner table. James liked Douglas personally, but he was labouring under very real grievances, and he ordered Douglas to break the pact with Crawford. Douglas refused, tempers were lost and James pulled a dagger and stabbed Douglas in the chest. Then he cried out for assistance, and guards came in to finish the earl off.

James's betrayal of the safe conduct he gave to Douglas aroused the most bitter feelings, not only among the Douglas family and dependants but also among the lords generally. Douglas's heir was his next brother, James, bishop of Aberdeen, who immediately threw off his clerical garb, raised an army of angry retainers and sacked Stirling. The king, however much he regretted his outburst, responded swiftly and mobilized a large army against the new earl and forced him to submit, at Castle Douglas in Dumfriesshire. The king granted Douglas a pardon and even restored some lands to the family, but he knew the final showdown between him and the Douglases was not far off.

Sometime in 1455 Douglas took up arms again, probably to bring on the final confrontation which he was confident he would win. He was supporting a man with a claim to the throne (for the Douglases never aspired to the throne themselves), who was Malise Graham, who had been banished to England in James I's time (see p. 98). The king met the Douglas forces in a battle at Arkinholm in Eskdale. On the Douglas side were three brothers, Moray, Ormond and John, lord of Balvenie. Against them and supporting the king were, among others, Earl Douglas's cousin and rival, George, earl of Angus, known as the Red Douglas to distinguish him and his branch of the family from the Black Douglases, and another Douglas cousin, Lord Hamilton. The king's army beat the Douglas army. Moray was slain, Ormond was captured and put to death. Balvenie got away and joined the earl who eventually reached England where he threw in his lot with the Yorkists.

James moved swiftly through the Douglas lands, reducing and capturing many castles, notably the great fortress of Threave, and receiving surrenders. The castles were brought low by the king's use of cannon. One which became famous throughout Scotland was Mons Meg. It had a range of two miles and required one hundredweight of gunpowder to fire it.[5] James had long been interested in artillery and recognized its supreme advantage in war.

The Black Douglases were finally crushed. The ninth earl was condemned in his absence and stripped of all his possessions and titles, which reverted to the king, bringing him considerable wealth. Now James really was master in his own kingdom, and he was to put the remaining four years of his reign to good use.

His parliament of 1455 approved measures which enabled the king's and the government's expenses to be paid out of rents and customs due to the crown. This was achieved by listing the possessions of the crown (and including in it the vast Douglas lands and revenues) and declaring what dues were to be paid from which. There was thus no need to raise direct taxes. It also approved laws preventing any lord from refusing to allow royal officials to enter their land to monitor the observance of the law. And the other feudal families decided that co-operation with the king was to their best advantage. The last of James's parliaments recorded that 'God of his grace has sent our sovereign lord such progress and prosperity that all his rebels and breakers of his justice are removed out of his realm.'

In 1460 James took advantage of England's difficulties in the Wars of the Roses. He determined to win back two possessions in English hands, Berwick-on-Tweed and Roxburgh Castle. In August James laid siege to the castle at Roxburgh, employing some heavy cannons. He was closely watching the gunners one morning, 3 August, when a cannon near him burst as it was being fired ('brak in the fyring', as a contemporary report put it). Great splinters of hot iron flew up and one struck him, mortally wounding him. It was a sad day for Scotland, and James was to be greatly mourned. Not least of the reasons for lamentation was the fact that his heir was a son, James, still aged only eight. The 'dark and drublie days' of a minority were back in Scotland again. It was hardly much consolation to Scots to hear, a few days later, that Roxburgh Castle was successfully captured from the English.

CHAPTER 8

THE
NOBILITY
TAMED

(1460–1513)

When James II was killed at Roxburgh, Scotland had been enjoying several years of firm government. It is in these times that we see the beginnings of Scotland's participation in the European revival of learning and art that men call the Renaissance. In 1450 Bishop Turnbull of Glasgow, a scholar with a wide following in Scotland and a high reputation in Europe, founded Glasgow University. This put Scotland on a par with England which had two universities (Cambridge and Oxford), and it gave a boost to the spread of learning among an increasingly education-conscious people. The new university was on the edge of the Highlands, in the western half of the country, and it offered education to people of the clans who might care to learn rather than fight or steal cattle.

Encouraged by both James II and his father before him, artists and craftsmen played an important role in Scottish life. James I had tried to stop craftsmen forming themselves into guilds or clubs, but he had encouraged them as individuals because he recognized the urge for creative people to express themselves in art forms. There were also interesting developments in secular and religious building. Castles, formerly little more than stone chambers of violence and bloodshed, treachery and despair, began to take on a more comfortable residential character. They started to look like palaces, fortified palaces it is true, but they became splendid homes. Crichton Castle in Mid-Lothian, the principal home of Lord Chancellor Crichton, was greatly extended and ornamented. Caerlaverock, the only concentric castle in Scotland, was remodelled, the most interesting feature being the remarkable machicolations round the tops of the Murdoch tower and the gatehouse which itself was converted into a residential tower.

A number of good laws were passed, with every intention on the part of both king and parliament that they should be observed (though they often were not). One law ensured that a tenant of land belonging to one lord did not lose the tenancy merely because the freehold ownership passed to another lord. The national economy, to which we return below (see p. 113), was helped by prohibiting the export of gold. Scottish men and women enjoyed a rising standard of living, reflected in the increasing use of more durable materials like stone and granite for house-building. The fifteenth century saw the first of the very tall houses in Edinburgh and elsewhere, which in later years were to become so characteristic. The century also saw the building of several huge towers and towerhouses in the countryside for people of substantial wealth and influence.[1] Even the leisure pursuits of the Scots earned the active interest of the kings. They tried to get people to practise archery and swordsmanship rather than play football or golf. James II introduced fines for playing football, the money from which was said to have been used to pay for drinks for keen people who spent the morning with bow and arrows at targets.

Perhaps the most encouraging thing of all was the growing co-operation between king and great lords. Once the showdown with the Douglases was out of the way and the king triumphant, James tried to build up a more loyal nobility by awarding titles to friends who owed him more than he owed them. In some cases he advanced existing titles. The earldoms he created did not carry with them huge wealth in land, for the Stewarts had appropriated much of that wealth, but the honours were worth having. He elevated the earls of Huntly, created the earldom of Morton, gave the earldom of Erroll to the hereditary constable of Scotland, Lord Hay, and also created three more earls, Argyll, Marischal and Rothes. The Argyll earldom was given to Colin Campbell, in 1457, and thus began the story of the great and powerful Campbells who were really inheritors of the MacDougall and Lorne 'empire'. Most of these lords, and their descendants, were on the whole to serve their kings well, as will be seen, with a loyalty and vigour that would have amazed (and possibly disgusted) the Douglases of the fourteenth century.

James was succeeded by his nine-year-old son James III, who was crowned at Kelso. The first years were quiet enough. His mother and his cousin, Bishop Kennedy, governed in his name through a regency council. One event troubled those first years. This was the rebellion of the earl of Ross, lord of the Isles, who made a pact with the exiled Douglas in England and with England's king, Edward IV. They agreed to 'stab Scotland in the back with a Celtic dirk', that is to say, the two Scottish lords agreed to accept Edward as overlord in return for help to invade the kingdom. Ross would keep the northern parts, Douglas would get his lands in the south restored. Edward was willing to go along with this ambitious plan so that he could frighten the regency council which had been assisting the cause of his enemies in England, the Lancastrian party supporting Henry VI (now deposed from the throne). The threat worked; the regency offered to come to terms with him, and in 1463 a fifteen-year truce was negotiated, and support for the Lancastrians was dropped.

The Queen Mother died in 1463, and Kennedy two years later. This left James, now fourteen, on his own. He was extremely vulnerable, but he thought he could manage without a council of regency and he made no new appointments. But in the background was a family on the 'up', like the Crichtons and Livingstones of the previous reign. They were the Boyds of Kilmarnock, headed by Lord Boyd, a landowner of some wealth. His brother Alexander was governor of Edinburgh Castle (an influential post, as Crichton had found in the previous reigns). The Boyd group, which was supported by a half-brother of Kennedy, Patrick Graham, bishop of Brechin, pretending to befriend the king, suddenly seized him one day in July 1466 and held him in Edinburgh Castle. Boyd had himself proclaimed king's guardian and soon afterwards chamberlain, thus becoming the most powerful man in the kingdom.

For about three years the Boyds ran the government. It was by no means a disaster; indeed, some good came of it. They arranged for

James to marry Margaret, a daughter of Christian I of Denmark, Norway and Sweden. They negotiated a huge cash dowry, but when it came to paying it, the Danish king had run out of money. So he pledged the Shetland and Orkney Islands (Viking possessions for centuries) as cover for the dowry. The dowry was never paid, and in time James was able to take over the islands and add them to Scotland's dominions.

While the king was under age, the Boyds were unopposed. There was no one to stand up to them. But they had abused the king's authority and had handled him roughly, and James could not be expected to pardon them. When he married the Danish princess he decided the time had come to take over his kingdom. This was the end for the Boyds. Lord Boyd and his son, Thomas, took the hint and escaped; Alexander Boyd was taken and put to death. That was one of the very few occasions on which James consented to the death penalty.

The young man who was now in command had been born into a family noted for its ambitious pursuit of power, its ruthlessness in acquiring it, its vindictiveness and its relish for hard fighting. James had none of these qualities. He hated violence. His contemporaries criticized his excessive leniency with offenders. Tall, dark-haired, described by one chronicler as one of the most beautiful princes of the age, James has nonetheless had a bad press from historians. To some extent it is deserved. They cannot all be wrong when they agree about some of his defects, such as his favouritism for people from humble backgrounds, or that he seldom left his capital, Edinburgh, and very rarely made royal visits or progresses in the country. And we cannot overlook the repeated requests of his parliaments that he should do his job properly.[2] James's interests in music, architecture and science found little sympathy among the lords, and this led him to seek the company of people of lesser birth but greater sensitivity. This alienated the lords who thought he was letting his 'arty' friends run his affairs. But contemporary historians also testify to James's energy and activity, and the ten years after the fall of the Boyds were free from troubles.

When the peace was broken, it was by members of his family, his two brothers, the earl of Mar and the duke of Albany. Both had grown into vigorous young men, keen on sports and fighting, with much in common with the sons of the great lords with whom they were often in company, hunting, practising archery, swordplay, wrestling, and having nothing in common with their brother the king. They were alive to the discontent among some lords who resented being shut out of the king's entourage. They hated his favourites, especially Cochrane, who was an architect and who designed the Great Hall at Stirling Castle and possibly that at Falkland, too, and to whom the king turned for advice on matters quite outside his experience – it is thought that Cochrane advised the king to raise extra money by debasing the coinage (see p. 114). Before long, Albany and Mar were actively plotting with some of the lords to change the government, bring down the favourites and perhaps even the king himself.

The brothers were indiscreet and James got to hear of their ideas. In 1478 he had them both arrested and imprisoned, Albany in Edinburgh Castle and Mar in Craigmillar, then a new L-plan tower-house-type castle with walls over ten feet thick, surrounded by a rectangular enclosure wall with round turrets at each corner. Mar died soon after his arrest and because the circumstances were never clearly explained, it was said he had been put to death by his brother. But that is to misunderstand the king; murder was outside of his capability. Albany escaped from Edinburgh, with the aid of a servant who broke his leg in the effort, and reached France after a series of adventures that included carrying the injured servant on his back for several miles. In France he tried to get support from Louis XI for a rising against James. Louis entertained him generously, even found him a French bride of high nobility, but he baulked at supporting a revolt against the anointed king of Scots.

Albany left France and tried his luck in England. Through the exiled Douglas, still quick to give trouble to Stewart Scottish kings, he offered Edward IV (who already had a truce with James) a deal whereby Edward was to be acknowledged overlord of Scotland in return for support for Albany's campaign to expel his brother from the throne. Edward drove a tougher bargain; he wanted a formal end to the 'Auld Alliance'; he demanded Berwick, and parts of Annandale and Liddesdale; he expected Albany to marry his daughter Cecilia. Albany probably accepted these terms, though how he thought he would get over the marriage part is not known. Edward then authorized an army to head for the Border and besiege Berwick, under his brother Richard, duke of Gloucester.

James III became aware of his brother's treachery but hesitated before acting. Then he called up an army to march to the relief of

Berwick. He set out from Edinburgh on the road through Lauder-dale, accompanied by his favourites, including Cochrane who is said to have been dressed in the most lavish costume of black velvet edged and decorated in gold thread. The force encamped at Lauder. Then unexpectedly, the king's plan was frustrated. Among the lords who had gathered at the encampment were the earl of Buchan (the king's uncle), the earl of Huntly and Archibald Douglas, earl of Angus. They represented the discontented nobles and they said they would go no further. Instead, they seized Cochrane and the other favourites, dragged them to the bridge over the river there and hanged them. Then they took the king back under guard to Edinburgh and confined him in the castle.[3]

Albany, meanwhile, was still besieging Berwick with Glouces-ter's help, and soon after the Lauder Bridge episode, Berwick fell.[4] Albany and Gloucester then marched on to Edinburgh. For a moment it seemed as if they would sack the capital, but Gloucester decided to let the Scots sort themselves out and he withdrew to England. In Edinburgh Albany found growing hostility to the lords among the people who wanted James released. So he pretended to champion his brother's cause and in September the king was set free. Once more, the king's good nature prevailed over his judg-ment and he agreed to be reconciled with Albany, and in public, too. For a while they appeared to be working together to govern. Albany was made lieutenant-general of the realm and consulted by the king on all state matters of importance. Yet he was continuing to plot behind his brother's back, in particular to further the aims of the conspiracy including Edward IV. It is said that James was told many times about Albany's treason but refused to accept it, until the evidence became overwhelming. Then he dismissed Albany from all his offices – but would proceed no further. In 1483 Edward IV died and his successor Richard III (Gloucester) was in no position to follow up his brother's part in the plot, for he had many troubles of his own.

Desperately, Albany, now determined to win the throne, joined up with Douglas again, and in 1484 (with the tacit agreement but without support of Richard III) they led an ill-prepared invasion army into Scotland through Galloway, stopping outside the walls of Lochmaben Castle to besiege it. Douglas believed the peoples in his old lands would rally to the cry 'A Douglas! A Douglas!' but when it came to the point there was no response and he and

Albany were routed. Albany fled to France and was killed in a tournament the next year. Douglas was taken and brought to James, but he refused to turn his head to look at him. If ever a man had grounds for revenge, it was James – and yet he did not seek it. He merely banished Douglas to the monastery at Lindores. Douglas had started his career in the church. It seemed fitting that he should end it there.

James had three more years left to rule, and they were unhappy. He had again spared the lords who had plotted against him, and now they were to bring him to his death. The disagreements between himself and many of them deepened, in particular those with the earls of Angus and Argyll. By 1488 they had made up their minds to get rid of him. His son James had reached the age of fifteen and was, they thought, capable of taking on the kingship, with their advice. They worked on him, attempting to influence him against his father. So far as is known there was no plot to murder the king, but they must have considered it, even if young James was not told. Angus and Argyll raised an army and enlisted the support of one or two other lords who had grievances, real or imaginary, such as the Homes and the Hepburns and Lord Gray. The king took the threat seriously and summoned the help of his loyal lords, including Huntly, Erroll, Archbishop Scheves of St Andrews and Elphinstone, bishop of Aberdeen. There was a clash at Blackness, near Linlithgow, but both sides broke off the engagement in order to parley.

The terms of the truce included leaving young James with the Angus–Argyll faction. But it was no sooner agreed than James had second thoughts. So he had reluctantly to go to war again to recover his son. Without waiting for all his supporters to reach him, he took a reduced force towards Stirling and at Sauchieburn, near the hallowed field of Bannock Burn, he challenged his enemies. But he was defeated, and he fled from the field. He took refuge in a miller's cottage but was accidentally betrayed by the miller's wife to a passing stranger who went in and stabbed the king to death. The stranger was an agent of Lord Gray, who had been on the look-out for the defeated king.

The victors of Sauchieburn thought they had everything their own way. But they overlooked two things, first, that young James would be overwhelmed with grief and remorse over his father's death and, secondly, that the whole nation would be appalled at the fact and the manner of his death. Young James vowed to wear an iron belt of chainlinks round his waist for the rest of his life as a penance. He also decided against vengeance upon the lords, but determined instead to rule Scotland straightaway, and to do so with firmness and justice. His reign certainly bore out this determination.

The murder of the king was to be deeply regretted for many reasons. He had been the greatest patron of the arts in Scottish history to that time. The flowering of Scottish artistic and literary achievement of his son's reign had its roots well planted in his. Remembering that James III was only thirty-six at his death, given a full span of life he would have been at the forefront of an even greater Scottish renaissance. It was he who commissioned Cochrane to build the Great Hall at Stirling, described as 'one of the earliest buildings in Great Britain to which the adjective "Renaissance" may with some fitness be applied'. The transformation of Linlithgow from a fortress into a royal palace began in his time. He was the first monarch actually to commission works of art in Scotland, and among these was an altarpiece for the Church of the Holy Trinity in Edinburgh, which featured a portrait of the king. The artist was Hugo van der Goes (1440–82), the Flemish painter. James also encouraged Scotland's literary emergence. Robert Henryson, sometime called Scotland's Chaucer, produced his *Testament of Cressed* and his *Morall Fabillis*, and was a mainstream European humanist. Gavin Douglas, one of the Douglases, and a leading poet, was inspired by James, and William Dunbar, another poet, began under James's patronage. James himself was an accomplished musician who played the lute well and championed church music. He collected manuscripts and encouraged the development of letter-writing in fine styles. If lords and big land-owners felt they had little support from James in their efforts to improve their positions, artists, poets and craftsmen had much for which to bless James's memory.

The respite in the Border troubles with England afforded by the Wars of the Roses enabled the Scots to advance in many fields. Peaceful times brought more trade, expansion in the burghs, in industries and in fishing. Aberdeen's fishing fleet was one of the largest and most prosperous in western Europe. And yet these good things involved money, and for much of the reign, as for that before and after it, the country endured a series of economic difficulties. Perhaps they were not unlike those that beset us today. People were spending too much in relation to what the country earned. James III had been miserly in his financial dealings but he was unsuccessful in getting others to follow his example. Laws were passed to regulate spending on comforts and luxuries. One controlled the amount of cloth used in costumes. But Scotland's money problems were not peculiar to her: almost every European kingdom was in similar difficulties. Gold and silver supplies were gradually drying up everywhere. Much of Scotland's reserve had been eaten up by the ransom payments on behalf of David II and the effects were still being felt a century later. Measures were tried to curb inflation, like regulating the amount of hard currency that could be taken abroad (in much the same way as today Britons are sometimes limited as to the amounts of cash they can take on holiday abroad). But in the end James had to resort to debasing the coinage. Kings had done so before, and would have to do so in the future, and he was no pioneer in this short-term remedy that generally had such disastrous longer-term results. Silver coins became more and more adulterated by being mixed with growing proportions of base metal. Cochrane is believed to have counselled James to issue special coins of copper for currency, 'black coins' or 'Cochrane's plaks' as they came to be called, but traders refused to accept them at their face value.

The decline in monetary values has been worked out.[5] In 1150 David I coined 252 penny pieces out of a pound of pure silver. By 1367 David II had thinned that out with debasement to 352 pence a pound. In 1393 it was 528, in 1440 it was 768, in 1451 it was 1,152 and in 1483 it had reached 1,680. By the 1470s the Scottish pound was worth only a quarter of the English pound, whereas in the 1360s they had been equal. Debased coinage pushed up prices and brough hardship. The problem was not solved in his time, nor in his son's, grandson's nor even great-granddaughter's.

James IV succeeded to the throne to preside over a very interesting turning-point in Scottish history. The last years of the 1400s were not merely the end of a century. They marked the close of the Middle Ages. They saw the disappearance of the feudal system as the order of society in most (though not all) European countries. They witnessed major changes in techniques of making war, as men learned how to control gunpowder and to use it decisively in battle or siege. Armoured knights on horseback were no match for cannon or musket. They also saw the introduction of printing and the benefits to civilization that resulted. The last years were also filled with the adventures of brave Spanish and Portuguese navigators and discoverers who showed that you did not fall off the globe when you reached the equator (as most people believed, and were encouraged to by the orthodox Catholic church), who demonstrated that the world was a far bigger place than the European-Asian landmass. The revival of learning and art was to spread excitingly throughout Europe.

Naturally, the Scots wanted to enjoy the new age like anyone else. In those times peoples expected their rulers to take the lead in new movements, and in James IV they had a splendid leader anxious to welcome the changes and direct them to Scotland's advantage. He had all the qualities they wanted. We may quote some from contemporary sources: 'courageous, more than a king should be'; 'of noble stature, and handsome as a man can be'; he spoke several languages, including Latin (very well), French, German, Italian, and he could also speak Gaelic; 'he moves about his kingdom to administer justice and to collect his rents'; 'the people no longer dare to quarrel so much with each other'; 'he executes the law without respect to rich or poor'; 'he is a very humane prince, he is much loved'.

James wore a long beard, although he never seems to have been painted except as clean-shaven. Beards were not fashionable at the time. He enjoyed 'manly' sports, especially hunting and hawking. He is said to have liked practising various craft skills and would sometimes be found in a blacksmith's forge hammering out red-hot iron on an anvil.

This accomplished king was popular for his entire reign. He dominated his kingdom from start to finish. He faced all problems boldly and, except in his dealings with England, with wisdom. He was greatly helped by the fact that most of the lords were on his side. The faction that had defeated and killed his father gave themselves high offices, but none were allowed to become too powerful. James was subtle in the ways he dealt with overweening lords. When Angus was found to have been plotting with Henry VII of England, James confined him in Tantallon Castle and confiscated his treasured fortress Hermitage. But to sugar the pill he gave him lands elsewhere to make up for its loss. Angus never plotted against him again.

Like most of his predecessors, James had confrontations with the Highland chiefs, especially the lord of the Isles, in this case the same John Macdonald, earl of Ross, who had vexed his father and grandfather. This time the king decided that the lordship itself must go. So long as the kings recognized the existence of a lord in the west with powers scarcely less extensive than their own, the safety of the rest of Scotland would continue to be at risk. The differences between the Highlanders, still Gaelic speaking and organized on the same social basis as they had been for centuries, and the rest of Scotland were as marked as ever. MacDonald, who had been let off lightly by the long-suffering James III after his involvement with Edward IV of England in the 1460s, opened up war again in 1491. He had been plotting once more with England, now under Henry VII. His nephew Alexander seized the royal castle of Inverness. He claimed it was to win back the earldom of Ross which Macdonald had forfeited. Then, unexpectedly, he was defeated by a force led by the MacKenzie clan. The king used this reverse as an opportunity to break the power of the lord of the Isles. He took the title away from Macdonald and assumed it himself, thus undermining Macdonald's hold over the clans and their septs. At the same time James gave the old chief a pension and let him live out his days at Paisley Abbey. James made several visits, not all of them peaceful, to the Highlands and islands to accept or extract submission from the various chiefs. It was no walk-over. Many chiefs bitterly resented James's attempts to create new sheriffdoms in lands where they had been prosecutor, jury and judge for generations. Though James was not to be troubled unduly from the Highlands after about 1500, the problem was not permanently solved. It is worth noting, however, that several of the chiefs and many of their men were disposed to fight – and die – with him at Flodden.

Among the victories against the Highlanders had been sea victories. James had decided to develop the Scottish royal navy as a key armament, and he was fortunate in having several extremely able and bold sea captains to serve him, notably Sir Andrew Wood and the Barton brothers. Wood had organized punitive expeditions against the islands with great success. He had already won national fame as a 'sea dog', a bold forerunner of the kind who were to serve Elizabeth I of England a century later. In 1489 he had twice attacked English privateer squadrons and forced them into Scottish harbours after a day-long running fight, although in both engagements he had been outnumbered. The exploits encouraged the king to embark upon an expensive programme of shipbuilding, with which he proposed not only to dominate the waters around Scotland but also to impress Europe. One ship was the *Margaret*, which had 21 guns, big for those days. But the star of the navy was the huge battleship, *Great Michael*. Begun in about 1506, it took four years to build. Practically every oak tree in Fife was said to have been used in its construction. It was 240 feet long (that is, nearly a third of the length of the *Titanic*, in 1912 the largest liner in the world!) and its walls were ten feet thick. It carried more than 300 guns, some of them as big as cannons. Over 400 men were needed to crew the ship, and she would also carry 1000 troops, if needed. It was the biggest ship in the world at the time. Ironically, however, the *Great Michael* was only used once in fighting by the Scots, and after the king's death it was sold to France.

James made his authority felt in other ways. He held many parliaments which handled a great deal of legislation. Some of them were held in Edinburgh which he was keen to strengthen as the capital of his kingdom, a process begun by his father. He constructed a new royal palace at Holyrood. He granted additional privileges to the burgesses. Though there were still to be judges and sheriffs travelling the countryside to try cases and hear lawsuits (James himself also travelled about as a judge and arbitrator), the supreme courts of the land were centred in the capital. In 1507 Andrew Myllar set up his printing press, the first in Scotland, in Edinburgh.

In his dealings with England, James displayed much less wisdom. This may stem from the fact that in the first years of the reign Scotland was subjected to many irritations by the English. Henry VII, while not actually at war with Scotland, nonetheless encouraged many warlike acts, notably the attacks by privateers on Scottish ships in the Firth of Forth (dealt with by Andrew Wood) and the support given to John Macdonald of the Isles. James retaliated later by supporting Perkin Warbeck, who claimed to be Richard, duke of York, one of the princes alleged to have been murdered in the Tower of London in the reign of Richard III. James welcomed Warbeck and found him a Scottish wife, Catherine Gordon, a daughter of his friend the earl of Huntly. He even launched an invasion of England, but it came to naught, and

Warbeck had to pursue his aims without Scottish help. Soon afterwards, James reached an accommodation with Henry VII, a truce which both men intended to keep, and it was sealed when in 1503 James married Henry's daughter, Margaret Tudor. This marriage brought James in line for the succession to the English throne. For the remainder of Henry's reign the truce was upheld.

Scotland's position among the nations of Europe had been growing so that by about 1500 her prestige stood probably higher than ever before. Many European powers considered Scotland as an important factor when making alliances. Towards the end of the 1490s the balance of power in Europe was shifting again, and this time it was France which became dangerously powerful. The king had designs on some of the Italian states. Spain, recently freed from the dominion of the Moorish Arabs and now enjoying a kind of unity under Ferdinand of Aragon and Isabella of Castile, reigning as joint sovereigns, was in equally 'empire-building' mood. Ferdinand's anxiety to check French aims was made clear in his diplomatic missions in many lands. In 1495 he sent a new ambassador to Scotland, Ayala, with the express purpose of persuading the Scottish king to detach his country from the 'Auld Alliance'. England, too, was working towards the same end. James played a waiting game, committing himself to no one. In the first years of the new century, he decided to make his mark as an influential European sovereign by organizing a crusade against the Turks, enlisting the support of France, Spain and England, as well as the papacy. The scheme fell through, but the pope, Julius II, recognized his efforts by describing him as Protector of the Christian Religion and presenting him with a sword with the pope's name etched on the blade. This became the Scottish Sword of State and is still one of the principal relics of the Scottish royal regalia.

When Henry VII died in 1509, Scottish–English relations began to deteriorate almost at once, through the arrogant stance of Henry VIII, James's brother-in-law and one of the worst kings ever to rule England. Henry was a bullying braggart. He claimed to be overlord of Scotland ('I am the very owner of Scotland', he was to say in 1513). He also made threatening noises against France. The French King used this to try to renew the 'Auld Alliance', more important to him than ever now because at the time a number of European states (including England) were ganging up together to form a Holy League against him. James was in a quandary. France needed his support and called upon ancient obligations. Francis I looked to James to invade England from the north. But James was married to the English king's sister and there was still the truce formed with Henry VII. Nor indeed did he want to go to war. Henry VIII, gambling on James being tempted to support France, goaded him by a variety of warlike incidents, such as encouraging privateers to raid Scottish seaports in the Forth. Henry also planned an invasion of Scotland but wanted to get James to attack first so that the latter would be seen as the aggressor. Henry ordered the earl of Surrey to marshal an army in northern England and to get it ready for a successful onslaught. He even sent to the Netherlands for the return of certain pieces of artillery that he had loaned. By the spring of 1513, Surrey was ready.

In July Henry left for France and six weeks later defeated the French at the battle of Spurs. It is probable that James heard about the defeat. He certainly knew that Henry had left for France. He called a council and discussed the situation with his lords, Angus, Elphinstone and others. With one voice they counselled him not to go to war. But the king's patience was at an end: so it appears was his wisdom. He summoned the levies of Lowland and Highland and sent for artillery. But it was a hastily prepared expedition that he led. Many of the troops were raw and badly equipped, though they were filled with enthusiasm and were to fight with tremendous courage. In mid-August they crossed the Tweed and forced the surrender of Norham, Etal and Ford castles. Then the king led them to Flodden Edge and set up a fortified camp. It was a strong position. Surrey came up from Alnwick to confront James, but on 8 September decided on a ruse. He crossed the Till, a tributary of the Tweed near Flodden, and manoeuvred into a position from which he could attack the Scots from the north. If they had wanted to retreat he was sitting with his forces across their only escape road.

And on 9 September battle was joined. The English forces were superior in every way. Their artillery had better range and was more effective (for James had sent his best guns to sea in the *Great Michael* and other ships to harry English ports). English foot-soldiers were armed with eight-foot bills (a wooden shaft with a long iron blade ending in a spike). These were more than a match for the Scottish fifteen-foot spears which, once the English had got to close quarters, were quite useless. The English gunfire caused havoc very early on, and when the Scots began to charge downhill they were already out of formation, each man fighting for himself and not as part of a team like the schiltrons at Bannock Burn. The battle turned into a massacre and all the courage in the world, which the Scots displayed, every man of them, could not avail. By sundown more than 10,000 were lying dead or dying on the field. Among them were the king, his illegitimate son who was archbishop of St Andrews, two bishops, fourteen earls and three Highland chiefs. Also among the dead were two sons of old Angus who nearly came to join his king but held back because of his age and infirmity. None of the Scots fought more magnificently than their king, who fell, pierced by many arrows, with a huge wound in his neck, scarcely a spear's length from his adversary, Surrey.

It was one of the most catastrophic defeats in Scottish history. It left Scotland with a new king less than two years old. It deprived the nobility of its leaders. It put Scotland at the mercy of the English. Its longer term effects were that the nation became disillusioned with the 'Auld Alliance'. The slaughter of the 'Flowers of the Forest', as the dead came to be called, had been brought about not for Scotland but for another land and its peoples. It was too high a price to pay for friendship. Reluctantly, people realized that Scotland and England would have to move closer together. Fortunately at this time neither Henry VIII nor Surrey felt able to exploit their success, and this ensured that there would be no 'take-over' of the ancient kingdom. Scotland would continue to be independent for a time, and when it did lose its independence it would not be as the result of war.

17 A groat of the time of King James III

18 The Great Hall at Stirling Castle. Designed by James III's architect, Cochrane, it is among the finest Renaissance buildings in Britain

19 Portrait of James IV, now in the National Portrait Gallery of Scotland

20 Now healthy with ripening corn, this field was once drenched with the blood of Scottish nobles and knights who fell at the tragic disaster of Flodden in 1513, where James IV was also slain

21 The inside of Parliament Hall in Edinburgh. The hammer-beam roof is nearly 120 feet long. Once the assembly place for the Scottish Parliament, from 1639 to 1707, will it ever again see Scottish members in discussion?

22 An engraving of John Knox, now in the National Portrait Gallery of Scotland

23 A miniature of James Hepburn, earl of Bothwell, painted in 1566

24 Hermitage Castle in Roxburghshire. This huge tower-house was once a Douglas stronghold (the original tower is inside the larger outer building). In the 1560s Hermitage belonged to Bothwell, and Mary Queen of Scots visited him there in 1566

25 A relatively little-known portrait of James VI when he was twenty-nine years old. Something of his suspicious nature can already be detected in his eyes

The Arch-Prelate of St Andrewes in Scotland reading the new Service-booke in his pontificalib assaulted by men & women, with Crickets stooles Stickes and Stones.

26 An engraving by Wenceslas Hollar of the riot that broke out in St Giles's Cathedral, Edinburgh, in 1637, when the archbishop of St Andrews attempted to introduce the Revised Prayer Book into Scottish churches

27 Portrait of the 5th marquis of Montrose, after Honthorst, now in the National Portrait Gallery of Scotland

Marquis of Argile

28 Portrait of the 1st marquis of Argyll, by an unknown painter, now in the National Portrait Gallery of Scotland

29 An engraving of 1679 depicting the murder of Archbishop Sharp. As he is being pulled out of his carriage he is shot by the mounted assassin beside the carriage door

30 Second only in importance to the Declaration of Arbroath, this is the Treaty of Union between Scotland and England, signed in 1706. The Act of Union came into force in 1707. The Scottish Commissioners signed in the left-hand column

31 The belated arrival of James Edward, the Old Pretender, at Peterhead in January 1716. By that time his cause was already lost. This is a Dutch engraving and James is described as James VIII of Scotland and III of England

32 Robert Burns—the well-known portrait of this much-loved national poet, the greatest in Scottish literature

CHAPTER 9

THE
PROTESTANT
REVOLUTION

(1513–60)

Once more a dead king of Scotland was succeeded by an heir in childhood, this time in infancy, for James V was but seventeen months old. His mother Margaret was made guardian and the baby was crowned at Stirling Castle. Among the council of advisers that governed in his name were the old earl of Angus ('Bell-the-Cat'), who was to die at about Christmas in 1513, James Hamilton, first earl of Arran and a grandson of James II, Alexander, third Lord Home and James Beaton, archbishop of Glasgow. The council was by no means united about which direction Scotland should be taking. Some were pro-French, others favoured closer links with England. As the reign proceeded the alignments hardened into political groups which were quite prepared to resort to violence to assert their policies, and this was to get worse from about 1525 onwards when religious argument became a new and very emotional dimension in Scottish politics.

Queen Margaret was English and attracted support from the pro-English faction, which included the new earl of Angus ('Bell-the-Cat's' grandson). But this Angus was probably pro-English because his arch-enemy James Hamilton, earl of Arran, was not.

Arran was supported by Beaton, and it is thought that they had very early on offered the regency to John, duke of Albany, cousin of the king and son of the Albany who had been killed in a tournament in 1485 (see p. 112). Albany took some time to consider the offer, and in the interval Queen Margaret married Angus. This move (rash, as it turned out, because she and Angus were miserably unhappy together) cost her the guardianship of the king. It also alarmed the rest of the council and Albany was urged to decide whether he would accept or not. It was a hard decision for him. He had spent his entire life in France, spoke hardly any English, Lowland Scottish or Gaelic, and had probably never visited his native land. Naturally he was greatly influenced by France and would want to preserve the 'Auld Alliance'. Eventually he accepted, and in the ten years which he served as regent he showed a creditable devotion to the interests of Scotland.

One of Albany's first acts was to compel Margaret to leave Scotland. She withdrew to Harbottle Castle in Northumberland and at the end of 1515 she gave birth to a daughter who in time was to marry the fourth earl of Lennox (Matthew Stewart) and become the mother of Lord Darnley. Angus may have gone with her but even by then the differences between them were apparent. The regent's action did not endear him to Henry VIII of England, her brother, and Henry tried to get the pro-English faction in Scotland to drive Albany out. But Albany was personally liked and he enjoyed much support in the council and the kingdom. In 1516 parliament declared him 'second person in the realm', for he was young James V's heir.

Albany's French environment, however, made it hard for him to understand his Scottish colleagues, despite their respect for him, and he was reluctant to give high offices to people he did not know well. French colleagues were given some of the posts. One was made warden of the East March, which is the equivalent of governor of Lothian. The previous holder had been Lord Home, whom Albany had had to put to death in 1516 for treasonable dealings with England. The Home family took their revenge when they murdered the Frenchman.

Albany returned to France for a visit in 1516 which was to last nearly four years. In that time he left Scotland 'rudderless', as it were, and the feuds between the great families were renewed. Perhaps the worst was a bloody street battle in Edinburgh between the Douglases and the Hamiltons, which the former won when they drove all the Hamilton adherents out. This was afterwards known as the 'Cleane the Causeway' battle. Albany, meanwhile, had cemented the 'Auld Alliance' with France in a treaty at Rouen in 1517, and from that time the lords in Scotland began to line themselves up for or against a pro-French policy. In most cases, however, the stands which they took were motivated not by what was good for Scotland but by what they considered would bring them the greatest personal advantages.

In 1522 – and again in 1523 – Albany led Scottish armies, supported by French troops and armaments, against England in fulfilment of the agreement at Rouen, as France was threatened by the emperor of the Holy Roman Empire who had Henry VIII among his allies. In both instances the Scottish commanders marched with their forces to the border – but would not cross it. They remembered Flodden. They also reflected that they were marching not for Scotland but for France, and they were not prepared for the sacrifices they felt in their bones they would be called upon to make if they attacked the English in England. Albany took the hint and told the French king, François I, not to expect much help from Scotland. It was a defeat for his pro-French policies and he retired from Scotland altogether.

The result could be expected. The pro-English faction came into its own. Margaret was invited back by the earl of Arran, who was ever willing to change sides. They brought young James V from Stirling, where he had been living for much of the time since 1513, to Edinburgh. There they paraded him wearing a crown before a crowd and took him to a special session of parliament at which friendly noises were made in the direction of England. Margaret, who had been trying to get a divorce from Angus, was persuaded to make up her differences with him, politically if not maritally, and for a while they co-operated. But Angus was hatching a plot to kidnap the king, and in 1525 he seized James and held him in comfortable captivity while he and his faction, no doubt supported with promises by Henry VIII, took over the government. It was the Boyds and James III all over again. Angus was divorced by Margaret, who married another Stewart. Angus remained in power, filling the high offices with members of his family and with his friends, until 1528 when James managed to escape from the Douglases at Edinburgh. He headed for Stirling where he knew he could count on loyal support. He managed to get word to the governor of the castle, who 'preparit the castell witht all neidfull thingis ffor his coming . . . drew down the portculeis and pat the king in his bed to sleip because he had ridin all night'.

Once safely in the castle and joined by friends, James decided to take the government in his own hands. He was only sixteen, but was full of self-confidence. The unsettled and often dangerous nature of his childhood and environment, coupled with his natural gifts of courage, vigour, cunning and ruthlessness, served to make him even at that age a formidable but suspicious personality – and a dangerous person to cross. He summoned a parliament which condemned Angus and members of his family to death, and ordered the forfeiture of their possessions. Angus had before the session fled to Tantallon Castle. There, with his brother George and a cousin Archibald he held out against the king, who besieged the great fortress with artillery. On the way to the siege the royal troops marched to the tune 'Ding Doun, Tantalloun'. But the castle did not 'Ding Doun': the king failed in the siege and as he withdrew his artillery train was captured.

By 1529 Angus had exhausted himself dashing to and from the castle to outwit the king's attempts to take it, and he surrendered it, fleeing across the border into England where he stayed for the rest of James's reign. The Red Douglases were to trouble James no more.

James next turned to the various Border lords who had been quarrelling between themselves. One family, the Armstrongs of Liddesdale, had been rampaging about their territory and that of their neighbours at will, bragging that they owed allegiance to neither king of Scotland nor king of England. But by a trick James captured the head of the family and hanged him. Other trouble-some lords, including the Bothwells and the Homes, were impris-oned. There followed such tranquillity in the border district that men long afterwards remembered it, saying that the king was able to graze flocks of royal sheep unmolested in forest land once thought to be the unsafest in Scotland.

The king also moved against the western Highlands and the islands where descendants of the MacDonalds were anxious to recover the lordship of the Isles. The territories had for some time been under the government of the earls of Argyll, acting for the kings, but James had taken a dislike to Colin Campbell, the third earl, so that when he died the governorship was not passed to his son but went instead to a MacDonald! This aggravated the new earl of Argyll and made him an enemy for the rest of the reign. In 1539, another MacDonald, Donald Gorm of Sleate, rebelled but his revolt collapsed when he was slain at a siege of his castle, Eilean Donan. The king followed up the end of the rising with a royal progress round north Scotland by sea in twelve ships armed with guns and carrying troops. He set out from the Forth, sailed up the North Sea, rounded the Orcades and Cape Wrath and went to most of the larger islands in the west, ending up at the mainland town of Dumbarton. All along the route he received the submission of clan chiefs and other lords. Some were taken as hostages for good behaviour; others gave up their sons. Among these were the chief of the MacKenzies, and the chief of the Duart Macleans, Hector. James formally took on the title lord of the Isles.

These demonstrations of royal power and intent to maintain order in his realm were received well by the ordinary people who had usually been the ones to suffer most in the feuds between the great families or in the fighting between the reivers in the Border district. James's stern and rapid campaigns against these trouble-makers were effective. The progress round the islands had been an excellent public relations operation, too, for it was the first time a Scottish monarch had actually visited many of them. If the chiefs did not relish being ordered to submit or deliver up sons as hostages, the ordinary folk were heartened to know that they had a king who so forcefully showed who was master in his realm. Not for nothing was James known as 'the poor man's king'.[1] James enjoyed the company of the people, even though to do so he generally disguised himself and pretended to be a farmer or a traveller. Some of his adventures have become legendary. Quite apart from any others, he is said to have seduced many innocent country girls, while among the upper classes he had a veritable seraglio of mistresses, including Margaret Erskine (their son was James Stewart, earl of Moray, Regent in the late 1560s), and girls from great families like the Elphinstones and the Beatons.

But if he won the hearts of the ordinary people, James certainly alienated his lords, and when at the end of his reign he needed them they did not respond. Many were actively conspiring with English lords to undermine the Scottish throne and some were receiving money from Henry VIII to make difficulties for James.

Henry had difficulties of his own at this time. He wanted to divorce his wife Katharine of Aragon so that he could marry Anne Boleyn. This had been refused by the pope and Henry had thereupon broken with Rome and taken England out of the Roman Catholic church. This coincided with the great Reformation to which we return later (see p. 129). In doing so Henry would have liked to get Scotland detached from Rome, too. He now had two good reasons for backing disaffected nobles who came to England for support. James, on the other hand, remained a Catholic and continued to accept the authority of the pope. He did not intend to let the new religious ideas disrupting so much of Europe at this time spread to Scotland and he supported the church in their efforts to prevent them. Pamphlets from the European reformers were banned in Scotland. Attempts to smuggle in translations of the Bible (by Tyndale) were severely dealt with. Men and women caught preaching or advocating the new ideas were ordered to be burnt. One preacher, Patrick Hamilton, one of the great Hamilton family, had already perished at the stake in 1528 for heresy. There were to be several others, some of whom were burned before the king's own eyes.

James felt his kingdom to be threatened not only by Henry VIII but also by those European states which had embraced the reformed faith, and might support further attempts made by Henry to conquer Scotland. He asked the pope to provide him with a yearly income of £10,000 – a huge sum for those days – with which to defend his kingdom. After much bargaining the pope agreed, but arranged its payment in a roundabout way, namely, by allowing the revenue to come from payments due to Rome from the Scottish church to be routed to the king instead. The device was to set up a College of Justice in Edinburgh which would provide a central civil court of justice, taking the place of the occasional meetings of the Lords in Session. This new body was to have fifteen judges (seven churches, seven laymen and a president who was to be a churchman) and they were to receive salaries. Thus was born the Court of Session, still the principal civil court of Scotland today – and still meeting in Parliament House in Edinburgh. The church was to fund the College, which it was thought it would be glad to do, in order actually to provide funds for the king to remain safe from attack by Protestant powers. The church wanted, however, to commute the £10,000 a year into one payment of £72,000, to be spread over four years, and this was accepted. It meant short-term cash in the king's pocket.

James's determination to keep Scotland Catholic and his widening differences with his lords, many of whom were considering adopting the new faith or had already done so, edged him closer to France. At the treaty of Rouen Albany had arranged that James should marry a French princess as soon as he was old enough, and in the 1530s James was willing to do this. He had, after all, his many mistresses! But he played hard to get by letting the French king think he was toying with the idea of marriage to Mary Tudor, Henry VIII's daughter. In the end François I agreed to endow a marriage between his daughter Madeleine and James with 100,000 French livres. They were married in 1537, but the young queen died soon after arriving in Scotland a few months later. James then married another French bride, Mary, the daughter of the powerful duke of Guise. These marriages cemented the 'Auld Alliance' and this angered Henry VIII. It also frightened Henry, for several European powers were getting together against him because of his break with Rome.

For the first time Henry tried to win James from his French alliance by negotiation and not crude bullying. He arranged to meet James at York for discussions and he travelled all the way there, said to be the first time he had ventured so far up in his kingdom. But James did not turn up. His advisers had counselled against the meeting. Henry was furious and in his anger he ordered the duke of Norfolk to take an army across the border. The army burned Kelso and Roxburgh. James responded by summoning his levies at Edinburgh and leading them southwards to the Border. At Fala Moor, however, less than twenty miles from the capital, the lords he had summoned and who had come with great misgiving, dug their heels in and said they would go on further. They were stricken with the Flodden complex: this was another invasion on behalf of France. So James had to call off the march.

Leaders of the church were dismayed. Led by David Beaton, archbishop of St Andrews and a cardinal of the Roman church (and nephew of James Beaton) they offered to help raise and finance fresh forces. In November 1542 the king led a mixed force of armed retainers of the church, mercenary soldiers and some loyal troops through Dumfriesshire to Lochmaben where they encamped. On the 24th James decided to remain at the castle, but sent the force southwards under the command of Oliver Sinclair, one of his favourities.[2] The force was badly organized, morale was low, and the lords objected to Sinclair being in command. The army blundered into a trap in the marshy ground of Solway Moss, between the Esk and the Sark, and was surprised and scattered by the English. Most of the Scottish lords surrendered rather than give their lives, and they were conveyed to Henry VIII. It was a disgraceful defeat. When the news was brought to James it was too much to bear and he died soon afterwards.

James had come to a sad end. He was only thirty, but he had accomplished much. His centralizing of the civil court at the College of Justice was a major advance in Scottish legal history. His skilful management of royal finances, aided it is true by the artful ways he got the church and other sources to make substantial contributions to the crown, enabled him to indulge in a splendid programme of architectural and building improvements to several royal residences and thereby to encourage artists and craftsmen. He initiated major works at Holyrood, Stirling, Linlithgow and Falkland, which certainly stand comparison with contemporary Renaissance building in other European countries. Falkland was perhaps the greatest of these works. There he kept his court in the same kind of splendour as many European sovereigns. He added two ranges of buildings to the palace, most of which were sadly destroyed by a fire in the 1660s. At Stirling Palace James commissioned the famous Stirling Heads, a series of carved oak medallions which adorned the ceiling of the king's presence chamber. These have been described as being among the finest examples of Scottish Renaissance woodcarving to survive.

James's ties with France, and the ideas he gathered during his visits there in the days when he was negotiating to marry Madeleine, led him to encourage French craftsmen to come and work on his projects in Scotland. One of these was a fine woodcarver, Mansioun, who probably masterminded the Stirling heads. Later on, Mansioun was employed by the burgesses of Edinburgh to construct new choir stalls for St Giles' Church. Certainly the old association with France was good for Scotland in one way – the arts flourished; France was in the full throes of her Renaissance and had many ideas to export. But after James's death Scotland endured several years of disorder and weakness, as we shall see, and the

Scottish Renaissance was short-lived. But if the Renaissance could not blossom in Scotland, the Reformation certainly could.

The Reformation was the greatest revolution in ideas in European history. Directly or indirectly it affected everyone. It was more than a protest against the authority of the Roman Catholic church and its doctrines, more than an attempt to reform the abuses that had grown up throughout the church over the centuries. It produced major political changes in many lands, influenced by the ideas and writings of reformers and humanists who carried much weight in political circles, put into practice by leaders who used these ideas for their own political ends. The Reformation had many dramatic, cruel and intolerant aspects. Not least of these were that individual men and women were ready to be burned to death for the furtherance of this movement, and that rulers were prepared to countenance the destruction of whole communities of people who supported it. More interesting still, perhaps, was that the fervour and determination of the reformers in their disputes and struggles with the Roman church and its secular supporters were more than matched by the violence and intolerance with which they disagreed among themselves.

In Scotland the Reformation was a religious and political revolution that ended the 'Auld Alliance' with France, brought Scotland so close to England that union became inevitable, turned Scotland from a Catholic to a Protestant nation and eventually produced an important development in the character of the Scottish people, a morality of high order that has never left them.

The Scottish church had begun in the humblest way. In its earliest history it was largely independent of Roman authority, chiefly because of the distance between Rome and Scotland and the difficulty in enforcing any conformity to Roman rules; and also because Christianity had arrived in Scotland through missionaries who came not from Rome but from Ireland. The earliest ministers or priests in Scotland were simple teachers and monks and there were no bishops, nor was there any of the organizational structure bishoprics necessarily entail. Then, after the Celtic church had lost the contest with the Roman church, in the middle of the seventh century, a church organization began to grow. The first bishoprics were created, and these were followed by descending grades of dignitary, gradually building up into a hierarchy that was already familiar in other parts of Europe. After Queen Margaret's time there appeared the first of the greater monasteries,[3] and with them a further hierarchy. Most of the dignitaries were appointed by the pope at Rome, or if they were chosen by the kings in Scotland the appointments had to be approved by Rome, which they were often not. These people were almost the only people with any education in the things that mattered, such as law, and this put them in a very strong position in the state. They were often members of the Great Council, and later of parliament, not as the king's choice so much as because they were dignitaries, with the right to their positions. The temptation to spend their time in state affairs, in improving their standard of living by gathering round them households of servants and assistants, and in improving the places where they lived, meant that they neglected their church duties which were, after all, principally directed to guiding other people in the ways of the Lord. In time, the organization of the medieval church, in Scotland as everywhere else, became top-heavy, as more and more 'jobs for the boys' were created. Soon, some prelates began to acquire more than one office which, of course, brought them more than one income, a practice called pluralism. Then they began to pass these offices down to their sons, so that in some cases the offices became accepted as hereditary. Worse, their absorption with money-making, pleasure-seeking and political in-fighting demoralized them. Discipline disappeared at the higher levels, and it was no exceptional thing to find clergy of all ranks taking mistresses and fathering bastard children, whom they attempted to legitimize in law for purposes of succession.

Lower down the scale, the day-to-day ministering to ordinary people was done by the parish priest. For the first few centuries the parish priest did his job effectively and with devotion, and received on the whole enough funds to do so. The priests were paid out of *teinds*, or tithes, a 10 per cent tax raised on the produce or other earnings of everyone within a parish, which went to the church and from which the priests received allowances. But some time in the reign of David I there grew up the undesirable practice of appropriation. This was an arrangement whereby parish teinds could be granted to greater religious houses, like monasteries or cathedrals, and used by them exclusively for their activities. These included great building programmes, improvement schemes for church property, development of church farm lands, foundation of schools and other worthy works. But teinds were also converted to fostering high living among the higher clergy – and many of them lived very well indeed. With careful management the teinds should have been enough to pay for all the schemes, provide allowances for the humble parish priests and even leave a little over for the occasional extravagance, especially as the revenues were frequently supplemented by gifts from a variety of sources. Knights going to the Crusades, for example, generally gave sums to the church in return for advance absolution from their sins before they went into battle, probably to die. Merchants gave sums in order to win goodwill locally.

But this accumulation of funds was not enough, and it became increasingly too little to meet the demands of the higher clergy who were growing more and more extravagant. This meant that the parish priest had his allowances reduced, or even cut altogether, and so found it impossible to make ends meet. Frequently he had to depend on charity. Some of the more enterprising priests, probably because they had friends in the right places, got out of their difficulties by taking on several parishes and thus getting enough to live on. But on the whole these 'lucky' priests spent so much of their time on non-church matters that the parochial needs of their parishes were overlooked. Some of the religious houses appropriated several parishes directly and of course the revenues from these poured in to their coffers. In the early thirteenth century Arbroath Abbey, for example, controlled more than thirty parishes, while in the early sixteenth century more than 90 per cent of the parishes in Galloway were appropriated. By 1560, two-thirds of the parishes of all Scotland were appropriated.

As the lot of the parish priest deteriorated, so did his capabilities. The standard of education of those who became parish priests slumped. What educated man would relish such uphill and unrewarding work? A report to the archbishop of St Andrews in the early 1500s stated that many parish priests hardly knew their alphabet. In the 1540s the provincial council of the clergy mentioned the 'profane lewdness of life in churchmen of almost all ranks, together with crass ignorance of literature and all the liberal arts'. The churches themselves were decaying, for there was neither the money nor the will forthcoming to repair them. Reports were made of riots, noisy gatherings and parties taking place in churches on Sundays at divine service, of non-attendance by parishioners, of vandalism and theft.

The position was, if anything, worse in the Highlands. There were far fewer religious houses or churches and not one of them was safe from raiders or robbers. Elgin Cathedral had been burned down by the 'Wolf of Badenoch' in 1390. Many of the buildings like Dunblane and Dunkeld were near the edge of the Highlands and were far removed from the areas they were meant to serve. Some of the sees remained unoccupied for long periods. This meant there were few baptisms, marriage solemnizations and so forth, and practically no teaching. The revenues of the Highland houses fell into the hands of great families who used the money for their own enrichment. Abbots and priors from both Highlands and Lowlands gradually became little more than financial administrators of private companies, who lived with their communities, the monks, on salaries, shut off from much of what was going on in the world outside.

The friars in the towns and burghs were somewhat less corrupted, since the very nature of their orders was that they went out into the streets, the homes and the fields among ordinary people to do their work. It was difficult to live expensively, have mistresses, neglect their spiritual duties and play with politics in the public gaze. Friars did not on the whole get rich, but their houses were to become targets for looting as much as any other church building during the Reformation revolution.

In the sixteenth century the question of the pope's right to grant bishoprics and other benefices, challenged several times before, was brought up again by James V. The papacy, anxious to keep Scotland within the fold of the Roman church, was ready to make big concessions. Some had already been made in James III's time. Now the pope granted James more or less open-ended leave to appoint whom he liked to this or that benefice. It was a disastrous concession. With scant regard for the needs of the various bishoprics or the spiritual welfare of his people, the king filled vacancies with his bastard sons, with Stewart cousins and with unsuitable friends.

This sorry decline in the state of the church must have been extremely distressing to ordinary God-fearing Scots to whom religion was the most important and pervasive factor in their lives. It disturbed some of the higher clergy, too, and several attempts were made to introduce reforms. But they were too little and too late. Nor did they get much support from the kings – understandably! When the provincial councils of the church tried to correct abuses, they were not supported by the popes in Rome. Popes were often willing to exempt dignitaries from their obligations, even to excuse them from observing canon (church) law, in return for funds. Three important meetings of the council were held in 1549, 1552 and 1559, under the presidency of John Hamilton, archbishop of St Andrews and half-brother of James Hamilton, second earl of Arran (old Arran's son). A variety of measures were agreed: bishops were obliged to make regular visits to churches and religious houses in their dioceses, preaching and teaching were to be more frequent and more vigorous, and decaying churches were to be repaired or rebuilt. The councils failed, however, to do much to improve the financial position of the parish priests. But it was nonetheless clear that the Scottish church did want to 'clean itself up', but without swinging over to the doctrines and practices of the Protestants in the process. The church did not want to give up celebrating mass, nor would it surrender the dogma that the pope was the supreme head of the church.

When James V died, the government was taken over by the second earl of Arran (who happened also to be heir to James's daughter, Mary). He was inclined to support the Protestant movement, because it fitted in with his pro-English policies. There was a growing body of lords anxious to come to terms of some kind with England (a few of them who had been taken at Solway Moss had already declared such intention). Arran arranged with Henry VIII that Mary, still an infant, should be betrothed to Henry's seven-year-old son Edward. To get to power, Arran had had to displace Mary of Guise, the Queen Dowager, a formidable personality, uncompromisingly Catholic and patriotically French. He had also had Cardinal Beaton, her ally, imprisoned. But after a while Beaton prevailed upon his guards to set him free and he won Arran over to the pro-Catholic side. The arrangement with Henry VIII was cancelled, and this brought down upon Scotland yet another invasion, with the customary burning of abbeys, churches and towns. It was known as the 'Rough Wooing' because it was carried out in furtherance of Henry's attempt to win Mary Queen of Scots as a bride for his son. The violence served for a while to make many Scots think again about an alliance with England, and they turned once more to France. That, of course, meant continuing to accept the Catholic faith. Mary of Guise returned to power. But she was hardly less overweening in her ambition to join Scotland to France than Henry VIII was to bring Scotland under English rule. She remained at the forefront for much of the minority of her daughter Mary, and became officially regent in 1554. Arran was compensated for the reduction of his influence in Scottish government with a French dukedom.

But if it appeared that Scotland and France were edging closer to union, under the surface forces were actually working in the opposite direction. In 1546 George Wishart, a Protestant preacher, was burnt at the stake in St Andrews. The Protestants there took revenge, seized the castle and murdered Cardinal Beaton. Arran responded by besieging the castle with help from a French force, and in 1547, after a heroic struggle and an amazing attempt by both sides to tunnel through solid rock to get in and out of the castle, the defenders surrendered.[4] Among those taken was John Knox, who was sentenced to spend two years as a galley slave in the French fleet.

This episode increased the general disillusionment in Scotland with France. The Scots still had not got over Flodden and they wanted nothing like that to happen again. Despite tough measures by government and church, including more persecution of Protestants and more burnings at the stake, the reform movement gathered momentum throughout the country, more strongly in some places than in others. Angus, Fife, the Lothians and Ayr were the main centres. More and more Scots were urging the end of bishoprics, and asking for a return to the simpler but more relevant teachings straight from the Bible. Religion and politics, however, were becoming inextricably entwined. The break with France would have to go hand-in-hand with a break with the Catholic religion. Then, in 1558, three things happened that made the Protestant revolution certain. Mary, the queen, married the eldest son of the French king, making union with France a certainty unless the anti-France party acted quickly. Mary Tudor, England's queen, who had tried to restore the Roman faith and who had therefore forbidden Scottish Protestant exiles to take refuge in England, died and was succeeded by her half-sister Elizabeth, wedded to the Protestant cause. And John Knox, who became the greatest figure in the Scottish Reformation, returned to his homeland to champion the Protestant movement and to win more than enough support for it through his unique oratory and preaching.

In the previous year, some of the Protestant lords had combined to form the Congregation of Christ, with the aim of applying 'our whole power . . . our very lives . . . to maintain . . . and establish the most blessed word of God'. They came to be known as the Lords of the Congregation and were a politico-religious party bent on breaking the French grip and on restructuring the church in Scotland. They were militant, with troops and retainers at their disposal, and in 1558 they welcomed Knox whom they hoped would by his oratory stir up support for their cause. And so it happened. Knox and his colleague-preachers inveighed against the government of Mary of Guise and against the beliefs and practices of the established church in the same sermons. After one particular sermon in Perth, a riot broke out and an angry congregation ran down the streets and burned down the houses of the Black Friars and the Grey Friars. It was but one episode of many of the same kind, and they signalled the outbreak of the Protestant revolution.

The Lords of the Congregation declared war on Mary of Guise and when she mustered an army, with French aid, to meet this challenge, they sought – and received – assistance from Elizabeth I of England. Elizabeth intervened because Mary Queen of Scots and her husband had dared to assume the title king and queen of England, Scotland and Ireland. Catholics did not recognize Elizabeth as queen of England because she was the child of what they considered an adulterous union between Henry VIII and Anne Boleyn. She sent military aid, and the regent and her French forces were defeated. England and France then agreed, at the Treaty of Edinburgh, to withdraw their forces and allow the Scots to sort their difficulties out for themselves. In her agreement to help Scotland Elizabeth had been careful to say that her aid was only 'for the preservation of the freedoms and liberties of Scotland, and to save it from conquest by France'.

In August 1560 the Lords of the Congregation called a parliament which formally abolished the authority of the pope in Scotland, forbade the celebration of mass, recognized the new faith as the 'true religion' for Scotland (endorsed in a statement called 'The Confession of Faith'). The rebellion was over and Scotland became a Protestant nation. The arrangement was not ratified by Mary, when she returned to Scotland in 1561 to take up her throne, but that did not alter the fact. For six years the new church had no real legal status: Scotland had a Catholic queen who had no intention of being otherwise, and a government containing a majority of Protestant lords and officials, equally determined not to change. Which side would triumph in the end?

CHAPTER 10

A
LASS
ON THE
THRONE

(1542–1603)

After the battle of Solway Moss, James V had taken to his bed in despair. His queen, Mary of Guise, had taken to her bed too – for a very different reason. She had given birth to a daughter. When James had heard that the baby was a girl, his despair had increased. How could a woman keep out the English and rule the turbulent Scots? This daughter would, he believed, be the end of his line. 'It came with a lass,' he said, referring to the marriage of Walter the Stewart with Marjorie, daughter of Robert the Bruce, 'and it will go with a lass.' He was punning on the words 'a lass' and 'alas'. A little later, still in his bed, he rolled over onto his back, saw all his nobles around him, gave a little smile of laughter and yielded up his spirit to God.

The baby daughter, for whose future James had feared so greatly, became Mary Queen of Scots. People have very different opinions of her. To some she is a sad, romantic and fascinating figure, more sinned against than sinning. Others see her as foolish, deceitful, headstrong and, probably, criminal. James was right when he feared she would not be able to govern the Scots, but he was wrong when he thought she would be the last of the

Stewarts. Her son became king of England as well as Scotland, and descendants of the Stewarts have sat on the British throne ever since.

Mary was proclaimed queen when she was six days old. Then, when she was nine months old, her mother, Mary of Guise, and Cardinal Beaton had her ceremonially crowned at Stirling. While her mother and her supporters contended with the regent, the earl of Arran, and his allies, and while Henry VIII sent his soldiers northwards in the 'rough wooing' of Mary for his son, the little queen was kept safe. Then in 1547 the Scots were again defeated by the English in the battle of Pinkie Cleugh; Scotland was too dangerous for a royal child the English would like to get hold of and, when Mary of Guise decided to send her daughter to France, the Scots did not oppose her. In 1548, when she was five, the child queen set off, with four little Scottish companions, all called Mary like herself and known as the four Maries. The ship which carried them had to sail all round Ireland to reach France, because the Irish and English channels were filled with hostile English ships.

Mary was welcomed by Henri II, the king of France, as a little queen, a 'reinette', as he called her. With the approval of the Scottish parliament, dominated as it was by the supporters of Mary of Guise, the queen of Scots was betrothed to Henri's heir, the dauphin, a child a year younger than herself. The ambitious Guise family saw Mary as their way to the French throne.

Mary was put in the care of her grandmother, the austere, religious duchesse Antoinette de Guise. She visited the French court, the most elegant and artistic in Europe, and studied with the French royal children. She was taught to ride, dance, sing, play an instrument, speak foreign languages and write poetry. She learned embroidery, too, and developed a taste for rich clothes. Then in 1558, when she was fifteen, she and the dauphin were married. She was tall – almost six feet tall – graceful, slender and auburn-haired. In manner she was self-assured, high-spirited and very charming. She was described as 'the best and prettiest little queen in the world'. Mary had almost forgotten Scotland. In the public marriage treaty, the independence of her kingdom was guaranteed; but secretly she signed over Scotland, as part of her dowry, to the kings of France.

That same year in England another Queen Mary, Henry VIII's Roman Catholic daughter, died and her Protestant half-sister,

Elizabeth, succeeded to the throne. And Mary Queen of Scots, made the first and most fateful of many mistakes. Encouraged by her father-in-law, she added the arms of England to her armorial bearings, alongside those of Scotland and France. It did not seem so terrible; after all, the kings of England had borne the arms of France without ever being able to substantiate their claim to ruling there. But it meant that Mary thought she, and not Elizabeth, should be queen of England. In Roman Catholic eyes she had a certain claim. Elizabeth, as the daughter of Henry VIII's second wife, Anne Boleyn – for whom Henry had divorced his first wife and taken England out of the Roman Catholic fold – was an illegitimate child, whereas Mary was directly descended from Henry's sister Margaret. Yet it was not a claim anyone was likely to fight for. Mary was Elizabeth's heir; it was foolish and tactless to become her rival as well.

The next year, very suddenly, Mary's father-in-law died. A lance pierced his eye when he was jousting. Besides being the crowned queen of Scotland with hopes of the throne of England, Mary was now queen consort of France. She was at a pinnacle of greatness – but the year continued sadly. A few months later, after a year of civil war in Scotland, Mary's mother died. Then Mary's husband, François II, the new king of France, contracted an inflammation of the ear. He had always been sickly and, within a few weeks, the inflammation spread into his brain and he, too, died. The sunny years in France were over. The time had come for Mary, who was just eighteen, to claim her difficult kingdom.

Mary landed at Leith on a cold, foggy day in August 1561. She had not been expected for another couple of days at least, and the Scots were not ready for her. Hastily they mustered a troop of cavalry and sent it down to the waterside. Mary, being used to the elegance of France, nearly wept when she saw how rough and ragged both men and horses were.

Later in the same day, a group of nobles escorted her to Holyrood. There, during her first night in Scotland, Mary discovered what a strange, puritanical and fervently religious society she had come into. She had only just gone to sleep when she was awakened by several hundred Scots singing psalms beneath her window – and singing them extremely badly. The lugubrious singing of psalms had become very popular in Protestant Scotland. French-bred Mary had come to rule a people whose religion, not to mention taste in music, was quite unlike her own.

On 1 September she made her state entry into Edinburgh. Her subjects gave her a better welcome than they had at Leith. She was grave and charming as she rode into the city with her four Maries; her white skin and her red-gold hair were set off by the black mourning she wore for her husband; and the people of Edinburgh were enchanted. The crowds called out to her as she passed: 'God bless that sweet face!' Elaborate pageants and masques were staged for her and the fountains spouted wine.

One suggestion for a masque, the burning of a Roman Catholic priest in effigy, had been abandoned, but a child gave Mary a Bible and a psalter, the insignia of Protestantism, at a formal presentation and when, the following Sunday, Mary went to hear mass at her private chapel, her priests were attacked. 'This is a fair commencement of what I have to expect,' Mary exclaimed – as, indeed, it was. The following Sunday Mary's mass was denounced from an Edinburgh pulpit. One mass was more fearful to him, said the preacher, in a phrase which sticks in the memory, than ten thousand armed men.

The preacher was, of course, John Knox, the most brilliant and fiery of the leaders of the Scottish Reformation. After nineteen months in the French galleys, chained to his oar, he had been freed through the intervention of the boy king of England, Edward VI – the son for whom Henry VIII had fought so hard to win Mary as a bride. Knox had been a royal chaplain at Edward's court for six months or so and then, when Edward died and his Roman Catholic sister Mary came to the throne, had gone to Geneva to sit at the feet of Calvin. He had returned to Scotland during the civil war against Mary of Guise and her Catholic supporters, lending his courage and conviction, as well as his gift for the pithy and memorable phrase, to the Protestant cause, so that he could bring the Reformation about.

When he preached, Knox could rouse his hearers to a frenzy; the congregation had rioted when they heard him at Perth (see p. 135). Yet he denied all blame; he was not, he said, responsible for the actions of the 'rascal multitude'. On one occasion, though, his eloquence misgave him. During the reign of the English Roman Catholic, Mary Tudor, he wrote a famous diatribe called: *A First*

Blast of the Trumpet against the Monstrous Regiment of Women. (*Regiment* meant regimen, or rule.) He was what would nowadays be called a male chauvinist pig! Elizabeth of England, who could have been such a useful ally, never forgave him for it.

When she heard of his attack on her private mass, Mary Queen of Scots called him to an interview. Trusting her own charm and her ready tongue, she always liked to meet her adversaries face to face. On Knox's arrival, she attacked him for rousing her subjects against her, and then for writing the *Monstrous Regiment.* He replied that, if she behaved well and the realm were not brought to disaster by her femininity, he would not disallow her rule on that ground alone. He would be 'as well content to live under Your Grace as Paul was under Nero,' he said unflatteringly, though he would not give in over the mass. Mary tackled an even more important issue. 'Think ye,' she said, 'that subjects, having power, may resist their princes?' 'If their princes exceed their bounds, Madam, they may be resisted and even deposed,' Knox responded. At one point Mary burst into angry tears, but she could not move him. They were both courageous and able people, fitting adversaries, but Mary's arguments were the weaker. Mary failed with Knox. Through many interviews, she never turned him a hair's breadth from his Protestant purpose. How did she fare with the natural allies of a monarch, her nobles?

The Scottish nobles at that time, Protestant as well as Catholic, were, almost to a man, self-seeking. They still had almost no conception of a national interest greater than their own individual interests, of which their queen might be the guardian and symbol. They were concerned only with the power of their own families and the very complicated web of family relationships from which such power derived. Many had ties with English noble families and some with the royal family of England, the Tudors. When, as often happened, they were temporarily outlawed from Scotland, or their estates were forfeited, they went into England for help and a refuge. English monarchs often bribed disaffected Scottish nobles to push English interests in Scotland. Most Scots nobles were not averse to taking such bribes.

When Mary looked among her nobles for loyal and able men, she saw very few. Nevertheless, she found two first-rate advisers. One was her half-brother, Lord James Stewart, an illegitimate son of James V who is better known in history as the earl of Moray, which he soon became. He was one of the Lords of the Congregation and already effectively in power. The other was also a Protestant – a subtle, clever politician called William Maitland of Lethington.

Mary declared her religious tolerance. She even decreed that the reformed church should have some of the revenues that used to go to the old Catholic church, before its monasteries and other foundations were destroyed. Then she sent Maitland to London. He had two tasks. First, he was to persuade Elizabeth to name Mary as her heir, despite the terms of the Treaty of Edinburgh and, secondly, to negotiate a suitable marriage for her.

Mary was not a wily politician like her cousin Elizabeth, who could use endlessly protracted marriage negotiations as an instrument of foreign policy. She did not, as Elizabeth did, regard her marriageability as a card so valuable that, in the end, she could never bear to marry and give it up. She was used to having powerful male figures, such as Henri II and her Guise relations, to advise and protect her. She wanted a strong and capable husband who would do the same.

She considered Don Carlos, the heir to the Spanish throne, but he turned out to be insane. Then she thought of the Archduke Charles of Austria. Both were Roman Catholics with large armies, which could be used to bring Scotland back to the old faith. Elizabeth did not want that kind of marriage for Mary. She countered by refusing to name Mary as her heir. Then she put forward her own candidate for Mary's hand. He was Robert Dudley, later earl of Leicester: Elizabeth's own favourite, the man she loved more than any other. The offer was an insult but Mary refused it politely.

She travelled through her kingdom, riding on the sands of Dee in men's clothes, hunting and hawking in the Highlands, singing, playing the lute and dancing. Her severer psalm-singing subjects were shocked by the fact that she danced. The earl of Huntly, known as the Cock o' the North, staged a minor rebellion and she put it down. Then, three and a half years after her return to Scotland, she began to behave in a very unqueenly way. She fell in love.

Early in 1565 Mary was dancing with her court in the castle at Wemyss, when she saw a beautiful eighteen-year-old youth. He had bright yellow hair, a face as delicate as a girl's and – wonder of wonders – he was even taller than Mary herself. He had easy, polished manners, enjoyed music and wrote elegant, courtly verses. He was soon Mary's boon companion. He travelled about Scotland with her, hunting and hawking, and played the lute at the musical supper parties she loved to give on winter evenings.

He was Henry, Lord Darnley, a prince of the blood and cousin to both Mary and Elizabeth. His father was the Scottish earl of Lennox and his mother was the granddaughter of Henry VII, the first Tudor king of England. An ambitious woman, she had brought her son up to marry Mary. She had had him trained in all the accomplishments which might please a queen.

Darnley, however, had defects of character. He was weak, vicious and untrustworthy. He cared for nothing but his own pleasure. Elizabeth of England knew it, as Darnley had spent some time at the English court. Some of the Scottish nobles knew it, and it did not take Mary long to find it out as well. By then, though, she was too deeply committed to Darnley to draw back. Her love probably led her into a secret marriage with him in March, only six weeks or so after she met him. By the end of July, when the public marriage took place, she knew he was not the strong helpmeet she wanted. Nevertheless, she pushed the marriage ahead, not waiting for the special dispensation from the pope which was necessary as she and Darnley were cousins and Catholics. Some people say she did so because she was headstrong and her passion could not wait, but her motive may have been very different. In those days, kings and queens who disliked their marriages often had them annulled on the ground that they had been contracted illegally. By not waiting for the papal dispensation, Mary could have been preparing the ground for just such an annulment.

She made Darnley an earl, then a duke and finally king Henry. He was almost on a level with Mary herself, and his arrogance knew no bounds. Mary's nobles hated him for it. The wedding itself was a strange one. Mary wore black as François's widow, and Darnley, although he was a Roman Catholic, refused to stay with her through the full nuptial mass. Afterwards, Mary seemed unhappy and changed, 'as if', wrote Elizabeth's envoy, 'she misliked her own doings'.

The marriage shifted the balance of power among the Scottish nobles in favour of the Lennox family, and Mary's friends left her. Moray, seeing himself eclipsed, withdrew from the court and was outlawed. He mustered an army and rebelled. Mary put on a man's steel helmet and breastplate and, with Darnley beside her in gilded armour, drove Moray out of the country in what is known as the Chaseabout Raid. Maitland of Lethington drifted away as well.

During the past months Mary had been turning to a different, lower class for support. She looked for men who would be more dependent upon her, and consequently more loyal, than her fickle nobles. Before her marriage, she had taken on a humble Italian musician, called David Riccio, as her secretary for foreign correspondence. Soon he became her adviser and then, as her brief love for Darnley cooled, her close companion.

At one time, Riccio had been Darnley's man almost as much as he was Mary's. But as Darnley felt himself pushed out, he began to hate Riccio. The nobles, who bitterly resented the rise of the Italian upstart, fed Darnley's jealousy. Riccio advised and influenced Mary, they said. Riccio sang and played to her. And it was Riccio who, when the young husband was away, played cards with her, sometimes until the early hours of the morning. 'Signor Davey', Elizabeth's faithful envoy wrote, 'governs all.'

Moreover, Darnley was being thwarted. In the heady days of first love, Mary had promised him the crown matrimonial, that is, that she would make him her heir. After marriage, she withheld it. Darnley blamed the influence of Riccio.

By the end of 1565 Mary, although she knew she was pregnant, was almost totally estranged from Darnley. Her disaffected nobles approached him about the formation of a bond, or brotherhood, with the twin aims of gaining him the crown matrimonial and bringing the exiled lords, notably Moray, back to Scotland. Darnley signed the document which bound them all. Moray signed it too, in England early in 1566. Maitland of Lethington, though he knew and approved of it, prudently did not sign. Riccio, the hated secretary, was not mentioned in it anywhere, but all the signatories knew he was their victim.

On the evening of 9 March 1566, Mary, by now nearly six months pregnant, sat at supper with six members of her household, including Riccio, in a small supper room, only 12 feet by 14 feet, next to her bedchamber in the palace of Holyrood. Darnley came into the room by a private staircase, which led up from his own bedchamber beneath. The party welcomed him with some surprise – he spent most of his evenings in Edinburgh, drinking and looking for girls. He took his seat beside Mary, and then a band of armed men, who had followed him up the staircase, burst into the room with drawn swords and demanded Riccio. The little Italian seized Mary's skirts, but his fingers were prized open, while Darnley held Mary back against the wall. Then the secretary was dragged down the stairs to Darnley's room and stabbed to death. His body had about sixty wounds. What remained of him was thrown out of the window into the courtyard below.

Mary was herself in very great danger. The use of such violence in her presence might easily have caused her to miscarry, and in those days women who miscarried nearly always died. Afterwards, she believed the plot had been against her own life, as well as Riccio's. If she and her unborn child had both died, Darnley would have been king in fact, as well as in name, whether he had the crown matrimonial or not.

Mary was always courageous in the face of danger. After the murder, she was virtually a prisoner in Holyrood; her disaffected nobles did not intend to let her go until she had both pardoned the murderers and agreed to the return of the exiles. She hated Darnley since the murder of her servant, yet she spent the next two days with him, cajoling and deceiving him until she had him on her side. On the Monday evening she escaped through the cellars with him, and together they rode through the night to Dunbar. She wheedled the names of the conspirators out of him and they, hearing of it, sent her the bond with Darnley's signature on it. Darnley, doubly treacherous, was doomed.

In June, Mary gave birth to the boy who would eventually, as James the Sixth of Scotland and First of England, unite the two crowns. When Elizabeth heard of it, she was almost jealous. 'The queen of Scots is lighter of a fair son,' she exclaimed, 'and I am but a barren stock.'

By now Mary wished her marriage over. Moray was her adviser once more, and he fostered her hatred of Darnley. Then Darnley learned that other lords besides Moray had been pardoned for their part in the murder plot. They would soon be about in Scotland again and want their revenge. Miserable and degraded, he prepared to leave the country. And Mary made ready for the second impetuous passion of her life.

During the last couple of years, a third man, besides Darnley and Riccio, had been close to Mary. He was the earl of Bothwell, a

145

turbulent Borderer whom she had known since her days in France. A bold and reckless adventurer, he had but a single virtue – loyalty to the crown. He never took English money and, although he was a Protestant, he had fought for Mary's mother against the Lords of the Congregation. It was he who had engineered Mary's escape through the cellars of Holyrood, and it was to his castle at Dunbar that she had fled with Darnley for refuge. Mary was filled with admiration for him. Perhaps he was the strong man she craved?

That summer, Mary told Moray and others that she wished to be rid of Darnley. Divorce was talked about. Maitland mentioned 'other means', without being specific, and Mary left the matter in the hands of her nobles. In November the second important bond of her reign was drawn up. Bothwell, Maitland and many others signed it, agreeing that Darnley should be 'put off one way or another'. This time, it was Moray who cautiously withheld his signature.

Just before Christmas, the infant James was christened in Stirling Castle. Darnley did not attend the christening, although he was in the castle at the time; his personal standing was too low. After Christmas, he left Stirling for Glasgow, a Lennox stronghold. He felt safer there and less humiliated. Then he fell ill. Before long, Mary visited him and persuaded him, with a promise of reconciliation, to return to Edinburgh with her. She could not risk his staying long with the Lennoxes and plotting against her. She arranged for him to convalesce in an old house, known as the Provost's Lodging, about three-quarters of a mile from Holyrood at a place called Kirk o'Field. It is covered now by the quadrangle of the University of Edinburgh.

The Provost's Lodging was a tall, narrow house, only containing a bedroom for Darnley, another beneath it for Mary, a presence room, kitchens and cellars. During the week that followed, Mary spent much time there. Darnley begged her forgiveness, blaming his mistakes on the inexperience of youth, and the two seemed to get on fairly well together. They arranged that, on the Monday, Darnley would be moved to Holyrood.

On the Sunday evening Mary and several of her nobles, including Bothwell, crowded into Darnley's room. They played cards and chatted with the sick man. Someone sang. Then, about eleven o'clock, Mary remembered that there was a ball at Holyrood, to celebrate the marriage of some of her servants. Accompanied by her nobles, she rode back to Holyrood. It was a gay, rather noisy group that left Kirk o'Field with torches flaring.

Mary did not return to Kirk o'Field after the ball. The hour was too late, so she slept at Holyrood. At two o'clock she – and everyone else in the palace – was woken by a tremendous explosion. The house at Kirk o'Field had been blown up. Two bodies, belonging to Darnley and a servant, were found in a nearby garden. They had been strangled.

No one knows what actually happened. When were the explosives put into the house, and where? In the queen's chamber, or in the cellars? Was Darnley strangled before or after the explosion? Most important, who was responsible?

The people of Edinburgh immediately suspected Mary's new favourite, Bothwell. In the weeks that followed, they pieced together a story something like this: Bothwell procured the gunpowder and had it taken to Kirk o'Field, where it was almost certainly stacked in the cellars – it would not have gone off properly in the centre of the house, where Mary's room was. He rode back with Mary to Holyrood at eleven o'clock, but soon left the ball there, changed into plainer clothing and returned to Kirk o'Field to give his final instructions. Then he slipped quietly back to Holyrood and his bed – from which he arose, seemingly as surprised as anybody, when the explosion was heard.

Darnley and his servant may have heard Bothwell's men and fled from them, only to be seen and caught by some Douglases, relations of Darnley and yet conspirators, in the garden. Women living in nearby houses said they heard Darnley pleading with them. 'Pity me, kinsmen,' he said, 'for the sake of Jesus Christ, who pitied all the world.' They did not pity him. They strangled him when the house went up.

The great question was, and always will be, what did Mary know about the murder plot? Had she guessed what Maitland's 'other means' of ending her marriage might be? Or had she been careful not to inquire? When she brought Darnley to Kirk o'Field, had she any inkling that she was luring him to his death? Had she 'looked through her fingers', to use a contemporary Scots phrase, at the murder of her husband?

After his death, she behaved very strangely. Instead of tracking down the murderers and avenging her husband's death, for several days she did nothing. She seemed to be in a state of nervous collapse. Europe's other queens, Elizabeth and Catherine de'Medici, both wrote to her in the strongest terms, telling her that justice must be done, and be seen to be done. Mary could not rouse herself. The people of Edinburgh put up posters on the walls accusing Bothwell of the crime. One poster even linked Bothwell and Mary, and implied that Bothwell was Mary's lover. Still Mary did nothing. Eventually it was Lennox, Darnley's outraged father, who brought charges against Bothwell.

Edinburgh, however, was full of Bothwell's men and Lennox was only permitted to bring six of his followers with him. He did not dare enter the city with so small a force. He could not make his case and Bothwell was declared not guilty. Mary's favour towards Bothwell never diminished and, at the next meeting of the Scottish parliament, he was given new lands. Some servants were captured after Darnley's murder, tortured and killed. Otherwise, Darnley remained virtually unavenged.

After parliament's sitting, Bothwell gave a lavish, and famous, supper party at an inn called Ainslie's Tavern and persuaded a large number of Scottish nobles and prelates to sign yet another bond, promoting his marriage to the queen. He took the bond to Mary, but she did not agree to the marriage. A few days later, when she was travelling to Edinburgh from Linlithgow, Bothwell met her on the way. He had a force of 800 men with him – far too many for her own small party to cope with. He turned her horse round and, docilely, she allowed him to lead her to his castle at Dunbar. She was so docile that people wondered if she helped plan the abduction. Whether she did or not, Bothwell was determined to marry her. When he had her, helpless, in his castle, he followed abduction with rape. After that, Mary had to accept him as her husband.

Bothwell was, however, already married; Mary herself had arranged his marriage just before the murder of Riccio. His wife, Lady Jean, was quite ready to divorce him – and in four days the divorce case was through. Bothwell led Mary triumphantly into Edinburgh and in mid-May, twelve days after his divorce and three months after Darnley's murder, the two were married. Once again, Mary went to her wedding in mourning for a dead husband. Once again, she did not have the full rites of her own religion; indeed, this time the service was Protestant. And, once again, she was sad and unhappy afterwards. She wanted nothing but death, she said, and called out for a knife that she might kill herself.

Mary had the strong man she had been looking for – but found he was too rough and rude to make her happy. And the Scottish nobles did not in the least want a dominant pseudo-king. As Bothwell's power grew, the nobles formed a league against him. Within weeks, they had gathered at Stirling. Mary and Bothwell left Holyrood for the greater safety of Edinburgh Castle, but the custodian would not let them in. Bothwell took Mary south to Borthwick Castle but, no sooner had they entered it, to wait, they believed, for their supporters, than it was surrounded by rebels. Bothwell slipped away to his own neighbouring castle of Crichton. A day or two later Mary and Bothwell fled to Dunbar, gathered their supporters, and then faced the rebel lords eight miles east of Edinburgh, at Carberry Hill. The rebel banner showed a green tree against a white ground, with Darnley's corpse beneath it and the infant Prince James kneeling beside it. Written across it were the words: 'Judge and defend my cause, O Lord.' For the first time, Mary realized that Darnley's murder and her re-marriage could cost her the throne.

All day she sat on a boulder, wearing a short red dress like any common woman, while the two sides conducted a medieval parley. Bothwell challenged the rebels to an even more medieval single combat – particularly appropriate as his own forces, seeing the superior size of the rebel army, were rapidly melting away! Then he tried to persuade Mary to return to Dunbar with him, to collect reinforcements. Foolishly, though, she preferred to trust herself to the rebels, who had promised to treat her as befitted a queen. Bothwell gave her the bond signed only seven months earlier against Darnley. Then he galloped away alone.

Mary crossed to the rebel camp – and realized immediately how her people's love for her had changed. The soldiers shouted insults at her: 'Burn the whore. She is not worthy to live.' Tears of humiliation ran down her cheeks. She was being treated, not as a young and beautiful queen, but as the willing bride of her husband's murderer.

The rebels took Mary, all dirty and bedraggled in her meagre red dress, to Edinburgh – not to the castle or her palace of Holyrood, but to one of their own houses, with guards posted both inside and outside her room. Her captors sat down to a hearty meal, but Mary was too distressed – and too afraid of being poisoned – to eat. The people of Edinburgh gathered outside. Mary appeared at her window, weeping bitterly, and called out that she had been betrayed. The crowd shouted back: 'Kill her, kill her!' 'Burn her, burn her!' Mary's nerves gave way. She appeared again at the window, still in her red dress, which was now torn to the waist, and wept bitterly, her hair hanging round her face. The crowd mocked and insulted her. 'Burn, burn!' 'Kill, kill!' they shouted. If they had got hold of her, they would have carried her off there and then to the marketplace and burned her to death.

Late the next day, the lords took Mary to a castle on an island in Lochleven. For fifteen days she hardly ate, drank, or spoke, such was her despair. During that time a silver casket, or box, containing various letters from Mary to Bothwell came into the hands of the rebel lords. Scholars and historians have argued ever since as to whether these very famous 'casket letters', as they were called, were really written by Mary, or forged. If she wrote them, they are proof that she conspired with Bothwell and others to murder Darnley. If parts of them, at least, were forged, they were a handy way of removing a queen who appeared to be a cruel murderess – everything the Edinburgh mob had accused her of being, and more. They were the weapon the nobles needed to remove the guilt of Darnley's death from themselves and put it on to Mary.

Then, in the middle of July, two months after her marriage, Mary told Elizabeth's envoy that she was pregnant. Soon afterwards, she either miscarried or gave birth to a premature baby. It might have been born dead, or it may have been smuggled out of the country and reared secretly abroad. According to one rumour, Mary had a daughter, who became a nun in France. The child was almost certainly conceived before Mary's marriage to Bothwell, and may even have been conceived before Darnley's death. If that were so, Mary's need to save her good name could account for a great deal – even the murder of her royal husband.

John Knox and other Protestant preachers railed against the imprisoned queen and kept the mood of the Edinburgh crowd dangerous. Then, while she was still weak from miscarriage or childbirth, the nobles took an abdication document to her and forced her to sign it, under threat of a public trial for Darnley's murder. Prince James took her place, with Moray as regent until James should be seventeen. Mary's part in Scottish history, a part so full of riddles, was very nearly at an end.

Bothwell tried to rally support for Mary but failed. He was

outlawed and fled to Denmark, where the king prudently imprisoned him. He went mad in prison and died six years later.

Mary's passion for him was soon gone. She knew that she had
made a second tragic mistake. After a few weeks at Lochleven, her
depression lifted, her courage returned, and the captive, dis-
crowned queen was dancing, doing her embroidery and light-
heartedly charming her jailers. One of them, a youth of eighteen
called George Douglas, was soon 'lost in a fantasy of love' with her.
In May 1568 he arranged her escape. Within a week, she had
collected an army of 6000 men, but she had no good general, and
when she met the forces of the Regent Moray at Langside, she was
easily defeated in 'one long quarter of an hour'.

Mary fled with sixteen followers. She rode day and night until
she had covered the ninety miles to Dundrennan. No doubt she
considered on the way whether to seek refuge in England or
France. She knew her French relations had lost patience with her
and, besides, France was embroiled in religious wars. She wrote a
lengthy appeal to Elizabeth, and then she crossed the Border into
England.

Elizabeth was in a very awkward situation. She had always supported Mary against rebels, in a kind of fellowship of queens. But
Mary had claimed to be queen of England. She had rivalled
Elizabeth. She could easily become the focus of all the religious and
other malcontents in the country. Elizabeth decided to put her in
prison and to keep her there.

For eighteen years Mary was a captive in one English castle or
another. It was quite an easy captivity. She could ride in the
countryside, dance, make music and dress like a queen. She had
her own household. But she could only receive visitors if her jailers
approved of them, and they monitored her correspondence. Her
youthful beauty soon went; often, she was sad and ill. But she
never abandoned her dreams of freedom, of restoring the Roman
Catholic religion – with help from Austria, perhaps, or Spain – and
regaining a throne. She never stopped plotting.

Her first idea was to marry the duke of Norfolk, the most
important nobleman in England and a Roman Catholic. Elizabeth
scotched that plan by having his head cut off. Later, she dreamed
of marrying Don John of Austria – but everyone knew she would
have to be rescued first, and that was impossible. If England had
been invaded, Mary would have been executed immediately.

Then in 1580 the pope and Philip II, the Roman Catholic king of Spain who was Elizabeth's greatest enemy, declared it was legal for a Roman Catholic to assassinate a heretic, or Protestant, ruler. Although this bann, as it was called, was aimed against the Dutch king, William the Silent, it endangered Elizabeth herself. She was reluctant to take any action against Mary, however, until William was indeed murdered in 1584. Then she agreed with her ministers that Mary's presence in the country was too great a threat to be allowed to continue.

Elizabeth had a very able minister, Sir Francis Walsingham, who had a role rather like that of a chief of police, or secret police, in a modern state. He laid a trap for Mary, which came to be known as the Babington Plot. Mary was being confined very strictly, with almost no communication with the outside world, when a man called Gifford, an agent of Walsingham's, offered to pass letters for her. They were to be got out of her prison, very conspiratorially it seemed, in the bunghole of a beer barrel. Various other agents, some of them Roman Catholic priests turned informer, constructed a vague plot to liberate Mary, re-establish the Roman Catholic church in England and assassinate Elizabeth. A rich, romantic and rather foolish young man called Thomas Babington was to be their leader. He wrote to Mary with plans so ludicrous that her secretary advised her not to answer the letter. But Mary was ready to clutch at any straw. In a series of letters, which all found their way into Walsingham's hands, she agreed to Babington's schemes.

She was arrested and taken to Fotheringhay, a castle in Northamptonshire. She was tried in the great hall there, before the leading nobles of England. By now a very sick, middle-aged woman, she limped in painfully. With great courage and dignity she defended herself, but she had no chance at all of proving herself innocent.

It took Elizabeth more than three months to bring herself to sign the death warrant. Then it was taken immediately to Fotheringhay and Mary, who had already gone to bed, was wakened to have it read to her. She was told she would die the next morning. She was not allowed to see her Roman Catholic chaplain, and she was told she could not be buried in France, as she wished.

Mary made her will and gave away her few remaining possessions. All night, carpenters hammered beneath her as they built the scaffold in the great hall. At six o'clock Mary rose and bade farewell to her servants. Then she prayed alone until the English lords came for her, between eight and nine.

She went into the hall of her execution with the symbols of her religion about her, a crucifix in one hand, a prayer book in the other, and two rosaries hanging from her waist. About 300 people watched as with difficulty, yet with total calm and courage, she climbed the scaffold, which was draped in black. She was offered the ministrations of a Protestant clergyman and refused them; nevertheless he recited prayers for her in English. She raised her voice against his in the Latin prayers of her own church. The black dress she wore was removed, revealing a dark red underdress, while her servants prayed in Scots, French and Latin, the tears streaming down their faces. The English clergyman fell silent.

Mary's women bound her eyes and hair, and then withdrew. Mary knelt in front of the block, recited a psalm in Latin, then felt for the block with her hands and laid her head upon it. She cried out three or four times: 'Into thy hands, O Lord, I commend my spirit.' The first blow of the axe only cut into the back of her neck. 'Sweet Jesus', her women heard her whisper. The second blow severed her neck. Like her descendant, Charles I, nothing in life became her like the leaving of it.

Elizabeth, when she heard of Mary's death, angrily blamed the secretary who had done as she bid him and sent the death warrant to Fotheringhay. She threw him into prison and fined him the huge sum of £10,000.

Mary's son, James VI of Scotland, wept when he heard of her end. His tears were genuine; but earlier the twenty-year-old king had let it be known that he could 'digest', to use his own word, his mother's death.

He had been in a very difficult position. He did not know his mother; he had not seen her since he was crowned, as a baby of thirteen months. Their interests had always been opposed. They had been titular heads of a king's party and a queen's party in Scotland, which had always been at loggerheads. While Mary lived, doubts could be cast on the legality of James' kingship and, as Elizabeth grew older and still did not marry, the chances of Mary leaving her imprisonment and succeeding to the English throne increased. James was not a disloyal son, but the consequences of such an event were almost too appalling for him, or anyone around him, to contemplate. The advantages for James of his mother's death were clear. But she *was* his mother. After the execution, Elizabeth tactfully gave him a loophole by writing to him to say that it had taken place without her knowledge and against her intentions. James accepted her explanation. 'I dare not wrong you so far as not to judge honourably of your unspotted part therein,' he wrote. James and Elizabeth understood each other perfectly. Other Scots wanted revenge, but for James the matter was closed.

James's early years were spent at Stirling Castle, where he was looked after by good and responsible people, the earl and countess of Mar. He was a highly intelligent boy, with a great love of books and learning, but physically weak and always rather nervous. Throughout his life he was subject to fits of unreasonable terror. His surroundings at Stirling were peaceful enough, but he dreaded the violence that he knew went on farther afield in Scotland. He had heard, too, about the murders in his mother's reign. When his grandfather, the earl of Lennox, was brought, bloody and wounded, into Stirling Castle to die, James, a five-year-old child at the time, was terrified.

We know now that, after the battle of Langside, Mary's rule in Scotland was over. The Scots of the time did not. She might escape from her English prison . . . she might be released . . . foreign armies might fight for her. Mary's cause still seemed worth backing to many of her nobility, and for years the violence continued. Moray, as regent for the boy king, sought to discredit Mary in the eyes of her Scottish supporters and her English jailers by exhibiting the 'casket letters' (see p. 150) (which implicated her in Darnley's murder) in London. The queen's party grew weaker.

Meanwhile, Moray set Scotland on the course towards peace and unity, which her rulers continued to steer for the rest of the century. In alliance with John Knox, he strengthened Protestantism and the Reformed church (the Kirk). He enforced the law restraining the warring nobles and giving protection to ordinary men and women. Consequently, they called him the Good Regent.

But Moray could do no more than begin his programme. He made a fatal mistake. He failed to curb the power of the Hamiltons, the rich Roman Catholic family which had fought for Mary at Langside, and the Hamiltons were determined to bring him down.

In 1570, when Moray had been regent for three years, he was

riding through Linlithgow towards Edinburgh when he was shot. Archbishop Hamilton, who had the Roman Catholic see of St Andrews, had a house in the High Street. He had lent it to James Hamilton of Bothwellhaugh, a relatively unimportant member of the family, but one with a particular grudge against Moray, for the murder. Bothwellhaugh had posted himself on a wooden gallery jutting out from the first floor. He had hung linen sheets over the gallery railing and from its roof. They probably looked as if they had been hung there to dry. He stood on a feather mattress, which deadened the sound of his boots, and poked the muzzle of his gun through a hole in the sheets. He fired at close range as Moray rode slowly through the crowded street. Then, as the mortally wounded regent was helped to a nearby house, he slipped out by the back way and escaped on a fast horse.

Bothwellhaugh galloped to the town of Hamilton, on the Clyde. The head of the family, the duke of Chatelherault (who had been the second earl of Arran), helped him escape to France. But the triumph of the Hamiltons was shortlived. When, soon afterwards, they raided the Border, the English, who had always given some support to Moray, chased them home and destroyed the palace, castle and town of Hamilton.

The next regent was the earl of Lennox. A weak and ineffectual man, he was appointed because he was James's grandfather. Fourteen months later when he, too, was shot, he was succeeded by James's guardian, the kind and peace-loving earl of Mar. But the real ruler of the country, it was becoming clear, was the head of the great Douglas family, the earl of Morton. For a year he led the king's party in skirmishes with Mary's supporters, known as the Douglas Wars, and then in 1572 Mar died – of a broken heart, it was said, because 'he loved peace and could not have it'.

Naturally, his successor was Morton. He became regent on 24 November 1572, the day the fiery Protestant preacher, John Knox, died. A few days later, gazing into Knox's grave at his funeral, Morton described him as one that 'neither feared nor flattered any flesh'. It was true. His forthrightness had given Knox, the humble farmer's son, the indomitable strength to battle with the greatest in the land.

Morton himself knew Knox as an opponent. Though Morton was a Protestant, the two men had quarrelled bitterly shortly

before Knox died. Bishops of the Reformed church were appointed
by the king (or his regent) and sometimes by the nobility. The
power to appoint bishops was often abused. A nobleman with a
see to dispose of sometimes appointed a bishop on condition that
he kept some, or most, of the bishop's revenues for himself. One of
the worst offending nobles was Morton. When he had the see of St
Andrews in his gift, he made no appointment at all for a while and
kept the revenues for himself. When, eventually, he did choose a
bishop, he paid him only a small stipend, still keeping the major
part of the bishop's income himself. Knox publicly denounced the
appointment of such 'tulchan bishops', as they were called: the
practice was 'anathema to the giver, and anathema to the receiver',
he said, and he refused to induct Morton's nominee.[1]

Morton was too fond of money. Nevertheless he was a loyal and
extremely capable servant to the young king. He was a good
soldier, too. The queen's party still held out in Edinburgh Castle,
with Kirkcaldy of Grange as their leader and Maitland of Lethington, Mary's old adviser, alongside him. Morton's first task as
regent was to take the castle. He made sure the defenders would
get no help from the Hamiltons by concluding a treaty with them
called the Pacification of Perth, and then he appealed to Elizabeth
for help. In May 1573 she sent twenty heavy guns northwards.
They pounded away at the castle to such good effect that, at the
end of the month, Kirkcaldy surrendered. Some weeks later, he
was hanged. Maitland of Lethington died in prison; otherwise, he
would have been hanged too.

Then Morton settled down to promoting Protestantism in the
country and peace under the law, in the tradition of Moray. Nor
did he forget that James might well become king of England as well
as Scotland one day. He maintained the English alliance. His
strong rule was good for the Scottish people, but it made him many
enemies among the nobles, whose powers were being eroded. His
harsh, arrogant manner did nothing to sweeten the pill and
unfortunately James, a nervous boy, detested him.

As the Hamiltons went down, the Lennox Stuarts, Darnley's
family, rose. They had a claim to the succession and, in order to
secure it, James's cousin Esmé Stuart, Lord d'Aubigny, came to
visit him from his home in France. Of Scottish descent but French
upbringing, he was a handsome, friendly and extremely charming
courtier – very different from the stern and violent men who had

always surrounded James. The thirteen-year-old king was delighted by him. Soon, he had developed such a fondness for him that it
astonished everyone, even d'Aubigny himself.

James gave d'Aubigny the abbey of Arbroath, which had been
forfeited by the Hamiltons and then, the next year, made him earl
of Lennox. The new earl had come to Scotland to win James's
favour. Now that he had it, to a greater extent than he had ever
dreamed of, he aspired to real power. The only obstacle in his way
was Morton. Very cleverly, he removed him. He bribed one of his
supporters, Captain James Stewart, to charge Morton with com-
plicity in Darnley's murder. Captain Stewart burst into a Privy
Council meeting, flung himself onto his knees before James and
made his accusation. Morton was imprisoned and tried. He was
found guilty of having known about the murder beforehand and
concealed his knowledge: a charge which could have been used
handily against many nobles at that time. He was condemned to
death and in June 1581 executed by the guillotine which he had
himself introduced to Scotland.

Lennox took over the role of regent, though no appointment was
made. When he came to Scotland, however, he had been a Catholic, and although he became a Protestant, the Reformed church
remained extremely suspicious of him. Perhaps, they thought, he
was really an agent for a foreign power? In 1582 a group of
Protestant extremists arranged the Raid of Ruthven. James was
invited on a hunting trip by the earl of Gowrie and then kept
prisoner by the earl at Ruthven Castle, near Perth, while Lennox,
recently created a duke, was ordered out of the country.

James, grief-stricken and angry, was determined not to remain a
prisoner long. One day, he slipped away from his captors and
rode, with two companions, to St Andrews, where his supporters
had gathered. With this escape, the seventeen-year-old king became politically adult. There was still one more pseudo-regent: the
swaggeringly confident third earl of Arran, who helped James
have the earl of Gowrie executed in 1584. Then the 'vieux jeune
homme' as James, with his wary, sidelong glance and his disillusionment, was described, took the reins of government very firmly
into his own hands.

The Kirk had proclaimed its approval of the Raid of Ruthven.
James decided he would let everyone know exactly where he, as
king, stood in relation to the Kirk. Soon after the death of the earl of

Gowrie, the Kirk's man, he passed what the Kirk described, in disgust, as the 'Black Acts'.

There was a powerful body of people in the Kirk who thought, in the famous words of Andrew Melville: 'There are two Kings and two Kingdoms in Scotland. There is Christ Jesus the King, and his Kingdom the Kirk; whose subject King James VI is, and of whose Kingdom not a King, nor a lord, nor a head, but a member.' James's view was very different. During his boyhood he had thought a great deal about the position of a king, especially in relation to God and God's church. As a child he had constantly been referred to as the Lord's anointed. He was not simply a member of the church; as king he was head of both church and state. He was God's lieutenant. In the 'Black Acts' he proclaimed his supremacy, and forbade the preaching of sermons against himself or the proceedings of his council.

He would maintain his authority, he declared, by appointing bishops. There was nothing new in this idea. Twelve years earlier, Knox had upbraided Morton for appointing 'tulchan bishops', but he had accepted the old principle that bishops should be appointed by the state. Andrew Melville wanted the Kirk to become Presbyterian, that is, to appoint all its own officials, both high and low, and to be independent of the state. Ultimately, he hoped, it would be more important than the state, the government would be a theocracy. Before that stage was reached, the Kirk could easily become an organized faction, a political party really, opposed to the state. James and the Episcopalians (those who wanted bishops) sought to avoid any such dangerous situation.

With the challenge from the Kirk averted, James' reign continued uneventfully. He published his first book, a collection of poems, in 1584, he had started writing poetry when he was fifteen, probably encouraged by Lennox, and had collected a group of poets round him. In 1586 he concluded an alliance with Elizabeth, which gave him an annuity of £4000. The next year his mother was executed, and in 1588 England was threatened by the Spanish Armada. James's position with regard to Spain and other major Roman Catholic powers had become very much simpler since his mother's death. He would have had to perform a very precarious balancing act indeed if she had still been alive: ensuring that he kept on terms with Spain as well as England, in case she should succeed Elizabeth on the English throne. As it was, he was able to take Elizabeth's side against Spain quite openly – though, at the same time, he discreetly allowed some of his Catholic nobles to side with Spain, just in case the Spaniards should succeed in invading England and win!

In 1589 James married Princess Anne of Denmark, a big, fair and rather stupid woman with whom he lived reasonably happily. They had several children, but only three of them, two sons and a daughter, survived infancy.

The period was not without incident. When James returned, early in 1590, from his marriage trip to Denmark, he had to deal with the affair of the North Berwick witches. These poor, demented women had used black magic in an attempt to raise storms at sea, so that James would be drowned on his homeward journey. They had done it, their trial judges were told, at the instigation of the earl of Bothwell, the nephew of Mary Queen of Scots' third husband, who wanted, it seemed, to rule in James's place. Bothwell was imprisoned, but escaped and was outlawed. Then he tried to terrify James – in the hope, apparently, of winning back his favour! One night he attacked the palace of Holyrood. On another night, he attacked Falkland Palace, and then he made a third attack on Holyrood and managed to reach James's bedroom. He was clearly as demented as the witches had been, but an extreme Presbyterian section of the Kirk supported him, describing him as a 'sanctified scourge' who would make James 'turn to God', that is, to their way of thinking.

In 1592 James did yield a little to the Kirk. He passed a law, promptly called by the grateful Kirk the 'Golden Act', which allowed the assemblies the Black Acts had forbidden. They could only be held at times and places agreed by the king, however – and he could manipulate those so that only the people he wanted could attend.

Bothwell was still at large. In 1594 he took refuge with his Catholic kinsman, the earl of Huntly, and the Kirk turned against him. James did what he had always hated: he took up arms and marched against Huntly's castle at Strathbogie. Both Huntly and Bothwell fled abroad.

During the 1590s the conflict with the Kirk went on, but James's viewpoint slowly gained ground. After a riot in Edinburgh, following a sermon preached against him, he managed to insist that ministers in major towns like the capital should not be appointed without his consent. Then in 1597 the Kirk appointed a commission to advise the king – not dictate, as Melville would have had it – on religious affairs. In practice, though, James influenced the commission rather more than it influenced him.

In the same year James persuaded the Kirk that he should appoint three bishops, who would sit in parliament. The Kirk would obtain representation in the law-making process and the bishops – parliamentary bishops, as they were called – would bring the Kirk within the structure of the state. Slowly and patiently, James had brought Kirk and state together.

As the century drew to a close, Scotland entered a new era of peace. James understood, as Moray had done, the importance of strong, just rule. In a book of advice for his eldest son, Prince Henry, James wrote: 'When ye have by the severities of justice once settled your countries, and made them know ye can strike, then ye may mix justice with mercy.' He worked hard to improve the standards of justice, to curb the excesses of the nobility and to give everyone the protection of the law. He had wanted to enable his people to live in peace, and he had succeeded.

Once the days of the regents were over, he had, like his mother before him, tended to bypass the nobility when he looked for advisers. He did not go so far as to elevate a low-born foreigner like Riccio. He chose well-established Scots of middle rank who would be dependent on him. He wanted men, he said, whom 'he could correct and were hangable', though none of them ever were hanged! He chose eight efficient men, who made excellent public servants, and were known as the 'Octavians'.

James had little enough in common with his nobles – or any other class. Timid, pedantic and unprepossessing in appearance, he moved among his people with some detachment. He described them with a kind of pawky humour. Of their endless family feuds, he said: 'They bang it away bravely, he and all his kin against him and all his.' Slowly and patiently, however, he was persuading them that such private wars were pointless.

Yet strange, violent incidents still occurred. In 1600 James himself was caught up in one of them, which came to be known as the Gowrie Conspiracy. He was invited to Perth by the two sons of the earl of Gowrie, whom he had had executed after the Raid of Ruthven. He went, ostensibly to see some treasure, and was led upstairs in Gowrie House by one of the Ruthven brothers. His attendants, down below, heard him scream out: his companion, he cried, wanted to murder him. In the scuffle that followed, both the Ruthven brothers were killed. Perhaps James was right: the two young men may have planned to murder him in revenge for the death of their father. Or perhaps he was oversuspicious, suffering from an attack of the nervous terror he was prone to. As the only account of what went on is the one left us by James himself, we shall never know.

When the new century began, Elizabeth of England was nearly seventy and clearly would not live much longer. James was obsessed with the prospect of succeeding her. He regarded the crown of England as the reward for his work in Scotland: a personal reward and an inestimable benefit for Scotland, safeguarding Protestantism and ending the Scottish–English wars. Although Elizabeth had never named him or anyone else as her heir, it seemed very unlikely that the English would turn down a king of proven ability, who brought with him the advantages of union, in favour of the obscure English nobleman who was the alternative. James made approaches to the earl of Essex, Elizabeth's favourite, and then, after Essex's execution in 1601, to Sir Robert Cecil, the son of Elizabeth's brilliant minister, Lord Burghley. Cecil had become the most powerful man in England, and he gave James the assurance he required.

James had only to wait . . .

CHAPTER 11
THE
UNION
OF THE
CROWNS
(1603–90)

Two weeks after the death of Elizabeth I of England (24 March 1603) James VI, who had become James I of England, made a speech at St Giles's in Edinburgh. 'Think not of me as ane king going frae ane part to another, but of ane king lawfully callit going frae ane part of the isle to ane other that sae your comfort be the greater.' Two days later he left the capital and headed south for London. On the way through England he received addresses of welcome, created many new knights (too many, some thought), hanged a thief without trial and talked freely about his rule by divine right, that he was answerable only to God. It was not a good beginning, and things deteriorated from that moment until twenty-two years later when he died, arguably murdered by his best friend, and certainly mourned by none. He had governed Scotland quite well for the last fifteen years, and then – suddenly – abandoned his people, visiting Scotland only once between 1603 and his death. What had come over him?

As he shambled out of St Giles's that day in April 1603, James, the thirty-six-year-old stuttering 'know-all', with a tongue too large for his mouth and none of the handsome features or graceful demeanour of his Stewart forebears, had already decided he would govern the two kingdoms from the southern capital. It is unlikely that he had ever been to England – certainly not to the rich and colourful London. When he got there he saw much to impress him. London was by far the biggest city in Britain, and already one of the largest in western Europe. The port of London was a hive of activity newly enhanced by the creation of the East India Company. New buildings, factories and warehouses were going up, mostly devoted to trade and commerce. Old St Paul's dominated the skyline hardly less dramatically than its successor (built after 1666 by Wren) would do. Westminster Abbey and Westminster Hall stood as proud examples of medieval architecture. Perhaps James saw something of the variety of merchandise in shops and marketplaces. He will also have seen sumptuous furnishings in many London houses. He will have compared Hampton Court and Greenwich enviously with the sparse décor of his own palace of Holyrood. He will have noticed how well off the nobles and gentlemen of England appeared to be, with their costly clothing, their coaches and their well-dressed retainers.

James will also have noticed that London streets were filthy, with garbage heaped up along the sides, that beggars roamed, and that the rough cobbled roads combined with the iron-banded wheels of coaches that traversed them incessantly day and evening to fill the air with a raucous din and clatter, making it impossible for people to hear themselves speak. He will have reflected that in this respect the city of London was no better than Edinburgh. With some pride he will have pointed out that London had no university, but that Scotland still had four (St Andrews, Glasgow, Aberdeen, Edinburgh) to England's two (Oxford and Cambridge). But England was much richer throughout. Its sterling pound was worth about twelve Scottish pounds. England had a population nearly six times greater (4.5 million to 800,000). James felt much safer in England. His new subjects, lords, gentlemen and people, would protect him. One or two would plot, but he need have no fear of baronial revolt or inter-family feuds. That sort of solution to problems had gone out in England nearly a century before. There were no Douglases in England. And James was to establish himself as absolute ruler of both countries, as we shall see.

The Scotland James left behind was not a rich land, nor was her industry and trade evenly spread across the countryside. The greatest prosperity was still in the east coast and the fertile Midland Valley. The spaces between and around, especially the high ground, were still agriculturally poor. Highlanders still preferred the easier life of cattle- and sheep-raiding, looting their neighbours' farms and homes, to the hard work involved in growing barley and oats, three years of harvests from the same fields, three years off lying fallow, the land deteriorating. It was still very difficult to travel about the countryside. The roads were rough tracks and there were not many of them. In most areas it was not safe to walk or to ride alone, for fear of robbery and violence. In the burghs it was different. Encouraged by the kings, they had grown over the years into wealthy communities, independent of the nobles who generally preferred life in the countryside. The merchants were often better off in terms of ready money, household furnishings and in education than the lords whose wealth lay in acres of land, and whose income was as often in kind as in cash.

The uniting of the crowns of Scotland and England did not mean union in politics and religion. It is understandable that James wanted these things, but his attempts to achieve unity were badly mismanaged. One of the first acts of his reign over both countries was to set up a committee to work out how the two parliaments could be joined. But the commissioners failed. There were too many differences between the peoples. Probably it was too soon for Scotsmen to forget the humiliations they had endured from the English, and the English certainly did regard the Scots as inferior. But if James could not persuade the two parliaments to work together or to make constructive proposals, he had already man-oeuvred his Privy Council in Scotland into controlling the country and dictating to parliament what measure he wanted. If a parliament appeared troublesome, he dismissed it. If he expected opposition from parliament to a particular measure, he declined to summon it. Gradually he filled the Privy Council with his own trusted allies and curtailed the right of parliament to nominate its own privy councillors. When he came to London James decided to govern Scotland through a representative and by means of written instructions to the Council. Once he said to the English parliament, 'Here I sit and govern Scotland with my pen: I write, and it is done.' This is an example of his insufferable arrogance, which perhaps more than any other of his unpleasant traits deprived him of friends. His first 'viceroy' was the duke of Lennox, a kinsman, and he was assisted by 'Tam' (earl of) Haddington and George Hume, earl of Dunbar. James still left much of the administrative work, however, to able men of middle-class birth.

James was no more successful in his efforts to unite the two countries in religion. During the last years of his rule in Scotland many of the ideas of the Presbyterians had prevailed in the Scottish church, whereby it was governed not by bishops and a hierarchy of prelates but by Kirk sessions of laymen and a General Assembly (a sort of parliament whose members were, among others, lords, representatives of burghs and ministers). This does not mean that only Presbyterians were ministers. There were still ministers who believed in the bishop-led hierarchy (Episcopalians) and there were even some bishoprics still functioning, but with little power. Presbyterians and Episcopalians differed on a variety of points of doctrine, of ritual and of usage of books for services, but they were agreed on the most important thing of all, the unity of the Scottish church. And of course they were both opposed to Roman Catholicism in any guise.

When he became king of both countries James wanted to bring the two churches into line, and he was determined that it should be the Scottish, and not the English, church that should make the required changes. It was a tidy idea but the king took little account of the wishes of his Scottish people. He also underestimated the growing influence of Presbyterian ideals among the people. By a number of cunning devices, however, he got the General Assembly to agree to the appointment of bishops. He strengthened the bishops' position by arranging for them to have seats in parliament. He tampered with the minutes of the General Assembly's meetings, at those parts where resolutions about bishops were discussed, so that everyone would get confused about what was and what was not agreed. He manipulated the Assembly by mixing up the dates of meetings, calling a meeting and then altering the date without notifying certain ministers whom he expected to oppose him during the session.

In 1606 James banished the most influential of all the Presbyterian theologians, Andrew Melville, who never accepted the king as supreme head of the church, holding that the church had no head on earth, and was responsible only to God. Melville had been resolutely opposed to bishops because they were likely to be agents for the king, while the General Assembly was free from any interference from the state. He thus represented a basic threat to James's position and the king knew he must rid himself of Melville before restoring the bishops to what he considered their rightful place in the church.

Finally, in 1618, James summoned a meeting of the General Assembly at Perth (which he did not attend), and with bribes and threats he got the members to agree to the Five Articles of Perth. One was particularly offensive to all members, and to all congregations of Presbyterians throughout the land, that communicants should kneel to receive the bread and wine at communion. To them, this was like worshipping idols, and they would not have it. Objections were shown most forcibly by a widespread refusal to attend services where ministers included this gesture among their rituals.

The king relented a little, not by changing the orders but more astutely by not pressing anyone to see they were put into effect. Perhaps James hoped the ideas would become more acceptable after consideration over a period. He was wrong, but thereafter he left the church alone.

The absolute rule of the king was irksome to many, but in some respects it was good for Scotland. It was very effective in suppressing disorder. The Border district was put under a mounted military police control which worked miracles. Raiders and thieves were rounded up and hanged or banished to serve in foreign regiments in wars on the Continent. Trouble in the Highland west was dealt with by putting the responsibility for keeping their people in order on the clan chiefs' shoulders. A sharp example of the new order was given when, in 1603, the Macgregor clan fought a battle with their enemies the Colquhouns near Loch Lomond. The king instructed parliament to confiscate the Macgregor lands and possessions – even the name Macgregor was to be erased, and not used again. The Macgregor chief was hanged at Edinburgh. In the Orkneys James's kinsmen Patrick Stewart, earl of Orkney and his son, Robert, were deprived of the earldom and its possessions and the islands brought under direct rule.

One of James's last acts was to try to get his son Charles married to a daughter of the king of Spain, in furtherance of his ambition to keep secure the Anglo-Spanish alliance he had been fostering. Charles went to Madrid, but did not get betrothed. Among his party was George Villiers, duke of Buckingham, James's favourite with whom he had been enjoying a homosexual relationship for some years.[1] Buckingham had behaved disgracefully in Spain, offending everyone he met at court, getting hopelessly drunk, and making silly and offensive remarks at formal meetings with Spanish ministers. Count Gondamar, former Spanish ambassador to England, went so far as to make arrangements to come to London to report all this to James. Now Buckingham knew that if Gondamar reached the king and told all, his position with James, whatever their personal attachment, would be irrevocably destroyed. Buckingham would be banished from court. Gondamar therefore had to be stopped from meeting the king, but the only way this could be done was by disposing of James. In February 1625 James was taken ill with tertian ague, not itself a fatal illness for a reasonably strong and fit man, as James was. The royal doctors recommended the standard treatments, but Buckingham intervened, and for some days the king was subjected to painful applications of poultices on his wrists and stomach, coupled with horrid-tasting medicines, none of which did him any good at all. When the doctors, Eglisham and Craig, both Scotsmen, protested, they were ordered to leave the court. Eventually James succumbed and died on 27 March.

When parliament tried to bring Buckingham to book on several charges, including his responsibility for the king's death, Charles, now king, rescued him by dissolving parliament. He was saved only for a while, however, for in 1628 Buckingham was murdered. It was widely accepted that James had been poisoned and that Buckingham had organized it. James died leaving religious and political problems boiling up beneath the surface of a seemingly calm realm, that were to burst through in the reign of his son. The Scots – and for that matter the English – hoped they would get a better and more tolerant king in Charles I. They were very soon to be disappointed, and it is hardly an exaggeration to say that Charles I's reign was a disaster for both countries.

If Charles Stewart was not blighted with his father's repulsive appearance and shambling gait, he certainly inherited the worst of James's characteristics, most particularly his obstinacy. Over the last years of his rule, James had been blundering from one insensitive or arbitrary act to another. This must have been known to his son who, after 1612, when his brother Henry, Prince of Wales, died, became heir to the joint throne and who thus drew closer to the centre of things at court and in government. And yet he appeared to have learned nothing from it. Sharing his father's belief in the Divine Right of Kings, Charles carried it to its extremity.[2] It pervaded everything he did north and south of the Border. He never recognized when he had gone too far, and he did not know how to back down gracefully. One historian put it well when he said that while James had divided his opponents by making changes gradually, Charles united them all against the crown.

Charles began his reign with scant consideration for the Scots. He hardly knew Scotland, and did not even trouble to visit it until eight years had passed. He went there in 1633 to be crowned at Holyrood, but the visit was not a success. His people were anxious to give him a great welcome, especially the burgesses of Edinburgh. But he offended them by being anointed with oil at the coronation, as earlier kings had done in Roman Catholic times. True, he established Edinburgh as the capital of Scotland but he ruined that gesture by making the kirk of St Giles a cathedral and appointing a bishop for it. He angered the Presbyterians by going about with his English archbishop of Canterbury, Laud, the 'high priest' of the English church which was drifting back towards Roman Catholicism. Then he alienated the lords who were disposed to support him by taking away possessions they had acquired in the previous century when the old church and its properties were swept away, by punishing those who disagreed with his policies (in some cases, by prosecution for treason), and by excluding Lords of Session from the Privy Council.

Charles departed from Scotland only a few weeks after his coronation, leaving behind a mountain of ill-will and resentment. This did not prevent him compelling the Scots, without reference to the General Assembly, to accept a new prayer book in place of the Presbyterian Book of Common Order (affectionately known as 'Knox's liturgy'). Drafted by Laud along with Scottish bishops who approved the English religious system, the new book was in Presbyterian eyes even worse than the English prayer book. Its reception in Scotland was stormy everywhere and led to riots, street fighting and widespread destruction of copies. It was introduced at a service on 23 July 1637 at St Giles's, attended by the archbishops of St Andrews and Glasgow and several members of the Privy Council, but hardly had the dean come to the end of the first page or two when a riot broke out. Books, shoes, hassocks and stools were hurled at him by the congregation, both men and women. One woman, Jenny Geddes, earned fame for her scream 'Sayest thou Mass in my lug [ear]?' as she threw her stool straight at the pulpit. The archbishop of St Andrews tried to restore order, but the tumult increased, and when the noisiest of the objectors were turned out of the cathedral, they hurled bricks and stones at the windows. News of the riot was brought to Charles who, instead of taking the hint, promptly ordered acceptance of the book to be imposed by force.

Feeling in Scotland was now running very high against the king and the government. The Privy Council in Edinburgh was seriously alarmed, and they agreed to hear objections from a committee of protesters, comprising sixteen members (four lords, four lesser landowners, four burgesses and four ministers). The committee became a regular body known as 'the tables', and it represented the opposition to the government in church and in state matters, since parliament had been effectively neutralized by the king. The opposition was further strengthened when early in 1638 an old covenant of 1581 was revived. This had been a national agreement signed by many leading Scot (including James VI) which undertook to resist any attempts to restore the Roman Catholic faith and its doctrines in Scotland. Now the National Covenant was renewed, signed by most of the influential men of Scotland, and then taken round the country to be signed by many thousands of ordinary folk. Supporters of the Covenant came to be known as Covenanters, and they represented an extremely powerful opposition party to the king. Before very long they were to take up the sword and fight for what they believed in.

The new Covenant was drawn up by two leading Presbyterians, Alexander Henderson, minister of Leuchars, and Archibald Johnston, a Lord of Session and later Lord Warriston. It stated that the signatories were opposed to the innovations of the king 'until they be tried and allowed in free assemblies and in parliament'. It was a defensive statement. That the signatories went to war about it was the fault of the king. The response to the appeal for signatures encouraged the organizers to become more demanding, and they pressed for a free parliament and a free assembly of the Kirk. The king began to see he might have to yield, but even as he did so he made covert attempts to divide the Covenanters and win some of them over to his side. A General Assembly was called to meet at Glasgow and Henderson was chosen as moderator, or president. It passed a number of major measures, including the abolition of bishoprics, throwing out the Five Articles, and finally rejecting the new prayer book. Some of the bishops were actually dismissed. Presbyterianism appeared to have triumphed, but the king refused to accept the assembly's decisions. Both sides knew that they must resolve the matter by force of arms.

The Convenanters had little difficulty in raising a substantial army. People flocked to join it. They chose as its commander the veteran of many campaigns with Gustavus Adolphus of Sweden in the Thirty Years War in Europe, Alexander Leslie. Charles, on the other hand, had great difficulties. He had little money to pay his forces and if he wanted more he would have to summon a parliament in England. But he knew that if he called such a parliament, the members would first demand considerable curbs to his arbitrary rule. He had been governing for ten years without parliament and grievances had been accumulating. Charles managed to marshal a force near Berwick and he got ready to enter Scotland. But Leslie confronted him. If a clash occurred now, it would mean civil war, and Charles could not count on much support from England. So he agreed to negotiate, but aggravated the Covenanters by insisting at the start that the Glasgow assembly had been illegal. He then agreed to a fresh assembly and a new parliament, both to be held in Edinburgh. It was clearly an attempt to play for time. The assembly and the parliament met, and the same resolutions were passed. Again the king refused to accept them and again he prepared for war. He had, meanwhile, summoned a parliament at Westminster and asked it for money. Parliament refused, preferring to press home their grievances instead, and so Charles dissolved it. The Scots moved across the Border under Leslie, defeated a force sent against them by the king and proceeded to Newcastle, where they cut off coal supplies to London and southern towns. More Scottish troops coursed through Northumberland and Durham and occupied both counties. In Edinburgh, meanwhile, the Scottish parliament had assumed powers of its own, and abolished the Committee of Articles.

The king was sandwiched between rebellious subjects at the highest level in both nations. He had perforce to give in to the

Scots, even to agree to pay them a substantial sum of money to leave the northern counties of England. Charles left England in August 1641 for a second visit to Scotland, this time to enlist support for the coming clash between himself and his English parliamentary opposition. When he arrived, he was pressed to endorse all the reforms passed by the Scottish parliament and to confirm the Kirk as Presbyterian. He had also to grant that in future all appointments in government should be made only with the advice and consent of parliament. It was a dramatic turnabout: divine right had given way to the will of the elected.

To some of the Covenanters, however, parliament had gone too far. One was the prominent member, James Graham, fifth earl of Montrose. This handsome, romantic personality, a born leader, courageous and moderate, had been one of the lords of 'the tables' and an early signatory of the Covenant. Before much longer, however, he was to lead those Scots who, while critical of the king, were not prepared to make war on him. To others, parliament had carried out its duties. They were not opposed to monarchy, nor did they advocate the king's removal. They desired that he should accept restraints. The leader of these was Archibald Campbell, eighth earl of Argyll, immensely rich and powerful, devoted to the Presbyterian cause, patriotic and resolute.

The king did not lack courage, nor did he give up easily. When he returned to London the Westminster parliament was in a very angry mood. Instead of trying to reach an accommodation with it, Charles went down to the House of Commons in January 1642 with a posse of soldiers to arrest the five leading members of the opposition. They were not there. The Commons took the gravest exception to this invasion of the sanctity of their chamber. There was no room for compromise any more. A few weeks later Charles left London for the north and, in August, he raised his standard in Nottingham. To begin with, what followed was a war between Charles and his English Parliamentarians. The Scots were not disposed to take sides. Montrose would not countenance war against his king. The Scots were concerned to see that the Presbyterian triumph remained unsullied. Yet they soon found they were not able to stay out of the war.

Once war had broke out, both Charles and the Parliamentarians approached the Scots for help. After consideration, the Covenanters threw in their lot with the Parliamentarians because they saw they would get a better deal that way. A treaty was agreed in 1643, called the Solemn League and Covenant, whose main provision was that the parties would do all they could to preserve religion in England (and Ireland) 'according to the word of God and the example of the best reformed Churches' (which meant the Scottish church). The Scots even wanted to give up the use of the Lord's Prayer and the Ten Commandments – 'old, rotten wheelbarrows to carry souls to hell', as someone put it. Interestingly, the forms of worship and the system of Kirk organization set out in the discussions held in London have lasted to this day in Scotland without basic alteration, although they disappeared in England very soon after the treaty.

It is a curious irony that while the Presbyterians had always regarded it as unacceptable for Charles and his council to try to impose an English church organization and ritual on the Scots, it was quite another thing for the Scots to use the imposition of Scottish Presbyterianism upon England as a main bargaining point with the English parliament. No doubt many Parliamentarians were aware of the irony of it, too, but at the time parliament's cause was so hard-pressed they had to agree. Leslie took an army of more than 25,000 Scots across the Tweed to the aid of the English parliamentary commanders, Thomas Fairfax and Oliver Cromwell. The combined forces routed the king at Marston Moor in Yorkshire in July 1644.

A few months earlier, Montrose had slipped out of Scotland when he saw the Covenanters were ready to join the Parliamentarians, and went to support Charles at Oxford, where he was made a marquis and appointed lieutenant-general of the Scottish royal forces, with a commission to raise an army in Scotland among those still loyal. Montrose headed for the Highlands where he exploited the long-held hatred of many of the clans for the Campbells (Argyll) and mustered a tough force ready to fight anyone anywhere under him.[3] In a campaign of less than a year Montrose won a series of victories over Covenanter armies, beginning at Tippermuir on the Crieff–Perth road. Then he descended upon Aberdeen and sacked the ancient city (for which he was never forgiven and which was to turn many Lowlanders against him thereafter). Montrose swung westwards and careered through Campbell country in Argyllshire, defeating Argyll at Inverlochy in Inverness-shire.[4] Turning south-east he chased Argyll and beat him at Kilsyth, near Stirling, and then marched to Glasgow, which he entered in triumph. He was ready now to march down through the Lowlands to avenge the defeat of Charles at Naseby in Northamptonshire (June) which had for practical purposes ended the Civil War in England. But on his way down he found he could get no support. At Philiphaugh near Selkirk, early in September, Montrose was surprised and defeated by David Leslie, Leslie's nephew, and his cause collapsed.

Meanwhile the Scots were finding that the English parliament was hedging over the establishment of Presbyterianism in England. This was because the civilians in the government were no longer in command of the Parliamentary party. They had handed over to the army, flushed with the successes of Marston Moor and Naseby, to Fairfax, Cromwell, Ireton and others who were not disposed to adhere to the Solemn League. They did not want a Scottish Kirk in England. At that moment the king surrendered to the Scottish army when it was in the Midlands, in the hope of saving his throne, for he knew that if he gave up to the English he would be compelled to abdicate. The Scots insisted on his agreeing to establish Presbyterianism in England in return for saving him, and moved northwards taking him with them back to Scotland. But he refused, and so the Scots delivered him to the English. It was no more than he deserved. The Parliamentarians imprisoned him at Carisbrooke in the Isle of Wight.

Very soon the Scots began to feel badly let down. They had provided military aid for Parliamentary forces, and indeed at both Marston Moor and Naseby had helped to win the day. They had given the king to his victors. Now the English were refusing to pay the Scots for helping in the war, which they had promised to do. Some of the Scots entered into negotiations with the imprisoned king, by which he agreed to give Presbyterianism a three-year trial in England if he were restored to power through Scottish help. The negotiations were, of course, secret; openly, the Scots approached the Parliamentarians and demanded that the king should be released and that the Covenant should be fulfilled. By this time there were divisions within the ranks of the Covenanters and when the duke of Hamilton led an army into England in 1648 in support of the demands, it was ill-prepared and meagrely supported. It had none of the fire and zeal of Leslie's crack forces. Along the Preston to Warrington road in Lancashire, Hamilton's army was attacked and crushed by Cromwell. Hamilton escaped but surrendered later, and was executed in London.

In Scotland Argyll took over the government, reached agreement with Cromwell that royalists should not hold office and undertook to leave the English alone to resolve their own problems. But when at the beginning of February 1649 the news came through that Charles had been executed in Whitehall after trial before parliament, the nation was outraged. With all his obstinacy, his insensitivity to other people's feelings, his devious plotting, his faithlessness, his betrayal of his people, it had never occurred to Scotsmen that their king would be judicially put to death – and by a foreign power, too. And yet, violent though his death was, it cannot be said to have been undeserved.

Argyll sensed the mood of the nation and immediately proclaimed the dead king's son, Charles as King Charles II. The young prince, who was in exile in Holland, was invited to return to Scotland provided, of course, that he would sign the Covenant. At this point, Montrose, in exile since his defeat at Philiphaugh, offered to take an army of mercenaries to Scotland to prepare to fight the army of the English Commonwealth government which everyone knew would soon be advancing on Scotland. Montrose landed in Caithness but was defeated by a Covenanter force at Carbisdale, south of the Kyle of Sutherland, and was captured. He was taken to Edinburgh, tried and sentenced to be hanged, drawn and quartered. It is said that the cart taking him to Mercat Cross where the gallows was erected passed the Edinburgh home of Argyll, and that the two men for a moment saw each other.

Charles accepted the Covenant, but had no intention of observing his promise. 'Presbyterianism is not a religion for gentlemen', said the young man who had already begun to take an interest in Roman Catholicism (for his mother was one all her life). Then the king crossed to Scotland. Within weeks Cromwell was marching to Scotland with an army, intent on forcing the Scots to hand over their 'illegal' king to him. The commander of Charles's forces was David Leslie, who had led the cavalry of Scotland at Marston Moor. He had been thunderstruck by the execution of Charles I. For several days the two generals stalked each other about the countryside of mid- and East Lothian until at the beginning of September (1650) Leslie made the mistake of thinking that Cromwell was retreating to the coast to embark in his ships. Leslie brought his force down from Doune Hill near Dunbar into the unfavourable ground below. 'The Lord hath delivered them into our hands,' cried Cromwell when he saw Leslie's forces coming down the hill on the 3rd, and straightway broke up the Scots as they floundered between the slope and the stream at the bottom. He then marched to Edinburgh and occupied the city as a conqueror. Gradually he wore down resistance to the Commonwealth in the Lowlands.

Meanwhile Charles had fled across the Forth and at Scone Argyll crowned him as king, on 1 January 1651. It was a gesture which meant that, so long as Charles adhered to the Covenant, Argyll would remain his true servant. The Scots assembled another army and prepared to meet Cromwell again. Then they decided instead to invade England in the hope of disaffecting enough English people to overthrow the Commonwealth. Argyll was incensed: he was prepared to accept Charles as king of Scotland but had no wish to upset whatever political arrangements the victors of the Civil War in England had made for themselves. Retiring in high dudgeon to his castle at Inverary, he sat and waited for what he knew would happen next.

The Scottish army, still led by Leslie, crossed into England but outside Worcester they were caught up by Cromwell who chased them into the city. A fierce battle ensued, but Cromwell triumphed. The 'crowning mercy', he called it. Leslie was captured but spared execution. Charles escaped abroad after a series of adventures that have become part of British folklore.

Cromwell was now master of England and Scotland. He left military garrisons in key Scottish towns. The Scottish parliament was kept dissolved. A new Privy Council was appointed, with English members; the Court of Session was replaced by a panel of English and Scottish judges. Thirty Scottish representatives were chosen to attend the Westminster parliament in 1654. Independence, fought for so desperately for so many centuries, was gone. And yet life under the Cromwell regime had many advantages – it was probably better ordered than the country had ever known. All the privileges of the English were to be enjoyed by Scotsmen. Liberty of worship was granted, though this did not please the more extreme Presbyterians. Scottish traders and merchants got concessions formerly reserved for English merchants (despite the union of crowns and the common citizenship arrangement). The military policed the country, particularly the more lawless districts, so effectively that it was said you could ride anywhere in Scotland with £100 in your purse – the first time for several centuries. Kirk sessions, synods, all the business of Presbyterianism, could be conducted without interference. Occupation forces needed buildings, forts, roads and other facilities and there was much work for Scots people, with proper pay. New manufactures were introduced. At Leith, the first glass-making factory was opened. The victorious fleets of the Commonwealth kept the seas relatively free for Scottish as well as English merchant shipping.

Cromwell died in 1658. To some it was a relief, but in hindsight it was a tragedy that he did not live on to consolidate his work, certainly in England. His son had no relish for the job which came to him by succession, and he retired. Britain floundered for a while, until in 1660 General Monck, whom Oliver had left as commander-in-chief in Scotland, invited Charles II to return to Britain and take up the throne, to preserve order and unity. Before leaving Holland, Charles agreed to continue with the religious toleration policy and to stick to the Covenant that he had signed in 1649. The Scots were delighted to have a king again, for to them it meant restoration of their independence – or so they thought. They showed their enthusiasm by organizing some of the most sumptuous celebrations ever held in Scotland. Wine flowed from the water fountain at Mercat Cross in Edinburgh; bells rang, bonfires burned, guns were fired – everywhere. It seemed that all would be well – but of course it did not work out like that at all.

Charles, let it be said, had no interest in Scotland. He is said to have thought that the Scots were mad. He never visited the kingdom in twenty-five years as king, and he regarded it as only a large county on England's northern extremity that gave the government a lot of headaches over a religion that he had said was unsuitable for gentlemen. He was quite content to leave the administration in the hands of commissioners whose motives he did not examine. One early act was to bring Argyll to trial in Edinburgh. Argyll had no chance: his judges were royalists and he had sided with Cromwell, and in May 1661 he was executed.

Within two years of his restoration, Charles had arranged many changes in Scotland. One was to revive the Privy Council whose members he chose, and without the advice of parliament. The council's secretary remained in London, issuing orders to the councillors in Scotland. This secretary was John Maitland, earl of

Lauderdale, (and great nephew of Maitland of Lethington, secretary of state in Mary Queen of Scots' time). For twenty years Lauderdale, who had once been a Covenanter but had changed sides, dominated Scottish government, filled state and church offices with family and friends, and eventually retired hated by most Scots for whose welfare he had consistently shown scant regard.

The story of Scotland in Charles's reign was largely a continuation of the struggle between Presbyterians and those who favoured restoring government of the church by bishops (Episcopalians). In 1661 a Scottish parliament packed with royal supporters met at Edinburgh and passed numerous acts, including cancelling all laws passed by the Covenanters' parliaments since 1639 and declaring the king head of church and state. The Privy Council, without discussion with parliament, announced that episcopacy was to be restored and that it should be the national form of government for the church. James Sharp, who had in 1660 been appointed archbishop of St Andrews and primate of Scotland, was confirmed in office. Sharp had been a Covenanting minister, at Crail in Fife, but had been bought off. This reversal of the Presbyterian position put Presbyterian ministers in danger, unless they compromised their deeply held beliefs. They were offered ministries within the episcopal organization, but of course many refused and fled instead into the countryside to hold services in barns, in the fields and in private houses for their congregations who refused to attend the episcopal church. Presbyterianism was especially strong in Galloway, in other parts of the Lowlands and in Argyll. The government responded by making it illegal to fail to attend Sunday services, and the penalties were severe. But this did not stop the irregular country meetings, known as 'conventicles'. In Galloway, about 3000 Covenanters took up arms and marched to Edinburgh to whip up support in the resistance to the new religious order. The revolt was broken, and thirty-three ministers and others were hanged. Other rebels were banished as slaves to plantations in the Barbadoes.

In 1669 Lauderdale took over the job of commissioner in Scotland. He tried a softer approach at first, and even allowed some of the ministers who had refused to accept episcopacy to return to their ministries. But there were still many who refused to conform. Some of them went so far as to refuse to accept Charles as the true king because he had betrayed the Covenant. Lauderdale met this with much sterner measures, but they did not deflect the Covenanters. So he tried to goad them into open revolt. In Argyll, for instance, he sent special forces to impose discipline upon the Covenanters, but they also had orders to pillage and burn, to take over homes, farms and estates. The money raised thus went straight into Lauderdale's pocket, but still the Covenanters did not rise in revolt.

Then something happened on the other side of Scotland. Archbishop Sharp was assassinated near St Andrews. The murderers were not thugs – they were victims of the brutality of some of Sharp's employees. They fled to the west and joined the embittered Covenanters. At the end of May 1679 there was a rising. The army formed by the Covenanters succeeded in defeating government forces sent against them, at Drumclog. In response, a fresh army of some strength was despatched under the command of the duke of Monmouth, the king's eldest illegitimate son. At Bothwell Bridge, on the Clyde, the Covenanters were defeated. The punishments were severe: 250 or more were banished to the Barbadoes, more than 200 of them perishing at sea when their transport ship sank on the way. Many others were hanged, including ministers. It was the end for Lauderdale. His rule had been disastrous, and the king replaced him with the heir to the throne, his brother James, duke of York – a devout Catholic.

The appointment of James Stewart as commissioner was a signal for further bad times for the Scots. This second son of Charles I had none of the charm of his elder brother, and was well endowed with the family obstinacy. No historian of Scotland can sustain a defence of James for his career as James VII (1685–8), and yet there is something sad about the disastrous way this man went about his business once he was in a commanding position within the kingdom. As a younger man he had been a very able sea commander, and his period of office as lord high admiral had brought him great credit. He had had a good marriage with Anne Hyde, daughter of the earl of Clarendon, a Protestant who managed the government of England in the early years of Charles II. He adored his daughters Mary and Anne, both of whom fell out with him over religion. The English parliament had spent years trying to cut him out of the succession to his brother's throne, but had failed. Yet the bitterness left behind had weighed heavily.

James arrived in Scotland determined to oppose Presbyterianism. There were still many ministers and Covenanters equally
resolved to resist him. They went on holding their conventicles,
the congregations fetching up armed with bibles in one hand and
swords or guns in the other. It was a situation of increasing
violence on both sides. Government attempts to squash the Covenanters were answered by exhortations to overthrow the government. Force was often met by force. Richard Cameron, a fiery
preacher from St Andrews, led a group of angry Covenanters into
Sanquhar in Dumfriesshire and nailed a document to the town
cross. It was no less than a declaration of war on the king. The
military was called out and troops hunted the 'Cameronians' (as
they came to be known) until they had killed them all. The
government followed up with the Test Act which compelled
ministers and anyone who worked for the state to renounce the
Covenant. This aggravated Episcopalians as well as Presbyterians.
Even the president of the Court of Session, Dalrymple, resigned.
He was condemned for treason, but escaped.

The struggle went on, and so did the fear and uncertainty that
affected all Scotland. In 1685 James succeeded his brother to
become James VII, and in no time declared his intent to restore
Roman Catholicism throughout the two kingdoms. He did not
swear the coronation oath to uphold the Protestant religion. His
first parliament in Scotland made it treasonable to be a Covenanter
and a capital offence to attend a conventicle. But people remained
Covenanters and went to 'illegal' services all the same. In 1687
James issued a letter of indulgence which granted toleration to
Roman Catholics and Presbyterians alike. It was not a high-minded
act, but part of a plan whereby, if he could encourage the growth of
Romanism he could, at the appropriate time, reverse the indulgence and stamp out Presbyterianism – and Episcopalianism as
well. But James had not thought it out well enough; he overlooked
the possible reaction to toleration of Roman Catholicism.[5] The
whole kingdom (except of course the Roman Catholics) united to
resist. As he had likewise aggravated the great majority of English
people, he could count on no support anywhere. His Protestant
son-in-law, William, prince of Orange, invited by English lords to
come and rescue the liberties of the English, sent a declaration to
Scotland promising to restore the nation's religious liberties. A
gathering of Scottish lords, landowners and burgesses met in

Edinburgh and invited William to take over the government until a national parliament should decide how the kingdom was in future to be administered. In their invitation they inserted a request that he must agree to abolish prelacy which they said had been a 'great and insupportable grievance and trouble to this nation, ever since the Reformation'.

There was, however, still some support for James, now in exile. This came from among the Episcopalians who did not want a king who might impose Presbyterianism on Scotland (for William was a Calvinist). Lord Dundee, who as Claverhouse had been the commander defeated at Drumclog (see p. 178), marshalled an army and took it into the Highlands to raise the clans in support of the exiled king. A battle was fought at Killiecrankie Pass and William's forces were annihilated, though Dundee was slain. The victorious Highlanders advanced upon Dunkeld but there met the fiercest resistance from a Covenanter force which wore them down until they melted away back to the mountains. It was the end of major resistance to William, though not all opposition was yet crushed.

There was another episode to follow, which has a high place in the annals of Scotland under the emotive title of 'the massacre of Glencoe'. In pursuit of their efforts to bring the Highlands to order, the government engineered a situation whereby the Macdonalds of Glencoe in Argyllshire (a small sept of the MacDonalds, hereditary enemies of the Campbells) were unable to swear the required oath of allegiance to William within a stipulated time, on pain of their lands and homes being burned and themselves put to the sword. The government decided to make an example of them. Orders were sent to a Captain Campbell (one of the clan) to 'fall upon the rebels . . . and put all to the sword under seventy'. And on the evening of 13 February 1692 the Campbells moved into the Glencoe pass. Robert Campbell actually dined with the head of the sept, who was totally unaware of the plot about to be murderously carried out. At about five in the morning the next day the Campbells rose quietly and crept towards the homes of the Macdonalds, and in a few swift minutes slaughtered thirty-eight people, including two women and a child of six. It was a frightful act and the king was directly responsible. He attempted to deny prior knowledge of the plot, but the documents showed otherwise and he was never trusted again in Scotland.

The settlement which followed the collapse of James's rule and the 1688 Revolution was more definite than anything tried since the onset of the Reformation, though it did not, as has often been said, give the church in Scotland freedom and independence from parliament or the crown, that is, disentanglement from politics. In the years between the Letter of Indulgence and 1690 the Presbyterians got themselves well organized. Many Episcopalian ministers were driven from their livings, particularly in Galloway. The lord chancellor, the Catholic earl of Perth, was forced to resign and leave Edinburgh. A parliament in 1690 succeeded in getting William to accept a measure that restored the Presbyterian system of church government and abolished the office of bishop. The same parliament also restored the rights of the burgesses of royal burghs to elect members to parliament, which strengthened parliament and the burghs.

But whatever goodwill Dutch William may have earned by agreeing to the restoration of Presbyterian domination was wiped out by his squandering of the lives and the resources of the Scottish people upon his fruitless war with Louis XIV of France, Scotland's old ally. France was a long standing and major trading partner of Scotland. Among many commodities, she imported herrings, coal, wool and cloth, and exported to Scotland salt and wine. All this trade vanished as long as William and Louis were at war, which was for most of William's reign (1688–1702). Scotland was already in the grip of a severe agricultural depression (see p. 183). It was difficult to see how the nation could survive.

CHAPTER 12

THE
PRICE
OF
UNION
(1690–1785)

In the last years of the seventeenth century the Scots found themselves drifting towards full political union with England, but it was a union that few people in Scotland wanted. They feared, rightly as it turned out, that it would be a 'take-over', to use a twentieth-century term. And when it did come, most of the advantages were stacked on England's side.

For a century and a half religion had dominated the lives, thoughts, acts, hopes and fears of Scottish people, more so than perhaps any other people in Europe of the time. Everything was considered in terms of religion and its role in their lives. Those who fought for the reformed faith in the sixteenth century had not been in the majority to begin with, but they worked diligently and fanatically to make Scotland Protestant, according to the teachings of John Calvin. The ideals of these Presbyterians stimulated a remarkable response among many Scottish people. Severe though its doctines were, and harsh as its disciplines became, Presbyterianism aroused the very deepest passions. It spread far beyond the belief that people were individually responsible to God, that their every act must be measured against that responsi-

182

bility. It spilled over into politics, domestic life and social activities. Even famines and crop failures were looked upon as punishments from God. Presbyterians saw it as their destiny to work to improve every aspect of society: public conduct, private lives, trade and industry, education, farming – all these received their attention. And over these years the ideals became ingrained in the character of the great majority of the Scottish people, and the discipline 'put steel into the backbone of Scotland'.

The Scottish economy of the seventeenth century was still agricultural. Crop and livestock farming were backward, when compared with England and some European countries, particularly Holland, and they were to remain so for much of the eighteenth century, too. Admittedly, much of the farming land was of poor quality, but farmers were still using out-of-date methods. They had not developed the idea of rotating crops, planting cereals one year and root crops the next in the same fields. Invariably there was distress when crops failed. In the 1690s a series of disasters struck at Scottish agriculture. Grain prices fell in Europe. Disease spread among the cattle in Lowland and Highland pastures. And in four out of five of the years 1695–9 crops failed throughout the land. Misery and poverty were rife; hardly a district did not suffer. Hunger was accompanied by disease, notably typhus which was a killer. Men dropped dead trying to eat grass in the fields. The best hope of survival was to get to a town which because of its wealth and its trade connections was able to import the foodstuffs it needed. Many burghs responded to the plight of the country people and helped out. In Edinburgh a temporary camp was set up for the starving 'immigrants' coming in from nearby farmlands. But despite these noble efforts, nearly a quarter of Scotland's population of about 1.25 million died in these last years of the seventeenth century.

The standard of living in the burghs was very much better. Burghs had been regarded as special areas for a long time. They received encouragement from many quarters and the burgesses had worked and traded hard to make them strong, prosperous communities. Aberdeen and Dundee, with harbours, had five-figure populations. Edinburgh, with over 30,000, had overcrowding problems, and these were being met by the construction of high blocks of flats, some as many as ten storeys tall – the first such buildings in Britain.[1] The richer people lived in the higher storeys, away from the noise and dirt and the smells. Glasgow, Scotland's second city, was fast catching up, growing along an orderly street plan that resembled that of Paris, with good, solid, stone houses and a splendid bridge, Bishop Rae's, across the Clyde. The city was soon to become the business centre of Scotland, especially when the tobacco industry began to thrive in the eighteenth century.

The Scots did not enjoy going to war with France, their traditional ally. English hostilities with France, which involved Scotland, had a damaging effect on Scottish towns, particularly those on the eastern side. French ships attacked merchant vessels as they left or entered ports, helping to cut off Scotland's trade lines with Europe. At the same time the English insisted on applying their notorious Navigation Acts to Scotland as firmly as to any foreign land, despite promises made at the time of the Union of the Crowns in 1603. This struck at Scotland's trading with the American colonies. Scotland's European markets had in any case been declining, especially in Holland where the Dutch were relying more on their own expanding manufactures, such as wool and cloth. The time had surely come for Scotsmen to seek new commercial opportunities elsewhere.

The Navigation Acts stopped goods being imported into England except in English ships, or by ships that belonged to the country producing the goods. This applied to English colonies, such as those in America. If a Scottish ship carrying wool goods ventured to New York, for example, it could not be unloaded, and if a Scottish captain tried to pick up a cargo of sugar from Jamaica to take home, he was prevented. Here and there Scottish traders had managed to get round the restrictions. A small trading settlement had been quietly allowed in New Jersey and another in South Carolina, but this was not enough to counter the strangulation of Scottish trade. In 1693 a group of Scottish merchants sought to promote trade with the coasts of Africa and other foreign parts by setting up a colony or two of their own. The Scottish parliament approved the idea, which was masterminded by William Paterson, the eccentric Scottish financial genius who was in the throes of founding the Bank of England for William II (III of England). A company was formed and the people of Scotland were invited to subscribe £300,000 to finance the colonies. A further £300,000 was expected from English merchants willing to invest because they wanted to crack the monopoly position of the great East India Company.

At this point William II betrayed the Scots again. The East India Company had become alarmed at the possibility of a rival trading company in its areas and lobbied the king to discourage the scheme. English merchants were pressurized to drop their investment promises; the king used his influence to prevent European bankers lending money to the company, and as he was ruler also of Holland he forbade Dutch ships to be sold to the Scots. The Scots, however, persisted in their plan and raised £400,000 in Scotland, estimated to have been about half of the available cash in the country at the time. The first colony was to be set up in the Darien area of the Isthmus of Panama. Darien stood between two oceans, the Atlantic and the Pacific, and the potential trade should have been enormous. But the Spanish had a claim to Darien, and one of William's reasons for frustrating the scheme was that he was trying to negotiate an alliance with Spain.

The first expedition to Darien set out in the summer of 1698, carrying with it the hopes and the savings of the Scottish people. A town was established in the Darien, and it was called New Edinburgh. But the venture was a disaster. The pioneers could not get used to the terrible climate and fever raged throughout the settlement. The Spanish then arrived with forces to turn the settlers out. In 1699 another expedition set out for the same site and tried again to establish the colony, and again the settlers were expelled by the Spanish, with great loss of life. The Darien scheme was abandoned. And when the full story of the collapse was known, the Scots were furious. Knowing they had been betrayed by the king, they vented their anger against England. To those who still argued for union opponents could with much justice say 'Are these the kind of people you want to join up with?' By William's death in 1702 most Scots were against union at any price, and were ready 'to sit down under all these losses and misfortunes and in a kind of glad poverty live on what remained'.

There was one final insult. The English parliament passed the Act of Settlement in 1701 which arranged that William's heir, his sister-in-law Princess Anne Stewart, daughter of James VII, should, if she had no children to succeed, be followed by Sophia, electress of Hanover, who was the nearest Protestant relative. The act declared that the monarch must be a Protestant in line with the

Church of England. The Scots were not consulted; it was simply presented as a *fait accompli*. The Scots would not have objected to Princess Anne, but a German electress was another matter. The act had been passed to ensure that never again should England have a Catholic monarch. There was a special need for this act because in that year James VII had died in exile and his son, James Edward, had immediately afterwards been formally recognized as King James VIII by Louis XIV of France. And James Edward was a Catholic. In Scotland there was quite a lot of support for James Edward, and many would have welcomed him rather than his half-sister as heir to William, but they would have demanded that he become a Protestant. Loosely, these pro-James Edward Scots are known as Jacobites, a word that later embraced all those elements that resisted union with England before it happened, and plotted to undo it afterwards.

No sooner had William died and Anne succeeded than the Scots made clear their feelings about the 1701 Act and about the increasing difficulties over trading. Queen Anne sought to smooth things over by appointing a committee of Scottish and English commissioners to negotiate union between the parliaments, but the committee failed to achieve anything. A general election was held in Scotland in 1703 and Anne hoped that the new parliament would see the proposals through. The election results produced a divided parliament. There were about 100 members in favour, about 70 Jacobites against, and some 80 or so members who were not yet committed. Some of these 80 did not want union, but they did not want James Edward either. The foremost of these was Andrew Fletcher, of Saltoun, a radical politician who had a most persuasive style of oratory. He wanted a really independent Scotland, a church free from too much doctrine and intolerance, and a constitution for Scotland that was well-nigh republican. The new parliament passed two important acts. One was the Act of Security, which provided that after the death of Queen Anne the Scottish parliament should determine who was to succeed, that he or she must be a Protestant, a member of the Stewart family and someone not chosen by the English parliament as their monarch, unless the choice guaranteed the same trading rights for Scotland as for England, and undertook to ensure freedom of religion and government for the Scots. If the act was not accepted by the queen, the Scots would not provide any taxes. The other act was the Act anent

Peace and War, which gave Scotland her own powers to make war, peace and alliances; Scots should not be committed to provide money or troops for wars waged by England without the approval of the Scottish parliament.

The two acts are regarded by apologists for the union as having been drafted not because parliament was against union so much as that it wanted to make the nation's particular grievances heard – as they had hitherto not been. But the acts were really a true interpretation of Scottish feeling, and this was to be borne out by the reactions once union was effected. In the 1680s Fletcher had been a leading advocate for union: 'we can never come to any true settlement (with England) but by uniting with England in Parliaments and Trade.' Now, Fletcher was a leading opponent of union.

The English government was much put out by the failure of the negotiations set up by the queen. It was a change of view, the result of their fear that in their war with France a separated Scotland would endanger their security. The two Scottish parliament acts added to their consternation. The English government retaliated with the needless kind of force usually displayed when a large organization is threatened by a small one. Union must be achieved now; every kind of pressure must be brought to bear. The English parliament brought through the Alien Act which stated that if Scotland did not accept the arrangements for the succession of the Hanoverian electress, and do so by the end of 1705, all Scots would be treated as aliens. Scottish-owned lands in England would be appropriated; Scottish exports of cattle, linen and coal (representing the bulk of their total exporting to England) would be stopped.

The English did not need to enforce the Alien Act. Other measures were beginning to bear fruit. Queen Anne appointed a new commissioner for Scotland. It was the duke of Argyll, and he was charged to persuade the Scottish parliament to start negotiating again. Argyll was at heart a patriot, but he was susceptible to bribes. He had a large following in Scotland, and the English thought he would have a major influence on the Scottish members. He was offered a peerage in the English House of Lords, with a Scottish peerage for his brother Archibald. Argyll was also offered promotion in the army, which appealed to him as he was set on a military career (eventually, he became a field marshal). Other influential lords also bribed were the duke of Queensberry and the earl of Glasgow. Meanwhile, interference with Scottish trading ships by English ships went on. Scottish ships were seized. The Scots retaliated. When the *Worcester*, an English ship, ran aground in the Forth in 1704, its captain was taken and hanged.

The negotiations, the backstairs dealing, the infighting among the politicians in both lands throughout 1705 and 1706 were extensive and complicated. One more thing happened to bring union closer. This was a proposal that the commissioners chosen to draw up the union treaty should be appointed by the queen, and not elected. The proposal was made by the duke of Hamilton – who had lands in England. A majority of Scottish parliamentary members was prevailed upon by bribes and other inducements to approve this idea, which guaranteed that there would be more than enough commissioners to approve the treaty. Some of the pro-English lords and others must have worked very hard, while the English government certainly opened its purse wide.

In April 1706, thirty-one commissioners from each country met in London. By mid-July they had hammered out agreement, and in it Scots were guaranteed the same trading rights that the English enjoyed. They were to receive about £400,000, a sum known as the 'equivalent', to help the economy and to compensate for losses over the Darien scheme. The Scottish church was to be left alone, so were the Scottish legal system and the courts. The burghs were to retain their privileges. Scotland was to pay a very high price for these things. The Scottish parliament was abolished; the royal succession was assured for the Hanoverian liné; the two countries were to be known as Great Britain and to share the same flag; the Scots were to have forty-five seats in the joint House of Commons (to England's 513) and sixteen peers in the House of Lords to England's 190. The ratio of populations was five to one (5.5 million English to just over 1 million Scottish), but the ratio of members in the Commons was over ten to one, and twelve to one in the Lords. English coinage, weights and measures were to be uniform in both lands. And although the Scottish Privy Council was intended to be kept, it was in fact abolished a few months afterwards.

The treaty was put to both parliaments. The Scottish parliament voted on it article by article. On 16 January 1707 it ratified the whole treaty. The Act of Union was to come into force on 1 May. The English achieved by a mixture of bribes, threats, tricks and hard bargaining what they had failed to do by force of arms for centuries.

The passage of the act through the Scottish parliament was very rough indeed. Petitions against it were organized in many areas and presented during the course of the debates, but were ignored. Every day crowds packed the streets around Parliament Hall in Edinburgh, and clamoured for its rejection. Few people in the capital wanted union; less than a quarter of the Scottish people wanted it. They thought that it would end Scottish independence – which of course it did, in the political sense. But the people were not asked. There was no referendum, no consultation. Only a small percentage of the population had votes, possibly as few as 2000, and they had already cast them for the parliament.[2] Many of the members opposed to union fought hard at the debates; tempers rose, angry scenes were commonplace, some were tempted even to draw their swords. The duke of Queensberry, the commissioner, who had been secretly paid £20,000 for his support, was stoned in his carriage. If the mob had known about the bribe, doubtless he would have been killed. Other pro-union members of parliament were jostled and catcalled. In Glasgow there were riots and the army was called out. In Dumfries copies of the proposals were burned in the streets. 'We are bought and sold for English gold,' cried the Jacobites. And within a few years the English statesman Harley was saying that England had indeed bought from the Scots the right to tax them. That was the view of the union held generally among English politicians.

It was not long before Scotsmen began to see what union meant in practice, how the English regarded the treaty in quite a different light from them, indeed from the spirit in which it was made. It began with a financial matter – taxation. The English wanted certain methods followed in tax collecting and they sent officials into Scotland to show how they were to be carried out. They soon made themselves unpopular. Another early grievance was the long delay in receiving the £400,000 'equivalent'. When at last it was brought to Edinburgh in sacks on twelve carts, the people stoned the troops guarding the train. There were to be many other instances of aggravation. Generally, they revealed what angered the Scots most – the patronizing attitude of the English towards their Scottish 'partners' whom they regarded as conquered subjects. Relations deteriorated further when in 1710 an Episcopalian minister was imprisoned for flouting the authority of the Scottish church. The Scottish Court of Session upheld the sentence. The minister appealed to the House of Lords in London, which reversed it. The Scots were greatly affronted. The treaty confirmed the integrity of Scottish law and church; judgments in Scotland should not be overturned in London.

In 1712 the Westminster parliament restored the old system of patronage in the church, whereby ministers were chosen not by their congregations but by the owners of the land on which the churches stood, that is, their patrons. Church lands in Scotland had fallen mainly into the hands of lords and lairds after the Reformation. Many of these people's descendants were out of touch with the religious feelings of ordinary Scottish people. The temptation was constantly there to put in friends, members of the family, or political allies, whether or not they were good ministers. The Presbyterians feared further encroachments on church liberties.

These and many other grievances shocked the Scottish members of both Houses at Westminster, and even some English members, too, and in 1713 a bill was introduced into the Lords to repeal the Act of Union. It very nearly passed, being rejected by only four votes. In the background the Jacobite party in Scotland viewed these events as helpful to their cause. They believed that growing discontent with the government – and by extension, the monarchy – bettered the chances that James Edward might return to take up the throne as James VIII. Actually, they miscalculated the amount of support they had. Discontent there certainly was; changes there would surely have to be. But many Scots who hated the union were not willing to fight and die for James Edward. When Queen Anne died in 1714, her heir George Lewis of Hanover (his mother Sophia had died a few weeks earlier) succeeded and his proclamation was welcomed in England and in many parts of Scotland. This shocked the Jacobites, who thought that all Scotland would instantly call for James Edward. The position was not even as simple as that. There were politicians who did not want George Lewis but would accept James Edward only if he would change his religion, and there were no signs that he was willing to do that. There were politicians who wanted George Lewis but wanted also to break up the union. There were politicians in England who preferred James Edward to George Lewis, and would accept the fracture of the union if that was to be the price. When Anne died some of these English statesmen and their allies were ready to take up arms to depose her successor.

James Edward was not known in Scotland, as he had lived nearly all his life in exile. But he was the son of the Stewart king whom the Scots had known. He had been brought up at the French court and had acquired pleasant manners and a kindly disposition. For years the Jacobites worked for his cause. They encouraged their fellow Scots to support it by massive propaganda: portraits and descriptions of him were circulated widely. Jacobites drank toasts in public company to 'the king across the water'. His name was whispered wherever Jacobites went. A first attempt by force in 1708, with French help, had failed. A bigger attempt in 1715 nearly succeeded.

When Queen Anne was known to have only a short while left to live, the Jacobites on both sides of the Border (the English Jacobites included the duke of Ormonde and Viscount Bolingbroke) made their plans for three risings to be staged in both countries. One was to be in the south-west of England, with the aim to seize Bristol and Plymouth and thence march on London where government forces would have been depleted by simultaneous risings in the other two places, the north of England and in Scotland. The risings were to break out more or less as soon as George Lewis was proclaimed George I. But there was much hesitation on both sides, co-ordination of plans and resources went awry, and the government was able to crack down upon the English end of the disaffection. Ormonde and Bolingbroke managed to slip out of the country.

In Scotland the principal commander of the Jacobite forces was the earl of Mar. He had signed the Act of Union, but he had also been a prime mover of the 1713 bill to repeal it. The government had not been able to squash the Scottish end of the rising. Mar gathered together a number of lords and Highland chiefs and at Braemar, his Aberdeenshire estate, he declared for James Edward, proclaiming him King of Scotland, England and Ireland. He then headed south with his forces, picking up volunteers from the clans (though not from all of them). Opposed to him were the government's forces in Scotland, amounting to less than 2000 men, but soon to be reinforced and led by the duke of Argyll, whose reputation as a military commander was by now high. Argyll's position needs to be made clear. He had helped to persuade the Scottish parliament to accept the Act of Union. He had then become disillusioned by the results and had backed the 1713 bill to repeal it. But he was not a Jacobite, and as a Presbyterian he feared that a Jacobite success would bring about a return to Roman

191

Catholicism. Now he advanced into Scotland, and as he came he received the support of Presbyterian elements in the Lowlands: ministers actually preached in favour of resisting the Jacobites. Argyll was also expecting support from his own extensive 'empire', which stretched from the Mull of Kintyre to Loch Creran and from the Firth of Lorne to Loch Tay.

After much manoeuvring on both sides, which included the successful frustration by Argyll of an attempt by Mackintosh of Borlum to capture Edinburgh, the two armies clashed at Sheriff-muir, near Dunblane, on 13 November 1715. Mar had about 7000 troops to Argyll's 3500. Mar's Highlanders drove a wing of Argyll's infantry off the field, but Argyll took a cavalry force and broke up part of the Highlanders. By evening Mar had withdrawn, but neither side knew which had won the day. The next day, however, Mar's forces began to desert. Other Jacobites who had joined up with supporters in the northern counties of England, led by Lord Derwentwater, were defeated at Preston, twenty-four hours after Sheriffmuir.

James Edward did not reach Scotland until a month afterwards. By that time his cause was obviously lost. The Jacobites expected him to bring an army: he arrived with half a dozen servants. He stayed only a few weeks, and early in February 1716, together with Mar, he slipped away to France. The 'Fifteen', as the rising came to be called, was over. The reckoning had to follow. Argyll had been as careful as he could with the blood of his own countrymen who were on the opposite side, and had urged the government to negotiate with the Jacobites. But the government distrusted him and replaced him with another commander to crush the last embers of the rising. When it was all over, some Jacobites who had been captured were executed, including their leaders Derwent-water and Kenmure. Lord Nithsdale was imprisoned in the Tower of London and sentenced to death, but escaped dressed as a maid-servant.

Three factors made it almost certain that the rising could not succeed. One was that the Jacobite leadership lacked drive. Mar was not a military commander of force; he hesitated, wasted time, often failed to seize opportunities open to him. He bungled Sheriff-muir. Another was that the Presbyterians were against it, and thus the Jacobites could never know what kind of support they could count on as they moved about Scotland. Lastly, since the death of

Louis XIV and his succession by his great-grandson, Louis XV, a boy of five, executive power was in the hands of the duke of Orleans, whose policy was not to support the Jacobites. No French forces would be available. The Jacobites were on their own, and they had not a chance.

If few Jacobites were put to death, many hundreds were sent to plantations in the West Indies. The government also tried to clip the powers of the clan chiefs by disarming them. Fines were imposed for possessing arms after a date fixed for surrendering them. Many Highlanders handed in old and useless weapons but kept the more effective ones for another day. In 1725 the government sent General George Wade to Scotland as commander-in-chief, with an army, to pacify the Highlands where resentment was still strong against the union. In a period of about fifteen years Wade constructed a system of roads that linked up various forts, such as Fort William, Fort Augustus and Fort George (just north of Inverness), and coursed through the mountains to Crieff and Dunkeld. About 250 miles of road were built, with forty-two bridges, but they were meant for the military to be moved about quickly, and not for the convenience of Highland farmers to shift their cattle and sheep. Whatever peace this activity brought, it did not improve relations between the two countries.

From the time of the Act of Union the affairs of Scotland had been the responsibility of a special secretary of State. After 1725 the post was dropped and Scottish affairs were put under the aegis of the home secretary. Taxes were imposed quite out of proportion to the ability of the country to pay. And in 1736 Edinburgh was the scene of serious rioting when a Captain Porteous, who fired on a mob which was protesting against the hanging of a smuggler, and who was sentenced to death by a Scottish court, was reprieved by the wife of George II, acting as regent while her husband was away in Hanover. The crowd broke into Tolbooth prison, pulled Porteous out and hanged him in Grassmarket. The government responded with an order to destroy the charter of the city and to imprison the provost. The duke of Argyll intervened and got the government to change the reprisals to a fine.

And so the years passed, and with them the bitterness grew, as the English continued to misinterpret the Act of Union and the Scots saw no advantages coming to them. In 1745, when Britain was at war with France, a British army was defeated at Fontenoy.

This roused the hopes of the Jacobites again, who thought the French would support another attempt to get James Edward to the throne. This time the Jacobites had a worthy leader. He was Prince Charles Edward (Bonnie Prince Charlie, as he came to be known for his youth and good looks), a man of courage, dash and personal magnetism. The French had already planned an assault on England in 1744, but it had to be abandoned when the invasion fleet was scattered by storms. Nevertheless, Prince Charles determined to go ahead and try his luck alone. In July 1745 he landed in the Outer Hebrides with seven followers. At first he was cold-shouldered. The MacLeods told him to go home. He replied that he had come home. Then he left for Moidart. Among those who threw in their resources for him on the way were MacDonald of Clan-ranald, Cameran of Lochiel, MacDonnell of Keppoch and Stewart of Ardsheal. From Moidart, Prince Charles went to Glenfinnan where, on 19 August, he raised his standard and enlisted the support of over 1000 troops, gathering or already encamped there. Two days later the Jacobite army set forth eastwards towards Loch Lochy. Within a month Prince Charles had captured Perth, defeated a government force beyond, and reached Edinburgh where he proclaimed his father as James VIII of Great Britain and Ireland. By this time over 3000 clansmen had flocked to the colours. The English troops under General Cope withdrew north.

Cope tried to raise fresh forces in the north-east but met indifference. From Aberdeen he shipped what troops he had to the north coast of Lothian, where they landed at Dunbar, and then marched towards Edinburgh. At Prestonpans, on 21 September, they met the army of Prince Charles and were defeated. Cope fled to England to warn Wade (now a field marshal) who was at Newcastle. Prince Charles spent the next month at Edinburgh assembling the Jacobite forces, as more and more clansmen came in. But it was clear that if the Highlanders were for him, the Lowlanders were not. Edinburgh remained strangely sullen while it was occupied by the handsome prince who was wasting valuable time, giving his enemies plenty of opportunity to marshal their forces.

Prince Charles led his forces, now numbering about 5000 or so, across the Border via the western route, and on 9 November he took Carlisle. He was aiming at the conquest of England – no less – and he believed his best chance lay in the effects of surprise coupled with the shock created by his rapid advances. He expected

Englishmen to rally to him, but it was unrealistic. It was not their quarrel. On 4 December he got as far south as Derby, less than 130 miles from London, and there he halted for a council of war.

Although Prince Charles did not know it, there was panic in London. George II is said to have started to pack his bags in preparation for abandoning England. The Prince may not have known, either, that Wade had assembled about 8000 men and was heading south to intercept, while George's son, William, duke of Cumberland, was rushing up from Staffordshire with another 10,000 troops. And in Scotland, the Campbells had begun to gather, ready to attack if Prince Charles should come into Argyll territory.

After two days his generals advised Prince Charles to withdraw. It was heartbreaking. If he went on he might well reach London unscathed, but how long, if at all, could he hold one of the largest cities in Europe with but 5000 men? The generals prevailed and on 6 December the retreat began, conducted with great skill by Lord George Murray. In January 1746 the Jacobites drew up outside Stirling and besieged it. When the government sent a force under General Hawley to relieve it, Prince Charles defeated it at Falkirk. But inexplicably he abandoned the siege of Stirling. Instead, he went northwards and set up his headquarters at Inverness. Meanwhile, the smell of defeat was beginning to pervade the Jacobite army, and desertions increased. Cumberland was on his way up the north-east, via Aberdeen, and was aiming for Inverness. By mid-April it was clear that the final confrontation must come soon. Few of the Jacobites believed they could win, but they admired their Stewart prince and the Highlanders loved a good fight. Poorly armed, hungry and uncertain, they drew up on the moor at Culloden.

Even today, 236 years after the destruction of the Jacobite cause at Culloden, the battlefield and the woods still contain something of the atmosphere of despair that enveloped them on that wet and gusty day, 16 April 1746. By lunch time, less than 5000 men, many of them exhausted and hungry after trekking through the mountains vainly searching for food, had taken up their places on the south-west of a wooded area that straddled the road to Inverness. There were only about a hundred cavalry, and only thirteen guns. Many more Jacobite forces had not arrived; they were still out foraging, or were guarding other roads and towns. The battle position was not a good one at all. The ground sloped gently upwards away from them, making it impossible to launch an effective Highland charge. The sleet was driving at the Jacobite lines from the north-east. Five or six hundred yards away were the enemy, nearly 10,000 of them, with about 800 cavalry which were to be used with devastating effect. Cumberland's army was fed and refreshed, and in fighting trim. Among his forces were many Scottish troops, notably Campbell's 21st Royal North British Fusiliers and the Argyll Militia. It had long been the policy of English governments to use renegade Celts in their armies against Scotland or Wales or Ireland, to play upon divisions within the ranks in these lands.

Prince Charles ordered the Jacobite guns to open fire but the rate was sporadic and little damage was done. Cumberland's artillery responded with terrible effect. Impatiently, the forward Jacobite ranks, receiving the brunt of the gunshot, waited for the signal to charge, and when it did come, it was too late to be effective. The left wing of Cumberland's front was broken by the Highlanders under Lord George Murray, but reserves came forward to plug the gap. The centre of the Jacobite lines suffered great losses, while on the left the Clan MacDonald force had harder ground to cross and were withered in their tracks by accurate volley-firing of enemy musketry. Both left and right Jacobite wings fought desperately, even hurling stones and clods of earth at the superior forces bearing down upon them, but they were edged slowly backwards. Then the withdrawal quickened. Cumberland sent the duke of Kingston's cavalry arm in pursuit, and the chase stretched out along the road and through the fields, all the way to Inverness. Highlanders were cut down and killed, and so were innocent bystanders in the villages.

The main battle was over inside an hour. Prince Charles, once he saw the day was lost, rode away to the south-west, into hiding. For a moment there might have been a chance of gathering for another fight, but it was too late, and the prince sent word to the clans to disperse and look to their own safety. And well they might for the vengeance of the English was systematic and terrible.

When it was clear that the Jacobites were giving ground, Cumberland ordered his army not to spare anyone, not even the wounded lying in the fields or woods. 'No quarter' were the words sent out, the most hated phrase in the English language to Highlanders ever since. Many hundreds of fallen were shot where they lay. Some were burned alive. Many prisoners were shot out of hand. Over 100 were taken across the Border into England, tried and executed, in flat defiance of the Act of Union which guaranteed the integrity of the Scottish law courts. Those that were not killed were pushed into gaols, many with their wives and children, there neglected to the point of death from starvation and disease. More than 1000 were sold as slaves to American plantations. Cattle, sheep and deer were cut down, crops ravaged and burned. More cattle were herded into Inverness and given away or offered at ludicrously low prices to Lowland farmers, some even to English farmers from the northern counties. Cottages, farms and houses were burned down in every district of the Highlands. When protests were made by Scotsmen who were not Jacobites but who thought the punishment of the Highlands had gone far enough, the protesters were dismissed or insulted. The provost of Inverness was kicked downstairs. Cumberland complained that he had actually been asked to show a little humanity. Not for nothing did he earn the nickname by which he is known throughout Scotland – 'Butcher'. The harrying of the glens, as it came to be known, was carried out with Teutonic brutality and thoroughness.

The devastation of the Highlands was backed by the London government and applauded by many Lowland and Presbyterian Scots who hated Highlanders more for their stubborn adherence to the Roman Catholic faith than their loyalty to the Stewarts. The government took its own measures of revenge, aimed at destroying completely the whole Highland clan structure. The chiefs were stripped of all their authority and powers. Hereditary sheriffdoms and other jurisdictions were abolished, and in so doing the government bracketed the jurisdictions of clans who had not supported the Jacobites. This angered everyone. The clan relationship, with all its faults, with its barons' courts and clan councils, 'formed the whole basis of Scottish law and order as well as local government', and the Act of Union had emphasized the integrity of Scottish law. Worse, nothing was put in its place. The clan chiefs were left with no powers, no pride, no purpose. The wearing of tartans and kilts, the playing of pipes, and the owning of weapons of any kind, were all forbidden on pain of death or long-term imprisonment. Even the speaking of Gaelic was prohibited. It was a systematic attempt to 'obliterate the Celtic mode of life', a policy followed by England also in Ireland and in Wales. The lands of the fallen chiefs were forfeited and turned over to factors, special managers who, it should be said, ran many of them much more efficiently than their owners had.

As for Bonnie Prince Charlie, after he had issued his advice to the clans to disperse and shift for themselves, he became the object of one of the biggest manhunts carried out by an English government up to that time, a search accompanied by further assault and killing of those who, though they may not have known where he was, nonetheless remained loyal to him. A price of £30,000 was put on his head, and yet this huge sum, equal to about 2 per cent of the cash available in the country, tempted no single Scot to betray him in the five months in which he lay in hiding. His adventures, the best known of which was his rescue from one of the islands by Flora MacDonald, who dressed him in a woman's clothes to avoid detection and smuggled him over to Skye, ended when he managed to hide in a French ship bound for Europe and get away, never to return.

The government's policy towards the Highlands hastened on changes that had already begun. For a long time the clan chiefs had leased much of their land to middlemen, called 'tacksmen' because tack meant lease. Some tacksmen worked the land, others sublet to tenants, often getting more rent or greater amounts of produce than the clan chief received from the tacksmen. Sometimes tacksmen were members of the family, or of families of ally chiefs. One of their roles was to call up the clansmen into military service when the need arose. But by the 1740s some chiefs had stopped leasing to tacksmen and begun to collect rents and dues through agents who only earned commission. Some chiefs also began to see that more money could be made by turning over their lands to sheep-farming, as Lowland and Border lairds and farmers had been doing for years. The process quickened after the 1745 rising, and it was encouraged by the government's laws against the clans. Chiefs no longer protected their clansmen and could no longer command the unquestioning loyalty they once had from them. Instead, by turning over the land to sheep-farming, or indeed to crops, they acquired wealth in the form of cash and this gave them a taste for good living, fine homes and expensive entertainments, such as enjoyed by lords, lairds and businessmen in the Lowlands. Many chiefs were attracted to Edinburgh, some even to London, to build or buy grand town houses and live it up in the social whirl. Generally, they were able to pay for the new life from their rents, especially after switching over to sheep-farming. But if they could not pay, they mortgaged their lands to others who would work them. Many willing lenders were not Highlanders, some were not even Scottish.

Life for the tenants (in the Highlands they were known as crofters) and cottars (farmworkers) became more and more harsh and uncertain in these conditions. If they wanted to stay on the land they had to produce higher and higher rents even though there was no chance of increasing the profitability of the farmland to meet them. So they had to increase their demands on their sub-tenants who could generally not afford to pay more. Then, in the 1780s, sheep-farming accelerated in Scotland when forfeited lands of the clan chiefs (taken after the 1745 rising) were restored to their owners or to descendants. The owners were tempted by the easier profits available from sheep. They started to evict tenants and crofters on a big scale, for the tenants were no longer needed. Only a small fraction could find jobs on the new sheep-farms. Some of them left quietly, turning to crofting in the wilder parts. Some went to the cities where the Industrial Revolution (see p.210) was creating a need for workmen in factories. Some emigrated to the colonies. But there were many who did not go so quietly. They thought they would be helped by their former chiefs or their new landlords. Many believed they had hereditary rights to stay. But the landlords insisted and brought in the military and the sheriffs and their officials to evict them by force. Their houses were burned down, often over their heads, and they were driven off the land. If they fled, they were pursued and if caught taken to ships for transportation to the colonies. 'The people were terrorized, utterly impoverished . . . the litany of their sufferings would fill volumes.' One book tells the terrible story better than any, namely Eric Richards' *The Highland Clearances* (1982).

Among the most notorious of these 'clearances', as they were called, were those of the countess of Sutherland, which began early in the 1800s and went on for a generation. Many thousands of tenants (one estimate was over 15,000) were 'cleared' from lands in the county to make room for sheep. The countess employed agents, she did not even live in Scotland. One of them, Patrick Sellar, was tried for manslaughter when some elderly tenants were killed when they were being evicted. He was acquitted by a court bribed by the Sutherlands. Some of the evicted crofters were offered almost useless lands on the coast in order to make a living as fishermen, but they knew nothing about fishing and were given no boats or nets. So they drifted towards the towns and, if they were lucky, they found jobs or, if they were not, they joined the swelling ranks of the destitute.

The Highlands became a sad and empty 'desert' which would have amazed the Caledonians of Calgacus' time. In 1854, when once again the authorities tried to recruit Highlanders to serve in the British army, this time in the Crimean War, only a handful of men were raised. 'Since you have preferred sheep to men, let sheep defend you' was the reply to a landowner who called for volunteers. And the emptiness of the northern Highlands today, despite valiant efforts by the Highland and Island Development Board, is still a lasting reminder of the 'clearances'. New landowners have moved in, some of them big spenders from Europe, and they are more interested in the land than in the people on it. And yet the depopulation of the Highlands can in the end only be solved by the Scots themselves – if they want to solve it.

CHAPTER 13

SCOTLAND REBORN

(1770–1980)

The rising of 1745–6 was a Highland enterprise. Few people in the Lowlands sympathized with its aims and most of those few did nothing to support the Jacobite cause. For one thing, the Jacobites were campaigning for a Catholic king and the Lowlands were a stronghold of Presbyterianism. If the Lowlanders did not relish the gradual smothering of Scottish national pride and feeling by the overwhelming power of England, with its military forces scattered throughout Scotland, its fortresses specially constructed to hold areas down (like Fort George, the curtain at Corgarff and others now demolished), its predominance in parliament, its tax collectors and customs officials, who made their own rules, they were not prepared to fight about it. And when the rising was crushed and punitive measures put in train, the Highlanders were in no position to resist any longer. The collapse of the second Jacobite rising marks in a sense the end of the ancient Scottish nation. The Scotland whose story we have traced so far, over thousands of years, died on that terrible wet day on Culloden Moor. And you have only to visit the fields and the woods today to feel inescapably something of that ending.

Yet in an end there is often a beginning. After Culloden the Scots had to choose between asserting themselves still as a nation, a people with an identity, or succumbing entirely to English pressure, to becoming just another large 'county' added to England's northern border, and a poor and discouraged one at that. The Scots chose to survive. It would have been a betrayal of their history to do otherwise. That they did so and remained a nation, albeit a changed one, was due to three things: the strength of their institutions, the church, the law and education; the influence of their history and the fundamental character of Scotsmen which that history had forged; and their belief that the English were out to destroy them, borne out by the non-realization of the promises made at the time of the union and by reflecting upon what had happened to both Ireland and Wales. And this determination to survive was soon to be manifested in an artistic and architectural renaissance, an agricultural revolution and an explosion of inventiveness and industry. To begin with, these took place in Scotland, but before long Scottish genius spread across the borders into England and out to the great British Empire to the good of both but to the detriment of the homeland.

When a nation loses its independence, its subsequent history seems somehow not to fit into the threads that went before. It becomes more difficult to sort out which important aspects or landmarks belong to the nation, are its achievements, and which come more properly from the 'take-over' nation. In Scotland's case, the nation was left with certain of its institutions, which were not to be altered or amalgamated, and we can trace how they have developed since the eighteenth century and what part they have played in the Scottish national advance. Some other major aspects of Scottish life were more directly affected by the union with England, such as agriculture, industry, science and invention, and to a lesser extent art and architecture, and these may be summarized. But what emerges perhaps more clearly than anything is the continued survival of the essential Scottish character, and of a Scottish nationalism in some form. In the years that have elapsed since the Act of Union, there has always been some individual or some movement to remind the Scots of their national heritage, whether it was Robert Burns and the electric effect of his poetry, or Walter Scott and his bestselling Scottish historical novels, or Queen Victoria deciding to make a country home at Balmoral, or King

George VI with his Scottish queen, Elizabeth, the present Queen Mother, or Harry Lauder with his songs in the Scottish vernacular, or piper Gordon Findlater playing the bagpipes as he led the Gordon Highlanders up the Dargai Heights in far-off Afghanistan, or the Society of the Friends of the People (whose battle cry was Burns's specially written song 'Scots Wha Hae') or the Home Rule campaign of the 1880s or the National Covenant of 1950. These are testaments to Scotland's hope and aspiration.

Less than ten years after the destruction of the Jacobite cause at Culloden, the Scottish determination to survive began to show in an upsurge of literature, philosophy, architecture and building, and social reform, in Scotland's Golden Age of Intellect. It was not to be the last cry of a beaten and vanishing nation, although no doubt many people south of the Border thought – or hoped – it was. It was an expression of the latent and indestructible vigour of Scottish creative talent, which was to manifest itself again in the nineteenth and the present century.

Historians writing about the ancient world are inclined to see a civilization's periods of advance mirrored in its architecture and buildings, and that is a valid exercise. It is particularly so in the case of Scotland. Within a decade of Bonnie Prince Charlie's occupation of Edinburgh, from which he mounted his ambitious campaign, the town council had started to consider a variety of daring schemes for expanding and improving the capital. Town planners of today generally tear out the heart of a city they want to 'improve' and fill up the space with structures that do not blend with what is left behind. The Edinburgh development was a scheme to construct a new Edinburgh as an extension of the old. The marshy ground of Nor' Loch, that lay to the north of the medieval jumble of tall and often lopsided buildings that made up the residential part of Old Edinburgh, was drained and reclaimed. Immediately to the north, on the ridge that ran parallel with the rocky escarpment dominated by Edinburgh Castle, the New Town was begun. It was laid out according to the plan of a young architect, James Craig, published in 1767. It consisted of an ordered grid of fine streets, squares, crescents and gardens. The key feature was Princes Street (originally called St Giles's Street), still one of the loveliest streets in the world.

The new town took a generation or so to complete, and when it was done, there was a reluctance on the part of many Scots to take houses in the exciting development. They thought it was too 'English'. This may have been the start of the great myth, still held fast by some, that Edinburgh is not Scotland but a foreign city imposed on Scottish soil.

One architect who designed houses for the new town was Robert Adam. Born at Kirkcaldy, he was the son of William Adam (architect of Edinburgh's Royal Infirmary and other famous buildings). Two of his three brothers were well-known architects too. It was Robert who gave his name to a whole new style of architecture, interior design and furniture, the Adam style, which swept across Britain and Europe to replace the early and mid-eighteenth century rococo style. It was a revival of the classical forms that Robert had absorbed during a long stay in Italy, when he examined and drew all manner of ruined buildings and artefacts in Rome, Pompeii and elsewhere. Though much of Robert Adam's work was done in England, it was he who influenced English architectural ideas, not the other way about, and Scottish architects ever since have exerted the strongest influence in British building design, in particular men like Robert Matthew, Ninian Comper and Rennie Mackintosh. Adam carried out numerous works in Scotland, some of them his best, such as the Register House in Edinburgh and Lauriston House in Glasgow. He designed more than 100 great houses. Lords and rich men, some Scottish, some not, employed him or his brothers and 'disciples' to build them magnificent stately homes in Scotland, like Auchinleck in Ayrshire, or huge castellated mansions, like Culzean. Smaller homes were also built in great numbers, most of them constructed in stone, of which there has been so much for quarrying in Scotland.

Glasgow was not to be left in the shade in this architectural revival, although the best of its great building works programme was to be in the nineteenth century. A disastrous fire in 1677 had laid waste much of the city and it was afterwards rebuilt wonderfully in Scottish stone by Scottish craftsmen and artisans, with wide streets and open squares. In 1768 the Broomielaw Bridge was completed and opened, a construction marvel at the time.

But in considering the grand buildings and the spacious street plans, we must never forget the other side of the coin in the cities, the slums. Some of these were distressingly bad, among the worst in Europe. The tenements (blocks of flats) of the notorious Gorbals district in Glasgow (visited by one of the authors extensively before

SCOTLAND REBORN

they were demolished in recent years) were raised in the early and mid-nineteenth century. They began well but were so overcrowded that soon they became a byword for all that was squalid in dirty, unlit housing, where violence, disease and poverty were rampant. It was said that in those days the average life expectancy in the Glasgow slums was less than thirty years, so prone to disease were the slum dwellers, who were workers in the mushrooming factories and industries, shipbuilding yards, cotton mills, ironworks, coalmines and so forth in the Clyde area. The dreaded and fatal cholera made its first appearance in Edinburgh in January 1832, and so many thousands died from it in the Edinburgh slums that a national day of prayer was held before the end of March. There was one tenement in Edinburgh that had five storeys, each with a dozen rooms, and which in the mid-nineteenth century accommodated no less than 250 souls – and had no plumbing.

In the countryside housing was no better for the working people. As late as the 1870s cottars lived very roughly indeed: a whole family of eight would be crammed into a 'miserable hovel' of only one room, with no windows. Cottages with two or three rooms were a luxury enjoyed only by a very few smallholders.

In the present century Scotland has pioneered many architectural and environmental schemes. The new towns of Cumbernauld and Glenrothes have been held up as examples to other development agencies. Traditionally Scots have not been houseowners, except of course the lords, the lairds, the businessmen and the burgh councillors, and Scotland still has the lowest rate of home ownership in western Europe. But in the 1970s the difference between public authority house building and private sector building figures has been narrowing and there are more people owning their own houses than ever before.

As Scotland's national revival was being anchored to the soil in stone and tile, it was also burgeoning in thought and writing. The mid-eighteenth century was an age of reason and debate throughout Europe, and Scotland was deeply involved in it, along with every other nation. It was a time in which Scottish intellectual life flourished as it had never done before, most of all in the new Edinburgh. The great French philosopher Voltaire described Edinburgh as an intellectual centre at least the equal of Paris, London and Vienna, while Thomas Jefferson, the architect of the American Declaration of Independence and the third president of the United

States, said that as far as science was concerned 'no place in the world can pretend to competition with Edinburgh!' Dominating the scene were David Hume, one of the greatest philosophers ever to emerge from Britain, William Robertson, the fiery Presbyterian minister who wrote histories ranking with the best of the century, Adam Smith, professor of logic at Glasgow, whose book *The Wealth of Nations* laid the foundations for the science of economics, the poets James MacPherson, translator of Gaelic verse which activated a Celtic revival, Robert Ferguson, Michael Bruce and John Logan, who inspired Burns, Adam Ferguson, historian and philosopher and Thomas Reid, head of the Scottish school of philosophy.

But there was an irony in the situation. As Edinburgh was revelling in being the cultural capital of Europe, many Scottish nobles were deserting their estates, or clearing them for sheep runs, and hiving off to London for some high living on the money they made from them. Many more of the most able Scotsmen, who were neither nobles nor great landowners, were leaving their homeland to make new lives in the expanding British Empire. Even the rich well of Scottish scientific genius (which had produced Napier, inventor of logarithms in the early seventeenth century) was being sapped by a brain drain to England and Europe. James Watt, for instance, experimented with the condensing steam engine in Glasgow, but perfected and manufactured it at Birmingham; John Hunter pioneered modern surgery and anatomy in two London hospitals and many other leading medical men, trained in Scottish universities, went to work for royal families and rich nobles in Europe. Some Scotsmen were even 'apologizing' for being Scottish, like James Boswell, Dr Johnson's friend and biographer.

Two men, more than any others, showed Scotsmen they need not apologize. Robert Burns, Scotland's national poet, rekindled the fire of Scottish nationalism and helped to restore to the Scots their self-respect and confidence, not least by writing poetry in the Lowland Scottish tongue. Walter Scott, poet and novelist, who invented the historical novel, gave Scotsmen back their history and restored their national pride. Burns called for Scotsmen not to leave their native land ('O! Never, never, Scotia's realm desert'), although his advocacy of equality among men was an encouragement to emigrate. Scott, perhaps unwittingly, showed Scotsmen that the highest ambition they could reach was to take the Scottish genius abroad and influence the development of the new British Empire that was growing in many quarters of the world. Scotsmen's pride was restored, but their opportunities were not, and the steady stream of emigration rolled on.

The blossoming of Scottish intellectual activity in the eighteenth century had well nigh spent itself by the nineteenth. This is not to say that Edinburgh was no more to be the home of men of genius who ranked among the greatest in Europe, or that Glasgow and other Scottish universities were not to produce leading scholars and scientists, for they did. But the comment of Voltaire was no longer valid. Perhaps this was because of the drain that had gone on uninterrupted for so long. Certainly it was because Scotland failed to produce enough intellectual leaders, in the same way that it has failed to produce leaders in other spheres (see p. 224). Scottish writers there were in the nineteenth century, but many of them made their name and fortune outside Scotland and in the English language; to mention but a few household names, Carlyle, Macaulay, Ruskin, John Stuart Mill. But it was not till the 1920s that a fresh literary renaissance in Scotland emerged. Perhaps its most dominating influence was Hugh MacDiarmid (Christopher Murray Grieve), poet and pioneer of Scottish nationalism of the twentieth century, who died in 1978, having devoted his life to regenerating the Scottish literary language by encouraging a return to the Lowland Scottish tongue, like Burns. Hardly less powerful were colleagues like Edwin Muir (with whom he eventually fell out), James Bridie, Compton Mackenzie and Eric Linklater. Although the Scottish revival has had its dormant periods, it is still going on and increasingly Scottish writers are producing their work at the Edinburgh Festival, where they have the chance of a world hearing.

The Edinburgh Festival is a landmark in the cultural regeneration of Scotland. Started in 1947, it has become the largest and most comprehensive arts festival in the world. Contrary to the opinion of some commentators, the festival has not been imposed by outsiders upon an unwilling native population: more than 55 per cent of those attending in 1978 came from Scottish homes, a third of them from outside Edinburgh. It is now Scotland's festival, and other cities wanting to make a success of their own festivals have come to Edinburgh to find out how it is done. Until recently,

Scotland did not have the writers, actors and musicians to make a real impact, but this has changed. There is now a strong Scottish national opera, attracting world attention, producing its own newspaper and filling theatres wherever it performs. The example set by Edinburgh has been followed in several other Scottish cities and towns. The Pitlochry Festival began as a humble enough group of modest events a few years ago and today has a programme lasting several days each year, including plays, art exhibitions, concerts and poetry readings.

Agriculture

Scottish farming methods were backward enough at the start of the eighteenth century to make crop failure more the rule than the exception, but by 1800 Scottish farming had become the most advanced in Europe. English and European farmers were visiting Scotland to learn from it. There had been a revolution, particularly in the Lowlands and the north-east counties. It began after the union, when because the two countries were, apart from the Jacobite risings, no longer at war, Scottish landowners and farmers visited England in numbers to see the great developments that had already taken place in English agriculture. They brought all kinds of new ideas back: Jethro Tull's drilling methods; rotation of crops; enclosure of fields with hedges and ditches (which was to supersede the old run-rig system); planting of trees to provide timber to act as windbreaks and supply fertilizer from leaf mould (the earl of Loudon put in over a million trees in Ayrshire); and the introduction of the potato (first grown at Kilsyth in the 1730s) as a new staple food. To these were added Scottish innovations such as Meikle's threshing machine, Small's two-horse swing plough (or iron) and Bell's reaper. There were also great advances in livestock farming. The now famous Ayrshire dairy herds and the celebrated Border sheep had their beginnings. Probably four times as many head of livestock were being sold annually in the 1790s as in the 1750s. Over half a million Scotsmen and Scotswomen (a quarter of the population) were employed on the land by 1800, the women usually working for part of the time. The figure was to decline to about 200,000 in the 1800s, because of falling prices affecting all Europe following the famines of the 1840s, the operation of free trade and the continued expansion of livestock farming at the expense of crop-growing. Then livestock farming itself was to be jolted by competition from abroad in the early 1900s. Under the postwar Labour government (1945–51), Scottish farmers were greatly helped by laws giving security of tenure and guaranteeing markets and prices. Today the official view is that Scottish agriculture is efficient and well able to compete in the Common Market, that the country is self-sufficient in lamb and in milk products and actually produces a surplus for export. Four-fifths of the 19 million acres of land in the country are given over to farming. Of that 12 million acres are grazing land. But a significant part of this success has been due to farmers and agriculturalists who have come into Scotland from outside, particularly from England and Europe, which highlights a need for Scotland to produce its own farmers in greater numbers.

Traditionally, the Scottish fishing industry was a prosperous one. In James IV's reign so much fish was taken from the sea for home eating and for export (especially to the Low Countries) that some foreigners talked about 'fishy Scotland'. Fish were among the nation's principal riches. To a great extent the trade declined after the Union of the Crowns, presumably because the authorities turned a blind eye to English encroachments upon Scottish fishing waters. But in the last century there was a tremendous upsurge, especially in herring fishing (which flourished particularly in Shetland). Aberdeen became the third trawling port in Britain. The upsurge did not last, and many fishing ports have declined. But in the last two decades, there has been a second revival, not as startling as the first, but healthy. Landings of fish in Scottish ports rose from over 5 million cwt in 1962 to over 9 million in 1971 and the figure is still rising.

It would be unrealistic not to refer to the great whisky industry in Scotland, when considering agriculture and industry. For a long time the Scots produced only the whisky they wanted themselves, but in the middle of the last century whisky made in Scotland began to attract demand from England, and then from Canada and the USA. That demand has not flagged, and today Scotch whisky is the highest quality whisky made anywhere. It is exported to the tune of more than 200 million gallons a year. Indeed it is actually one of the United Kingdom's biggest single dollar-earning exports.

200 years of Scottish industry

The Industrial Revolution was a movement that brought sweeping changes in methods of producing goods. It substituted machines for men and women and it took work out of homes and small workshops and into factories. The revolution began in Britain in the 1740s and 1750s, earlier than anywhere else, and throughout its course, which is generally considered in three phases, Scottish engineers, scientists and inventors played leading roles. The first phase, from the 1740s to the 1830s, was highlighted by the development of the steam engine into a practical power unit for driving machinery, the work of James Watt. The steam engine revolutionized many industries, such as spinning, weaving and milling. By 1800 there were steam engines in many factories in Scotland. In 1802 a steam engine was used to power the first steamboat in the world, the *Charlotte Dundas*, built by Symington for the Forth–Clyde Canal. By that time there were more than 500 commercial vessels operating in the great river mouth. The most famous harbour was at Greenock. In 1790 the Forth–Clyde Canal, built by James Watt, had been opened. All this brought prosperity to Glasgow, making up for the decline in its tobacco industry that followed the breakaway from the British Empire of the thirteen American colonies that had supplied the leaf. Glasgow became the second greatest city in Britain, and has remained so to this day. It had about 12,000 people in 1707, 200,000 by about 1830 and well over a million now.

Linen and cotton manufacture were among the major industries of eighteenth century Scotland. In 1780 the linen industry produced more than 13 million yards of good quality linen. By 1795 cotton manufacture had overtaken linen. David Dale, an enterprising weaver from Glasgow, had set up a special village at New Lanark for cotton manufacture, with factories and blocks of flats for the workers. He was employing about 1400 people. There was similar industrial expansion on the east side of Scotland, too, notably at Aberdeen and Leith, and at Dundee where the jute industry began early in the nineteenth century.

Industrial expansion brings more goods and more kinds of goods, but they have to be moved about. Coinciding with this expansion was a revolution in transport. The old roads, little more than dirt tracks, narrow and full of potholes, could not cope. Rivers were not suitable. Here, Scottish innovations dominated. John Macadam of Ayr invented the road surface still known after him, made of small stones compacted in layers to form a hard-wearing surface. Macadam eventually became surveyor of roads for England, Scotland and Wales, supervising the surfacing of many thousands of miles of roads in all three. Sir John Rennie built the docks at Leith, enlarged the Clyde for more shipping, and then went to London to construct a new London Bridge. Thomas Telford, who started his working life as a stonemason at Langholm in Dumfriesshire, became the greatest civil engineer of his day. He worked in Scotland, England and Wales, designing, building and rebuilding roads. In Scotland he laid down over 900 miles of them, particularly in the Highlands, with hundreds of bridges. His greatest achievement in Scotland was the 61-mile-long Caledonian Canal, from Fort William to Inverness, linking the Atlantic Ocean to the North Sea. It was opened in 1822 and was the foremost of a considerable network of canals and waterways in Scotland engineered for the swift passage of goods.

Meanwhile the first ironworks of modern times to be of any size was established at Carron in Stirlingshire in 1759, using Highland timber for its furnaces. In 1776 the works produced a new light gun, with a chamber for the powder, called the carronade. These excellent guns were used chiefly in ships, and they contributed to the great victories at sea, particularly those of Nelson. By about 1800 the Carron works was the greatest armament factory in Europe.

In the early nineteenth century the textile industry began to run down. Linen had already taken second place to cotton, and after the upheavals of Napoleon's empire building in Europe and his destruction at Waterloo, the Scottish cotton industry began to stagnate. It was to be dealt its death-blow after the American Civil War (1861–5) during which the supply of the raw material that the industry depended upon was cut off completely, because the North blockaded the ports of the South. Other textiles, however, flourished, including jute, the principal industry of Dundee for a time. Coupled with this, Scotland had developed iron and steel industries and had gone into shipbuilding, coalmining and heavy engineering, which attracted many workers away from the textile industries because the pay was better.

The second half of the nineteenth century and the years to the

211

First World War saw tremendous advances in industry, particularly on Clydeside and elsewhere in the Midland Valley. They were helped along by a cluster of Scottish inventions: Robert Napier virtually founded the marine engineering industry and built the first Cunard steamships and the first ironclad battleships; James Nasmyth invented the steel hammer; James Neilson invented the hot blast furnace which enabled raw coal to be used for iron smelting so that the blackband ironstone deposits in Lanarkshire (which contained a mixture of iron and coal) could be used for ironwork but with need of much less coal. Railways, too, began to develop in Scotland, and by the end of the century almost everywhere in Scotland was within twenty miles of a station or boarding point, most places as little as ten miles.

In the 1880s steel production on the Clyde began to displace iron for ships and heavy engineering products, and this extended the Clyde's period of prosperity well into the present century. But Scotland was too dependent on a limited range of industries: textiles, iron and steel, shipbuilding and coalmining. Industrial prosperity in Scotland was hard hit by the economic recession of the 1920s, as it was in England. This 'slump' began in the USA, the world's leading industrial nation, and the effects were felt everywhere. The collapse of the economy of Scotland was real and widespread. In 1933, for example, less than 60,000 tons of shipping were produced, compared with three-quarters of a million tons in 1900. Unemployment reached staggering heights: a quarter of the country's work force was out of a job. So, too, the Scottish contribution to the total industrial output of all Britain plunged.

It was not until after the Second World War that Scotland slowly began to recover its self-confidence – again – and it has been a hard process. Underlying the prosperity generated by the Industrial Revolution in Britain in the late eighteenth and throughout the nineteenth century, there was a steady sapping of the benefit accruing to Scotland. This was because Scotsmen were emigrating – to England, to the Empire and to the USA at a rate that prevented the growth of the strong and lasting demand for consumer goods which there was in richer countries, where the emigration rate was far less. Scottish emigration has continued almost – but not quite – up to the present. At last there are signs that it is being stemmed. Fewer young people are rushing out of Scotland as soon as they have left school or got their university degrees or college certificates. Part of this is due to active attempts to stop the population decline by government encouragement for new industries in Scotland, such as aluminium smelting, petrochemicals, plastics, electronics and business machinery, the modernization of the traditional industries. New towns have been built too, many of them examples to the world in the quality of their town planning and environmental amenities. And, of course, the offshore oil industry has brought a considerable spin-off to Scotland in the form of a demand for services and equipment for the drilling teams.

The great challenge to Scottish industry, however, is not so much the need for diversification, nor to salvage what remains of the country's former eminence in shipbuilding (Clydeside ships are still the best in the world but they are too expensive and they take too long to build). It is for Scottish industry to find its own leaders. At present the greater part of investment in Scottish industry comes from outside, from the Westminster government and from foreign capital (American, Dutch, Japanese, German and English). Not enough is coming forward from Scottish men of wealth and adventure. Investment in their own industries give Scots the opportunity to take control of their own business affairs, to become leaders within their own land again, and help make it worth while for Scotland's best people to stay at home and work in the Scottish interest. As we bring this book towards its close, it is heartening to discover signs that this challenge is being accepted.

Science and invention

The Industrial Revolution was helped along in the nineteenth century by a marked upsurge in scientific discovery and invention, affecting every area of domestic and industrial life. Most notable and far-reaching advances were made in such things as electric power, mechanical power through internal combustion and the development of new fuels, especially oil and its products. Many of the discoveries were 'brain-children' of Scotsmen: William Murdoch (from Auchinleck) had introduced lighting by coal-gas in the first years of the century; James Simpson (from Bathgate) first used chloroform as an anaesthetic in 1847 and brought about one of two revolutionary developments in surgery (the other was the discovery of antiseptics, also made in Scotland, but by an English-born professor, Joseph Lister); James Clerk Maxwell (from Edinburgh) discovered electromagnetic radiation and so prepared the way for wireless telegraphy and, in due course, television – another Scottish invention made by John Logie Baird, of Helensburgh; Charles Lyell (from Kinnordy) was the father of modern geology; and William Thomson, later first Lord Kelvin of Largs, OM, who spent over fifty years as professor of natural philosophy at Glasgow University was the greatest natural scientist of the nineteenth century, second only to Isaac Newton in the range and importance of his scientific and theoretical innovations, as well as the inventor of the mirror galvanometer, the household electric meter and the tide predictor among a host of original ideas. In the present century radar was invented by Sir Robert Watson-Watt (from Brechin) which helped the Allies to win the Second World War while Sir Alexander Fleming (from Loudoun) discovered the bacteria-destroying mould penicillium which helped to save the lives of so many soldiers, sailors and airmen. And behind all these 'stars' have been – and still are – numerous Scottish scientific and medical men who, if they have not risen to the top of the charts, as it were, nonetheless have made important, sometimes pioneering, contributions in their fields.

The Scottish church

The Act of Union left the Presbyterian settlement of 1690 unaltered, and the Church of Scotland, or the Kirk, remained dominant. In 1712, however, the Westminster parliament restored patronage (that is, congregations were deprived of their right to choose their own minister, a fundamental Presbyterian principle). Presbyterians and Episcopalians drifted further apart because the latter backed the Jacobite cause while the Presbyterians were for the Hanoverian succession. Rifts also began to appear among the Presbyterians. Some wanted more state support for the jurisdiction of the church which, in those days, covered many matters that would today go before a civil law court. Some wanted to take the church back to the ideals of Calvin. Some wanted complete freedom from any control by parliament. And as the eighteenth century went on, groups began to break away and form new sects. The first breakaway was in 1733. Another, the Relief Church, which refused to receive any support from the state, was formed in 1761. There were more, and towards the end of the century those which had broken away developed an energetic missionary zeal, spreading their faith among the people of the new industrial towns, where there were few churches of any kind, and even to the heathen peoples in the newly discovered parts of Africa and elsewhere. These people were called Evangelicals and they promoted Sunday schools, stricter codes of behaviour in families at home, and public condemnation of 'sinners' at church services in front of the congregations, which must have been a frightening experience. The difference between the Evangelicals and the more moderate Presbyterians widened, especially as the moderates were not keen to go out and teach, and seemed content to go on tolerating patronage. In 1843 the Evangelicals decided, after deep consideration, to break away altogether from the Church of Scotland, that is, to become dis-established, and more than 400 ministers (about 40 per cent of the total in the church) left. They formed a new church, the Free Church of Scotland. The breakaway was called the 'great disruption', and it is worth noting that such was the sincerity of their convictions that these ministers were quite ready to give up their salaries and their manses throwing themselves upon 'such provision as God in his providence may afford'. God did afford, too, and within five years the public, from highest to lowest, had raised enough funds to build several hundred new churches and pay the ministers salaries.

This Free Church attracted more breakaways. In 1874 patronage was abolished, but that did not help to heal the break. Some of the 'Wee Frees' (as the Free Church was called) did drift back to the Kirk, but it was not until 1929 that the majority of the Wee Frees agreed to a union with the Kirk. When they did it was they who set the tone of Scottish religion thereafter. Since 1929 the Kirk has been the biggest church in Scotland, though it is clear now that, with nearly 800,000 members, the Roman Catholic community is not far behind. Today the Kirk is divided into some 2000 parishes and each has a Kirk session comprising the minister and several laymen (elders). It exercises a powerful influence in every part of the country and national life, far greater than the influence of the established church in England, and concerns itself deeply with all public issues, in individual parishes and in assembly sessions. Nearly 40 per cent of Scots belong to the Kirk and attend their local church. There are still some Wee Frees out on their own and there is a small Episcopalian community, some other Protestant churches and a Jewish community. But the Kirk predominates, and it is possible that some of the leaders Scotland needs will be found from its ranks.

Education

Until the 'great disruption' of 1843, the educational system in Scotland had been linked to the church. Ordinary education in Scotland was generally taken care of by the church or with its help. However poor people were, they managed to have their children taught. As early as the 1690s the Scottish parliament had ordered every parish to see that it had a school for its children, and the responsibility for doing so was given to the lords and richer landowners, although it was often found hard to enforce. In Burns's time Scottish people were remarkably well informed on many subjects, religion, politics, history and current affairs. Many people, even those living in one-room hovels, had books and the level of literacy was extremely high. Some private benefactors founded schools. David Dale set one up in New Lanark. It was huge, catering for more than 600 children of both sexes, whose parents were working in his mills. For a long time, Scotland had more schools than any other country in Europe.

We have seen that for centuries Scotland had four universities while England had only Oxford and Cambridge. In the eighteenth century it was not possible to read mathematics or many scientific subjects in England at all, and many Englishmen had to come to Scottish universities to study these subjects. The Scots were also pioneers in further education outside universities. When he died in 1796, John Anderson, who had been professor of physics at Glasgow, left his money for the foundation of the Andersonian Institute, the first technical college in Europe. The institute became the nucleus of the University of Strathclyde, in 1966. Both sexes were admitted. One pupil in the early 1800s was David Livingstone (see p. 219), whose thirst for knowledge had already been demonstrated when, as a boy working in the local mill at Blantyre, he could be seen studying Latin or history from books propped up on his machine. And David Stow founded the first Teacher's Training

216

College in the United Kingdom at Glasgow, to help provide teachers for the growing demand for learning. In the Highlands much of the teaching was taken on by the Scottish branch of the Society for the Propagation of Christian Knowledge (SPCK) which, by the 1800s, had founded more than 200 small schools, where children were taught in English and in Gaelic.

Despite this devotion to learning, in the nineteenth century there were many children who, for one reason or another, did not go to school. Benefactors helped by founding 'ragged schools' for poor children: one was opened in Aberdeen in 1841 and another in Edinburgh a few years later. But it was not enough. Nearly half the children of Glasgow were said to have remained untaught. In 1872 the Scottish Education Act made education compulsory for all those between five and thirteen, and schools were to be supported by government aid and managed through special boards, consisting of ratepayers. By the end of the nineteenth century only one child in 1,300 was getting secondary education in England, but in Scotland it was one in 200. Young people were, in fact, being taught well beyond the capacity of Scotland to provide them with careers. As a result many thousands emigrated, some in the end to take managerial jobs in the Empire. For a long time Scots filled the best administrative jobs there, and, to some extent, in England too.

The style of education in Scotland differed from that in England: it was authoritarian and based on learning by rote. No attempt was made to influence or shape a child's character; that was left to its parents and the Kirk. Scots had more knowledge than Englishmen, but only in limited fields. The strict Calvinist morality discouraged interest in, or talent for, the arts, thus depriving pupils and students of part of the richness of life. Over the years, education outside Scotland has developed a wider, freer and more critical attitude among its pupils. There are, happily, signs of change in the Scottish system. A recent introduction is a pre-University year of learning which leads to a Certificate of Sixth Year Studies, and which is open to everyone who has passed the Higher Certificate (comparable in standard with the 'A' levels of the English General Certificate of Education) and taken in two subjects in which pupils have to show an aptitude for individual research as well as demonstrate the results of the more traditional learning by rote.

Scotland also has four new universities, Heriot-Watt, Strath-

Clyde, Stirling and Dundee. The first two grew out of earlier colleges of advanced technology.

The Scottish legal system

One of the terms of the union was that Scotland should keep her own law courts and her own system for administering justice. Scottish law was different from that of other countries, and it is still so today. In Scottish criminal law, for example, there are three possible verdicts; guilty, not guilty and not proven, whereas in England only the first and second. As far as laws concerning 'public right, policy and civil government' have been involved, the tendency has been for these to be the same for both countries, though special provisions are made for the peculiar requirements of each. On the whole Scottish law, which is based on Roman Law (but with some borrowings from English law) and which is more like the systems prevailing in western Europe, is more compassionate and at the same time more logical, and in many areas there has been a gentle shift in English law towards the Scottish approach.

The Scottish legal profession is quite separate from the English. Scottish lawyers cannot practise in England unless they have special qualifications and English lawyers cannot practise in Scotland. This has meant, so far as the legal profession is concerned, that there has been no drain of Scottish specialists out of the country to England. Scottish lawyers are able to keep their part of Scotland 'Scottish'. In addition, the Scottish legal system has been fortified in its continuation in existence as a separate institution within the United Kingdom by the various legal and juridical writings on Scottish law, notably the *Institutes* of John Erskine (1773) and the *Commentaries and Principles* of George Joseph Bell (1829). The Scots do not have Magna Carta, the Petition of Right or Habeas Corpus, but the right to a fair trial and freedom from arbitrary arrest are well protected. In many respects the Scottish criminal trial procedure is fairer, not least because the preliminary hearing before the magistrates (or coroner) is not made public before the hearing in front of a superior court, if that follows. The position is different in England, as was sensationally demonstrated recently (1979) in the case of *R. v. Thorpe* and others.

The Scots outside their own land

Economic distress, uncertainty about the future and deep depression about the changes in Scotland's status combined to drive many able and energetic Scots to leave their homeland and seek new lives and fortunes abroad. Many others, as we have seen (see p. 199), were driven off the lands worked by them and their ancestors for generations, notably in the Highlands. Some Scots emigrated because they were fired with the spirit of adventure, and not because of pressures. Thousands of Highlanders were recruited into new Highland regiments to serve in the British Army abroad, where, since the 1750s, they have won exceptional glory, with numerous VCs and other battle honours. The eighteenth century was an age of adventure; new parts of the world were being opened up; new lands were being brought under British rule, and they required men of courage and ability to administer and police them, to build up trade, to explore their hinterlands and clear routes through difficult countryside, to teach native populations, to bring Christianity to them and to cure or assuage their illnesses and diseases. The opportunities were limitless and, along with others, Scotsmen took them. And when, at the end of the nineteenth century, Britain ruled nearly a quarter of the surface of the earth, Scotsmen and their descendants predominated in every important sphere.

The record is an impressive one, but we can only sketch it briefly. Alexander Mackenzie, a Stornoway-born merchant, travelled to Canada, explored the west and, in 1789, discovered the river named after him and became the first European to cross the Rocky Mountains to the Pacific. Stirling-born James Bruce, British consul in Algiers, explored central Africa, discovered the source of the Blue Nile and opened up Abyssinia. Lachlan Macquarie, born on Ulva, off Mull, was governor of New South Wales and built the colony into the best Australian state. Mungo Park, born at Foulshiels, explored West Africa and in 1796 reached the Niger river. He described his adventures in a bestselling book, *Travels in the Interior of Africa*. David Livingstone, born at Blantyre in Lanarkshire, became a doctor and went to Central Africa as a missionary; he discovered the Victoria Falls and Lake Nyasa, and crossed Africa from west to east. Following Mackenzie's pioneering travels in Canada early in the 1800s, Lord Selkirk created a scheme for

Scots to emigrate in large numbers and make new lives there. Scots were really the creators of British Canada, and the foremost statesmen of Canadian history have nearly always been Scottish or of Scottish descent.

Many Scots also emigrated to New Zealand and founded Dunedin, a replica of Edinburgh (*Dunedin* is the Gaelic word for Edinburgh). George Rutherford, a wheelwright from Perth, settled in Motueke in 1842; and his grandson, Ernest Rutherford (later Lord Rutherford of Nelson, OM), split the atom in 1919 and became the foremost nuclear physicist of all time. Sir James Barrie, the celebrated Scottish author and playwright, once wrote that the Scots were a race of people 'the wind of whose name has swept the ultimate seas'.

Adminstrators in the new lands of empire were more often from Scotland than from anywhere else: their names ring down the years – Dalhousie, Brisbane, Elgin, Minto, Dufferin, Tweedsmuir. And at not such elevated levels could be found lesser known but equally able and industrious Scotsmen in key roles, bringing to their work that blend of Scottish Calvinist morality, respect for law and equality, and a strong sense of purpose.

Scottish political reform and nationalism

The Industrial Revolution brought enormous wealth to the traders, factory owners and proprietors of coal mines, but it was at a very high cost in suffering for ordinary working people, and over a long time. The old relationship between landowner and tenant or farmworker, one of protection in return for work and rent in the form of produce, did not apply between factory boss and worker. Factories and mines needed workers, men, women and even children, in vast numbers, and owners were easily able to employ the labour they needed and at extremely low rates. People had to work twelve or more hours a day, for six days a week. There were no breaks: you could have your meagre wages cut if you were caught talking or whistling. In some mines, conditions were appalling: children had to crawl on hands and knees dragging trucks filled with coal away from the coalface, as if they were pit ponies. Some carted it about in baskets, on their backs, in loads of over one hundredweight up flights of steps over 100 feet tall. Many children grew up terribly deformed because they did not get enough to eat to sustain this back-breaking work; many died in accidents, or of disease, or simply through exhaustion. Factory life was hardly better. People worked on their bare feet on waterlogged floors; the working temperatures were as hot as engine rooms. But nothing was done. The owners had absolute power and no one had yet thought of forming a trade union. To protest would cost you your job.

Towards the end of the eighteenth century a new mood was sweeping the western world. The American Colonies had challenged the British government's right to tax them without giving them representation in the Westminster parliament. They went to war – and won. Five years after Britain acknowledged defeat, the French Revolution broke out. It was inspired by men of lofty ideals, great oratory and high skills in writing. It was guided by men of liberal ideas, in search of a new age, the kind of society Robert Burns and many others were clamouring for, summed up in the French Revolutionary ideals: liberty, equality and fraternity.

In Scotland the new ideas found a ready response in all areas. Working conditions had to be changed, but such was the political system that no one was able to get grievances properly aired in parliament or among the councils of those who governed. One of the things the French Revolutionaries preached was that every man should have a vote. We have seen that in Scotland by the 1780s less than 1 per cent of the people had a vote in the counties. In the burghs it was worse, for the councils chose the fifteen members who represented the burghs in parliament, and councillors were not elected by burgesses but by one another, a sort of closed shop. Many big towns had no members in parliament at all. A campaign for the reform of parliament was started in Scotland and it was widely supported. (Similar campaigns were being organized in England and in Wales.) It began as the Society of the Friends of the People, which to those in power at the time sounded very revolutionary. Branches were opened in many districts. Influential people helped. Burns was moved to write his great song 'Scots Wha Hae' in support, and risked his popularity with the upper classes.

The government was becoming more and more unpopular; it was also frightened, and it retaliated with severity. It took powers through parliament to arrest and imprison people involved in campaigning for reform. There were riots in several cities. Effigies of prominent statesmen were burnt. One of the most vigorous campaigners was Thomas Muir, a lawyer from Edinburgh. He and several others were taken and sentenced after a most unfair trail to fourteen years transportation to the convict settlements in Australia. Muir escaped, went to France and died there. He became a martyr to the cause of reform.

The war against Napoleon put a temporary end to the agitation, as all Britons joined together to resist the great emperor's ambition to rule all Europe. But when Napoleon was finally defeated at Waterloo, the fight for reform began again. In 1820, five years after Waterloo, some 60,000 Scotsmen supported a move to set up a provisional government, and this time the Westminster government, once it had broken the movement, dealt leniently with the ringleaders. Meanwhile, the campaign for reform was gathering speed in England and Wales too, and it was getting support from many members of parliament. In 1832 the Great Reform Bill was passed at Westminster, and it was swiftly followed by the passage of the Scottish Bill for Parliamentary Reform. Seats were distributed more fairly, and the vote was given to all who rented houses for £10 or more a year in towns and in the country to owners of houses or land worth more than £10 a year, or tenants who were paying £50 a year or more in rent. It was a great beginning, and a year later the Burgh Reform Act gave the vote in burghs to the £10-rent-paying tenant and broke the weird burgh election system.

From then onwards Scotland obtained much the same benefits as those won by the English in a succession of social and parliamentary reforms. Agitation for improvement in working conditions and in pay was constantly kept up by active Scotsmen, notably Keir Hardie, the Lanarkshire-born champion of the miners who helped to found the British Labour Party and was the first Labour candidate at a general election. But many Scots were resentful about the unbalanced political representation of Scotland at Westminster. There was no Scottish secretary of state and Scottish affairs were not given enough parliamentary time. A vigorous but peaceful campaign was organized for Home Rule, that is, separate parliament in Scotland to manage domestic affairs.

In the 1880s the campaign grew, and it succeeded in getting the government to appoint a secretary for Scotland. The Liberals, led by William Gladstone, already promising to give Home Rule to Ireland, backed the Scottish demands too. Gladstone was, after all, a Scot. Several bills were introduced, but they did not reach the statute books, although one, in 1894, was passed by 180 to 170 votes. It read: 'it is desirable while retaining intact the power and supremacy of Imperial Parliament, to establish a legislature in Scotland for dealing purely with Scottish affairs.' The present-day Scottish National Party seeks no more than that now.

In 1907 a Scottish Grand Committee was set up to examine all bills about Scotland brought before the Westminster parliament. Its powers were widened in 1948 to include second readings and Scottish Estimates. But Scotland's problems are not always best understood by officials living and working in London. Governments have increased the responsibilities of the secretary of state for Scotland. He has a seat in the cabinet; his department handles home affairs, health, agriculture and education for Scotland. But of course it is not the same thing as political independence. In 1950 over 1.25 million Scots signed a new Covenant calling for a Scottish parliament within the United Kingdom. The Scottish National Party, founded in 1928, began to dominate the political scene in the 1960s when Winifred Ewing won the seat at Hamilton in a by-election. It was not the party's first victory, but it was first in the latest chapter of successes in the movement towards political independence, or devolution as it came to be called. In the general election of 1974 SNP won eleven seats. A national referendum on whether Scotland should have a parliament was held in March 1979, and the result was indecisive, for the government wanted a 'Yes' vote of at least 40 per cent, whereas only 31 per cent said 'Yes'. The 'Yes' vote was greater than the 'No' vote, and so the tide rolls on. Two out of three major parties in the 1979 general election were pledged to give Scotland a parliament. In the General Election of 1979, the SNP lost nine of its seats, but the movement has not declined.

But is devolution the answer to Scotland's immediate problems? There is a tremendous revival of Scottish confidence in Scotland, but would not the result of self-government be excessive government? Already there are 432 regional and 1034 district councillors. A parliament at Edinburgh would mean another 150 elected representatives while there are seventy-one already at Westminster and those seats would remain. That makes nearly 1700 people elected to look after the interests of only 5 million people, and this takes no account of the civil servants and local government officers who staff the bureaucracy. Scotland needs better government certainly, a better deployment of resources, but it does not need *more* government. The revival of belief in Scotland's future, already manifest in the artistic renaissance, and capable of great and exciting development in other fields, could be stifled by the heavy hand of administration.

There seem more urgent matters for Scots to tackle than Home Rule. One is, and has been for centuries, how to keep the best people working in the Scottish interest, without tying them into a parochial strait-jacket. If Scotland's leaders leave their country, as the old nobility used to do, so that their assets – financial and otherwise – are employed elsewhere, other leaders will continue to come in from outside. It would be sad indeed if the Scottish heritage and traditions were to end up in little more than a folksy tartan culture, part of the tourist trade.

Scotland's challenge today is not so much to win Home Rule (that can come later – for come it must in the end) as to take charge of its own business affairs, to produce its own leaders, statesmen and financiers devoted to Scottish interests. Can the Scots pull something out of the hat? Can they revitalize Scotland from within? Their long history and their remarkable contribution towards the advancement of mankind fully equip them to meet this great opportunity.

RULERS
OF
SCOTLAND

Kenneth MacAlpin (843–60)
Donald I (860–3)
Constantine I (863–77)
Aedh (877–8)
Eocha (878–89)
Donald II (889–900)
Constantine II (900–43)
Malcolm I (943–54)
Indulphus (954–62)
Duff (962–7)
Colin (967–71)
Kenneth II (971–95)
Constantine III (995–7)
Kenneth III (997–1005)
Malcolm II (1005–34)
Duncan I (1034–40)
Macbeth (1040–57)
Malcolm III (1057–93)
Donald Bane (1093–4)
Duncan II (1094)

Donald Bane (again) (1094–7)
Edgar (1097–1107)
Alexander I (1107–24)
David I (1124–53)
Malcolm IV (1153–65)
William the Lion (1165–1214)
Alexander II (1214–49)
Alexander III (1249–86)
Margaret, the Maid of Norway
　(1286–90)
First Interregnum (1290–2)
John Balliol (1292–6)
Second Interregnum (1296–1306)
Robert Bruce (1306–29)
David II (1329–71)
Robert II (1371–90)
Robert III (1390–1406)
James I (1406–37)
James II (1437–60)
James III (1460–88)

James IV (1488–1513)

James V (1513–42)

Mary Queen of Scots (1542–67)

James VI (1567–1603)

Rulers of Scotland and England

James VI and I (1603–25)

Charles I (1625–49)

Commonwealth (1649–60)

Charles II (1660–85)

James VII and II (1685–8)

William II and III (1688–1702)

and Mary II (1688–94)

Anne (1702–14)

George I (1714–27)

George II (1727–60)

George III (1760–1820)

George IV (1820–30)

William III and IV (1830–7)

Victoria (1837–1901)

Edward I and VII (1901–10)

George V (1910–36)

Edward II and VIII (1936)

George VI (1936–52)

Elizabeth I and II (since 1952)

CALENDAR
OF
PRINCIPAL EVENTS
IN
SCOTTISH HISTORY

(*c.* 6000 BC – AD 1980)

c. 6000 BC first hunter settlers from Europe reach Scotland
c. 4500 BC earliest Neolithic farmer settlers from Europe arrive
c. 3400–*c.* 3200 BC
       period of settlements at Maes Howe
c. 3000 BC beginnings of settlement at Skara Brae
c. 2500–2400 BC
       Beaker folk begin to reach Scotland
c. 2000–*c.* 700 BC
       period of Bronze Age in Scotland
c. 800–700 BC
       Scottish Iron Age begins: arrival of first Celts from Europe: first
       hill-forts
       First phase of Jarlshof settlement
c. 700–*c.* 600 BC
       Finavon vitrified fort
c. 300 BC first stone forts (duns)
c. 200 BC earliest settlement at White Caterthun
c. 100 BC first stone *brochs* built (including Mousa)
55 BC first invasion of southern Britain by Caius Julius Caesar

227

c. late 1st cent. BC–*c.* 2nd cent. AD occupation of *souterrain*
at Ardestie

1st cent. AD

Greenknowe houses

AD 43   invasion of southern Britain by Aulus Plautius

AD 55   Caratacus, British chief, defeated and handed over to the Romans

AD 60–61 Boudica's revolt

78   arrival in Britain of new governor, Julius Agricola

80   Agricola crosses into Scotland

82–3   Agricolan camps north of Forth built

84   battle of Mons Graupius, at Bennachie

85   Agricola leaves Britain

AD *c.* 100 beginning of wheelhouses at Jarlshof

121   stone wall from Tyne to Solway started by Emperor Hadrian

142   earthern wall from Forth to Clyde begun

208–9   Emperor Septimius Severus invades Scotland north of Forth

4th cent. AD

Picts starts major raids upon southern Britain

c. 400   St Ninian founds church and school at Whithorn

c. 449   Hengist and Horsa in southern Britain

500s   Scots from Ireland come to Dalriada

c. 550   St Mungo founds church at Glasgow

563   St Columba lands at Iona

597   death of Columba. Arrival in Kent (England) of St Augustine

c. 600   Aethelfrith of Bernicia defeats Aidan of Dalriada at Dawston

c. early 7th cent.

Pictish church founded at Birsay

Aberlemno stones carved

664   Synod of Whitby

685   battle of Nechtansmere: victory for Picts over Angles

780s   first Viking raids on Scotland

c. 800   Iona plundered by Vikings

843   Kenneth MacAlpin of Dalriada unites Dalriada and Pictish kingdom, thus founding Scotia

860   death of Kenneth

end 800s Orkneys taken over by Vikings

937   Constantine II (and other chiefs in Britain) defeated by Athelstan of England at battle of Brunanburh

1018   Malcolm II wins battle of Carham and annexes Lothian from England; Strathclyde comes into Scottish orbit soon after

1040–57 Macbeth king: rules well

1040–65	Thorfinn the Mighty rules over Viking dominions in Scotland
1057	Macbeth slain at Lumphanan. Accession of Malcolm III (1057–94)
1069/70	Malcolm marries Margaret, of Anglo-Saxon royal family
1071–2	William I of England invades Scotland
1080s	Margaret founds Dumfermline Abbey
1098	Magnus Barelegs acquires western islands (Viking rule)
c. 1100	Edgar founds Edinburgh Castle
early 1100s	feudalism introduced into Scotland by Alexander I and David I. Castle Sween, earliest Norman-style stone castle in Scotland, built
1124	accession of David I (1124–53)
1138	battle of the Standard (at Northallerton)
1140–64	rule of Somerled in Argyll and islands
1173–4	William the Lion's invasion of England, and capture; he recognizes Henry II as overlord
1189	Scotland accepted as independent by Richard I of England
c. 1200	earliest mention of a parliament in Scotland
1230	Rothesay Castle besieged by Vikings
1263	battle of Largs (2 Oct.)
1266	Western islands acquired by Scotland
1274	Alexander III summoned to coronation of Edward I of England: attends
1286	Alexander killed at Kinghorn, near Burntisland, Fife
1290	Margaret, the Maid of Norway, dies on way to Scotland
1292	John Balliol selected as king of Scotland by Edward I
1296	treaty with France begins 'Auld Alliance' (as it came to be known)
	Balliol deposed by Edward
1297	rising of William Wallace; victory at Stirling Bridge
1298	Wallace defeated at Falkirk
1305	after years of guerrilla war, Wallace captured and executed
1306	Robert Bruce assumes Wallace's role: crowned king of Scotland
1314	battle of Bannock Burn: glorious victory for Scottish arms
1320	Declaration of Arbroath
1329	death of Bruce; Scotland recognized by papacy as independent nation
1330	death of 'Good Sir James' (Douglas)
1332	death of Randolph, earl of Moray
1333	Scots defeated at battle of Halidon Hill
1346	David II defeated by English at Neville's Cross: captured

1348/9	Black Death (returns with great severity, 1361)
1357	David II returns to kingdom: harsh terms imposed by England
1371	death of David II; succeeded by nephew Robert Stewart, son of David's sister Marjorie Bruce
1388	battle of Otterburn
1396	Clan Fight at Perth
1398	Robert III creates his son David first Scottish duke (of Rothesay)
1402–20	regency of the duke of Albany
1406	James, heir to Robert III, captured by pirates on way to France and handed to Henry IV of England; kept for 17 years
1409	accommodation between Albany and Archibald, fourth earl of Douglas
1411	battle of Red Harlaw
1412	University of St Andrews founded
1424	James I returns to Scotland
1425	Albany's son, Murdoch, who had been regent since 1420, executed
1430	Borthwick Castle begun
1437	James I murdered
c. 1450	Mons Meg (large cannon) made
1451	foundation of Glasgow University
1455	battle of Arkinholm. Fall of the Black Douglases
1460	Siege of Roxburgh Castle; James II killed by bursting cannon, but castle taken a few days later. Beginning of Ravenscraig Castle, first fortress designed specifically for firearms in UK
1470s	Robert Cochrane builds Great Hall at Stirling Castle
1472	Orkney and Shetland islands annexed by Scotland Bishopric of St Andrews becomes archbishopric
1482	Favourites of James III taken and hanged at Lauder Brig
1488	battle of Sauchieburn, and death of James III by violence
1493	final confrontation between king and Lord of the Isles; lordship abolished
1495	University of Aberdeen founded
1496	education legislation in Scottish parliament
1503	James IV marries Margaret Tudor, d. of Henry VII of England
1506	keel laid of *Great Michael*
1507	Andrew Myllar sets up first printing press in Scotland
1513	disaster at Flodden Field (9 Sept.); James IV and most of his nobles killed on battlefield
1514–24	regency of Albany
1518	'Cleanse the Causeway' battle in Edinburgh

1528	Patrick Hamilton burned as heretic
1530s	major works at Falkland Palace initiated by James V
1532	foundation of Court of Session
1542	battle of Solway Moss. Death of James V soon afterwards
1546	George Wishart burned at stake. Cardinal Beaton murdered
1547	Siege of St Andrew's Castle. John Knox captured and sent to France to serve as galley slave.
	battle of Pinkie
1559	Knox returns to Scotland
1560	Reformation Parliament. Protestantism established as national faith
1561	Mary Queen of Scots returns from France to take up throne
1565	Mary marries her cousin Henry Stuart, earl of Darnley
1566	Mary's secretary, David Riccio, murdered
1567	Darnley murdered at Kirk o' Field. Mary marries Hepburn, earl of Bothwell
1568	battle of Langside. Mary flees to England
1568–70	regency of James, earl of Moray. (Moray assassinated, 1570)
1571	Regent Lennox slain
1572	death of Knox
1582	Ruthven Raid
	Edinburgh University founded
1587	Mary Queen of Scots executed in England
1592	Parliament recognizes Presbyterian government
1600	Gowrie Conspiracy
1603	Union of Crowns of Scotland and England. James VI leaves Scotland
1606	Andrew Melville banished
1610	Episcopacy established
1618	Five Articles of Perth
1625	James VI (and I of England) dies, ?murdered
1633	Charles I visits Scotland for first time
1637	Scottish Prayer Book forced upon Scots
	riot in St Giles' Cathedral, Edinburgh
1638	National Covenant drawn up and signed
	Episcopacy abolished
1639	First Bishops' War
1640	Second Bishops' War
1642	Civil War begins in England
1643	Solemn League and Covenant
1644	Leslie joins Fairfax and Cromwell at Marston Moor
1645	Montrose's campaign on behalf of Charles I; defeated at Philiphaugh

1649	Charles I executed in London: Scots, horrified, proclaim Charles II king
1650	Montrose executed.
	battle of Dunbar
1653–8	Cromwell régime
1660	Charles restored to both thrones
1661	Episcopacy restored
	Argyll executed
	James Sharp appointed archbishop of St Andrews
1666	Pentland rising
1669	Lauderdale appointed Commissioner in Scotland
1679	Sharp murdered
	victory of Covenanters at Drumclog
	Covenanters crushed at Bothwell Brig by Monmouth
	Lauderdale removed
1680	James Stewart, duke of York, appointed Commissioner for Scotland
1680	Sanquhar Declaration
1681	Test Act
1685	James becomes James VII (James II of England)
1687	Letter of Indulgence
1689	William of Orange invited to take over government of Scotland from James VII; war between William and supporters of James.
	battle of Killiecrankie
1690	Highlanders defeated at Dunkeld
	Presbyterianism re-established
1692	massacre at Glencoe
1693	Scottish company formed to promote trade in Africa and elsewhere
1698	first expedition to Darien
1699	second expedition to Darien
1701	Act of Settlement passed at Westminster
1702	death of William of Orange. Accession of Anne Stewart
1704	Act of Security passed
	Act anent Peace and War
1706	Duke of Argyll appointed Commissioner for Scotland
1707	Act of Union between Scottish and English parliaments ratified by Scottish parliament, which then dissolves itself
1712	patronage restored
1713	bill introduced in Westminster to repeal Act of Union; lost by 4 votes only
1714	Anne dies. Succeeded by cousin George Lewis of Hanover
1715	first Jacobite rising. Battle of Sheriffmuir

	James Edward, Old Pretender, reaches Scotland
1716	James Edward leaves Scotland after collapse of rising
1736	Porteous Riots
1745	second Jacobite rising. Bonnie Prince Charlie lands at Moidart and collects forces. Takes Perth and at Prestonpans, near Edinburgh (21 Sept.), defeats government forces. Prepares to invade England. Marches down as far as Derby
1746	battle of Culloden. Destruction of Jacobite cause and virtual end of the ancient Scottish nation
1747	feudal jurisdictions abolished
1760	foundation of Carron Iron Works
1763	Small's swing plough
1767	Craig's plan for new Edinburgh published
1768	Glasgow's Broomielaw Bridge opened
1769	Watt's steam engine patented
1773	*Institutes* of John Erskine
1784	Meikle's threshing machine
1790	Forth and Clyde Canal opened
1793	Thomas Muir sentenced to transportation to Australia
1796	Andersonian Institute founded
	Robert Burns dies
1801	Mushet discovers blackband ironstone
1802	*Charlotte Dundas*, first steamboat, built
1822	Caledonian Canal opened
1828	Neilson's hot blast furnace
1832	Scottish Bill for Parliamentary Reform
1832	cholera epidemic in Edinburgh
1833	Burgh Reform Act
1839	Nasmyth's steam hammer
1841	first 'ragged school' opened, at Aberdeen
1843	The Disruption
1847	James Simpson discovers anaesthetic properties of chloroform
1872	Education Act
1874	patronage abolished
1885	Secretary of State for Scotland (office of) re-established
1889	county councils established
1894	Home Rule for Scotland Bill passed in Commons, but dropped when government fell
1900	union of Free Church and United Presbyterian Church
1907	Scottish Grand Committee set up
1928	Scottish National Party founded
1929	union of United Free Church and Church of Scotland

1947	Edinburgh Festival founded
1950	National Covenant for Scottish Parliament drawn up and signed
1966	Winifred Ewing elected SNP Member for Hamilton in by-election to Westminster
1974	11 SNP MPs elected to Westminster in general election
1979	referendum on devolution in Scotland; small majority in favour
1979	9 SNP members lose Westminster seats in general election
1981	Scotland's unemployment figures reach 15 per cent of total workforce

NOTES

Chapter 1: From Stone to Iron

1 Euan MacKie, *Scotland: An Archaeological Guide*, London, 1975, p. 237.
2 C. Renfrew, *Before Civilization*, Harmondsworth, 1976, p. 133.
3 The Mycenaean civilization flourished on the mainland of Greece *c.* 1500–*c.* 1200 BC.
4 Long, rectangular halls of timber, with rows of posts inside to support the roof, such as those whose remains have been discovered in Denmark.
5 Celtic priests who were spiritual leaders of British resistance in the first years of Roman occupation, in the first century AD, and who by virtue of their being educated sometimes assumed the military leadership.

Chapter 2: Celts, Caledonians and Romans

1 The Suburra was a well-known Roman slum, near the Forum.
2 Celtic chariots were an advanced form of vehicle. The remains of one were found in excavations at Llyn Cerrig in Anglesey in 1943–5. It had had wheels with spokes.

3 The word was first used by Roman authors at the end of the third century AD. Some years ago, bodies of some Scythians (from whom the Celts stemmed) were found in ice and snow in Siberia. They were getting on for 3000 years old. Bluish tattoo marks were found on some of them. This could be where the Celts got the idea.

4 A dun, most commonly found in the south and west, was a stone-walled enclosure, whose wall was up to 15 feet thick, and as tall. There was a passage through the wall. Timber huts and houses were erected inside.

5 J. K. St Joseph, 'The camp at Durno, Aberdeenshire, and the site of Mons Graupius', *Britannia*, IX (1978), pp. 271–87.

6 A. R. Burn, *Agricola and Roman Britain*, London, 1953.

7 When Boudica finally met the Romans in battle, somewhere near High Cross in Leicestershire, her force of about 100,000 was utterly routed by less than a tenth of that number of Romans, and about 75,000 of her force was cut down and killed as they attempted to flee from the battlefield. Their escape routes were blocked by families and friends encircling the field, who had come to watch what they thought would be a great British victory. Cf. Tacitus, *Annals*, XIV. 34, trans. by Michael Grant, Harmondsworth, 1956, pp. 319–20.

Chapter 3: The Coming of Christianity

1 Dumbarton probably meant 'dun of the Britons'.

2 This is a rectangular gravestone of *c*. AD 450, and is probably the oldest Christian monument in Scotland. It was dedicated to 'Lord Latinus, of thirty-five years and his daughter of four'.

3 Though this in turn affected the dates of Lent and the order of Sundays throughout the Christian year.

Chapter 4: Scotland becomes a Nation

1 The Gokstad ship was discovered in a mound 162 feet wide, 16 feet high, in 1880, and the Oseberg ship in a mound 120 feet wide and nearly 20 feet high, in 1903.

2 Alternatively, it is suggested that Ingibjorg was Thorfinn's daughter.

Chapter 5: Conflict with England

1 A dialect that was not the same as the English then spoken in the southern part of England, but a 'Northumbrian English' which with

modifications survived as the language of Lowlanders for centuries.

2 The Declaration of Arbroath of 1320, for example, was strongly supported by the church.

3 The effectiveness of William's work in England is well shown by the extensive details in Domesday Book, compiled *c.* 1085–6.

4 The Normans and their allies erected many motte castles in Scotland. The best-known are Duffus in Morayshire and the Bass of Inverurie in Aberdeenshire. They can be seen clearly today (without, of course, the wooden parts).

5 The sees were St Andrews, Dunkeld, Moray, Aberdeen, Ross, Glasgow, Galloway, Brechin, Dunblane and Caithness. In *c.* 1190 Dunkeld was divided into two, the new see being Lismore in Argyll. Further changes and additions were made later on.

6 Clause 59: 'We will act towards Alexander, king of the Scots, concerning . . . his privileges and his rights . . .' The rights relate to the Scottish kings' claim to parts of northern England and freedom from allegiance to the English king. (J. C. Dickinson, *The Great Charter*, London, 1955.)

Chapter 6: Scots will be Free

1 By the sixteenth century there were many hundreds of burghs in Scotland.

2 The present (twenty-fourth) Earl of Erroll is the twenty-eighth Lord High Constable of Scotland.

3 This storm could have been expected, for it was the time of the autumnal equinox.

4 They did so until 1472 when the Scottish Parliament formally annexed Orkney and Shetland to the crown.

5 Wallace was born in Scotland but his family had come from Wales. Wallace was a rendering of Le Walys (Welshman).

Chapter 7: Stewart and Douglas

1 Robert was heard to cry out that an epitaph should be carved on his tomb to the effect 'Here lies the body of the worst of kings and the most miserable of men.'

2 'Tyneman' means Loser. Douglas had supported the Percies of Northumberland in their revolt against Henry IV and had been defeated at both Homildon Hill (1402) and Shrewsbury (1403).

3 'The seal of Robert, duke of Albany, governor of Scotland.'

4 Henry Wardlaw, bishop of St Andrews, who founded the university,

had been tutor to James before the latter was captured by English pirates in 1406.

5 Mons Meg is a name arrived at in later years from Mollance, the Scottish version of Malines, in Flanders, where the gun was forged in c. 1450, and Meg is short for Margaret. This gun is still to be seen today at Edinburgh Castle.

Chapter 8: The Nobility Tamed

1 E.g. Affleck, Borthwick, Comlongon, Elphinstone, to mention a few.
2 In 1473, 1478, 1479, 1484, 1485 and 1487.
3 Archibald Douglas was thereafter known as 'Bell-the-Cat' because of the story about the mice who wanted to hang a warning bell round the cat's neck. Douglas had been quite ready to warn James of the nobles' discontent by hanging the king's favourites!
4 Berwick has remained English ever since, though some Berwick residents regard themselves as neither Scottish nor English, but independent Berwickers.
5 See Professor W. Croft Dickinson, *Scotland: From the earliest times to 1603*, London, 1981, p. 232.

Chapter 9: The Protestant Revolution

1 John Knox wrote: 'He was called by some a good poor man's king.' He also said that to others James was a 'murderer of the nobility'.
2 Oliver Sinclair was a junior member of the family of the earls of Caithness and Orkney.
3 Queen Margaret had founded Dumfermline, and others established after her included St Andrews (Augustinians), Kelso (Tironensians), Melrose (Cistercians), Dryburgh (Premonstratensians).
4 The two tunnels through the rock can still be explored today, during normal opening hours.

Chapter 10: A Lass on the Throne

1 *tulchan*: A calf's skin stuffed with straw to cause the cow to give milk. A tulchan bishop looked like a real one, but the revenues from his see went elsewhere.

Chapter 11: The Union of the Crowns

1 The king wrote to Buckingham at Christmas, 1624:

> . . . I cannot content myself without sending you this billet, praying
> God that I may have a joyful and comfortable meeting with you and
> that we may make at this Christenmas a new marriage, ever to be kept
> hereafter. For, God so love me, as I desire only to live in this world for
> your sake, and that I had rather live banished in any part of the earth
> with you, than live a sorrowful widow-life without you. And so God
> bless you, my sweet child and wife, and grant that ye may ever be a
> comfort to your dear dad and husband, James R.

2 Even at his trial by Parliament in 1649, at which his very life was at
  stake, Charles continued to assert it.
3 It was not entirely due to the magnetism of his personality, for the
  Highlanders were tempted with the promise of considerable booty for
  their pains.
4 During this campaign in the west, Montrose's ally, Cockilto MacDonald, a renegade Highland leader who had a reputation for murder and
  pillage in Ulster, severely damaged the ancient castle of Sween, one of
  the few castles of stone built in Scotland in the twelfth century.
5 When Presbyterians – indeed, most Protestants in Britain in the seventeenth century – spoke of toleration of religious beliefs, they did not of
  course include Roman Catholics. Catholics were regarded as outcasts
  in many quarters.

Chapter 12: The Price of Union

1 Even in the seventeenth century, Edinburgh could boast one of the
  longest and finest main streets of Europe.
2 In 1788, only 2600 or so people had the vote in Scotland. In Bute, the
  only elector was the sheriff.

239

INDEX

Glasgow Cathedral, 40
glass making at Leith, 176
Glencoe, Massacre of, 180
Glenfinnan, 194
Glenrothes, 205
Glenshee, house at, 18
Gokstad, Viking ship, 46
Golden Acts, 159
Golden Age of Intellect, 203
Gowrie, earl of, 157, 160
Graham, Sir Robert, 99
'great disruption' (1843), 215, 216
Great Michael, 117, 119
Greenknowe, house at, 17, 18
Grooved ware, 7, 9
gunpowder, use of, 114

Haakon of Norway, Viking chief, 74–5
Hadrian, Roman emperor, 25–6
Hadrian's Wall, 25–8
Halidon Hill, battle of, 85
Hallstatt people (Hallstatters), 12, 13
Hamilton, John, archbishop of St Andrews, 155
Hamilton, Patrick, preacher, 126
Hamiltons, the, 123, 154–5, 156
Hampton Court, 163
Hardie, James Keir, 222
Harlaw, battle of, 94–5
Hastings, battle of, 55
Henri II, king of France, 138, 139, 142
Henry VIII, king of England, 122–8, 133–4, 138, 139, 140
Henry, Prince of Wales (eldest son of James VI of Scotland and I of England), 160, 167
Henryson, Robert, poet, 113
Hermitage Castle, 115
Highland and Island Development Board, 200
Highland Clearances, 199–200
Highlands after Culloden, repressive measures (such as

Clearances), 198–200
hill-forts, 14, 22
Holyrood House, palace of, 117, 128, 139, 144–5, 146, 147, 149, 163
home rule, campaign for, 222–4
Hume, David, philosopher, 206
Hunter, John, 206

Inchtuthil, Roman fortress, 23
Industrial Revolution, 210–13
Ingibjorg, queen of Malcolm III, 48, 50, 55, 56
Inverlochy, battle of, 172
Inverness, 87, 195
Iona, monastery at, 40
Irish Celtic church, 42
Iron Age, 4, 11, 12–16, 17–18
iron and steel industries, 211–12

Jacobite rising (1715), 191–3
Jacobite rising (1745), 194–8
Jacobites, 186, 189, 190, 192–8, 201, 203
James I, king of Scotland, 93, 95, 96–9; arrests clan chiefs, 98; captured by English pirates, 93, 96; murdered, 99
James II, king of Scotland, 100–8; killed at Roxburgh, 104–5
James III, king of Scotland, 108–13; murdered, 112
James IV, 113–20; crusade against Turks, 118; killed at Flodden, 120; marries daughter of Henry VII of England, 118
James V, king of Scotland, 121, 123–8, 132, 133, 137
James VI, king of Scotland (and I of England), 145, 146, 149, 153–61, 162–8
James VII, king of Scotland (and II of England), 178–80
James Edward, Prince (claimed to be James VIII of Scotland), 186, 190–4
Jarlshof, 17